"Unlock the power of franchising! *Franchise Your Business* provides an easy-to-understand, well-defined guide for assessing fit and applying franchising to your business."

—CRAIG DONALDSON, FORMER PRESIDENT OF HARRIS RESEARCH (CHEM-DRY AND N-HANCE FRANCHISED BRANDS) AND SERVICE BRANDS (MOLLY MAID, MR. HANDYMAN, AND PROTECT PAINTERS)

"*Franchise Your Business* offers the step-by-step, RIGHT way to franchise a business. I have always believed that knowledge is power and with this book, the power and reward of a successful franchise system is at your fingertips!"

—DEBBIE SHWETZ, CO-FOUNDER OF NOTHING BUNDT CAKES

"For anyone who is thinking about entering the mine field of franchising, Mark's book is an absolute GPS that I recommend to guide them through it."

—DON NEWCOMB, D.D.S., FOUNDER OF MCALISTER'S DELI AND CO-FOUNDER OF NEWK'S EATERY

"*Franchise Your Business* is the definitive how-to book for anyone trying to expand using other people's money, written by someone who has helped hundreds of companies do it. It's a great and highly informative read. Mark helped us successfully franchise our business, and this book will help you too!"

—NICK FRIEDMAN, CO-FOUNDER AND PRESIDENT OF COLLEGE HUNKS HAULING JUNK

FOAL

"When I left my corporate life and became an entrepreneur, I discovered an amazing method to growing my business—franchising! Since this discovery, I have created three successful franchise brands with more than 500 units in the US. *Franchise Your Business* shows you how to use franchising to elevate your business far beyond your wildest dreams."

—PETER ROSS, CEO AND CO-FOUNDER OF SENIOR HELPERS

"Mark Siebert gives you a thorough understanding of franchising as an expansion strategy and the steps you need to take to do franchising right! Especially valuable is Mark's take on the franchisee-franchisor relationship, which is the key to a franchise's long-term success. Honest and insightful, this book is an absolute must-read for anyone who is exploring alternatives for growing their business."

—SCOT CRAIN, VICE PRESIDENT, FRANCHISE RELATIONS OF
AUNTIE ANNE'S SOFT PRETZELS

"*Franchise Your Business* is a solid recounting of the many facets of franchising that we have learned over the years working with Mark. If you are thinking of franchising your business, or have recently started the process, read this comprehensive guide!"

—DAVE PAZGAN, PRESIDENT OF 101 MOBILITY

"Whether you are trying to grow your business or just looking to get a better understanding of the franchise model, you will certainly come away from this book with a deeper understanding of the power of franchising as a growth engine."

—PATRICK WALLS, PRESIDENT OF CAPRIOTTI'S

"Mark Siebert unpacks his wisdom and expertise to guide you through the franchise business model. Anyone interested in learning about the dynamics of franchising will benefit greatly from this book."

—BRIAN MATTINGLY, PRESIDENT AND FOUNDER OF WELCOMEMAT SERVICES

"This book is an essential read if you are considering franchising as a growth strategy for your business. Mark boils down his 30 years in the business with client examples and secrets for success, sharing key elements for successful franchisee relationships, open communication, and supporting the financial success of the franchisee."

—SCOTT LEHR, SENIOR VICE PRESIDENT OF
INTERNATIONAL FRANCHISE ASSOCIATION

"*Franchise Your Business* is an invaluable resource for any successful entrepreneur who wants to explore franchising as a growth strategy. This book paints a high-definition picture of franchising that delivers the exact information and insights I spent countless hours trying to find and understand. If you think franchising is a possibility in your future, start here."

—P. ALLAN YOUNG JR, CEO OF SHELFGENIE AND
OUTBACK GUTTERVAC FRANCHISE SYSTEMS

"Mark Siebert has written *the* guide for the start-up franchisor or for anyone considering franchising their existing business. We learned a tremendous amount about franchising in working with Mark. Much of that wisdom is imparted in *Franchise Your Business*. I highly recommend reading this book."

—JEFF PLATT, CO-FOUNDER AND CEO OF SKY ZONE FRANCHISE GROUP

Franchise
Your
Business

THE GUIDE TO EMPLOYING THE
GREATEST GROWTH STRATEGY EVER

Mark Siebert, CEO of iFranchise Group

FOREWORD BY JOHN LEONESIO, FOUNDER OF MASSAGE ENVY

Entrepreneur
PRESS®

Entrepreneur Press, Publisher
Cover Design: Andrew Welyczko
Production and Composition: Eliot House Productions

This publication is designed to provide accurate and authoritative information in regard
to the subject matter covered. It is sold with the understanding that the publisher is not
engaged in rendering legal, accounting or other professional services. If legal advice
or other expert assistance is required, the services of a competent professional person
should be sought.

Library of Congress Cataloging-in-Publication Data
Names: Siebert, Mark, 1955–
Title: Franchise your business: the guide to employing the greatest growth strategy
ever/by Mark Siebert.
Description: Irvine, California: Entrepreneur Media, Inc., [2015] | Includes index.
Identifiers: LCCN 2015036135| ISBN 978-1-59918-581-1 (alk. paper) | ISBN
1-59918-581-4 (alk. paper)
Subjects: LCSH: Franchises (Retail trade)
Classification: LCC HF5429.23 .S55 2015 | DDC 658.8/708--dc23
LC record available at http://lccn.loc.gov/2015036135

Printed in the United States of America

20 19 18 17 16   10 9 8 7 6 5 4 3 2 1

Contents

PART ONE

Exploring Franchising

PART TWO

Developing Your Franchise Company

PART THREE

Building Your Franchise Empire

CHAPTER 10

CHAPTER 11

Foreword by
John Leonesio
Founder of Massage Envy

If you have an entrepreneurial spirit like me, my guess is that every time you see a business you look at the model and say to yourself, "How could I make that better?" Or if something is being done extremely well, you think, "How can I incorporate that idea into a business?" Like me, "in every problem or solution, you see an opportunity."

And, if you are like me, you do not have an off switch. Your career is not about work. It's about passion and the desire to build something that's enduring. Something that can also help other people become successful—for many, for the first time in their lives.

The education I got on how to run my first business was priceless, and I never, ever get tired of teaching it to others. My journey, like many entrepreneurs, started with a concept, evolved into a model, and grew into a franchise.

I had been in the health club business for 30-plus years, and I was tired. I was tired of vying with local gyms, mega fitness chains, and all the new concepts to get the consumers' attention. Tired of constantly striving to be different as the market was getting more and more crowded. In the health clubs we operated, we offered massage therapy as one of our services. I consistently received feedback from our members that if it was more convenient and more affordable, they would get more massages. This stuck in my mind.

I left the health club business in 2000 and began to work on a massage concept that had been in the back of my mind for a long time. With the help of my former massage therapy director and with no clear industry leader, no chains to follow, and no model to replicate, we set out to invent an entire model.

I have always said that I don't change a product or service, like massage or chiropractic therapy; I just change how it is delivered to the consumer. Ask consumers what they want. And if you can deliver it and make a successful business model out of it, everyone wins.

In early 2002, I opened my first Massage Envy and immediately knew we had found a successful model. With that success, my vision became bigger than just a few locations. Massage Envy was going to change the way that therapeutic massage was delivered around the world. Yes, the world!

But there was a problem. Without the capital needed to grow, my fear was someone would capitalize on our model and be the first to market what we had created to the masses. We already had dozens of clients asking how they could get their own Massage Envy clinic. So I knew that if I wanted to build the brand, I had only one option. That option was to franchise the model . . . and so it began.

Like everything else I have always done, when venturing into a new business I seek out the best and brightest. I found long ago that they can help shorten my learning curve and help me avoid costly mistakes. I was learning the massage business. But I was honestly clueless about the franchise business.

In 2002, I met Mark Siebert. I had one location, an SBA loan, and only a vague knowledge of franchising. And to be honest, at that point I did not even know if I wanted to franchise my model. It all seemed so overwhelming. Mark and the team he had assembled at the iFranchise Group soon calmed my fears, provided strategic direction, and helped me bridge the knowledge gap. I knew I was in great hands as I transitioned from operator to franchisor in just one year.

In early 2003 we began franchising, and now, 12 years later, I am working on my fourth franchise concept. Combined, these four concepts will generate more than $1.5 billion in annual sales and have more than 1,300 locations. What a journey!

In this book, Mark shares many of the secrets, strategies, and principles that have been at the core of many successful franchise programs—mine included. If you, like me, are pursuing a dream that involves rapid growth, the lessons in this book will provide you with a road map that can help you achieve that dream. It can also assist in avoiding costly mistakes that, unfortunately, many new franchisors tend to make.

At the same time, Mark cautions business owners to carefully consider whether franchising is the right strategy for them and their business. There are many ways to expand a sound business. Even if a business is a strong candidate for franchising, that does not mean it is the only option. The decision to franchise needs to fit both the business model and the owner's personal goals, depending on where they want to take the brand.

The early chapters of the book take the reader through the process of understanding the core elements of franchising and issues to consider when evaluating franchising as a growth strategy. As Mark points out, franchising can be used as the sole strategy for growth, or it can be used in conjunction with other growth strategies such as company-owned locations.

A common theme throughout the book is the importance of building strong relationships with franchisees and ensuring that their success remains of paramount importance to you as a franchisor. A good franchisor will be a leader, coach, teacher, and communicator of best practices throughout the franchise system. A good franchisor welcomes franchisee input and, at times, criticism. A good franchisor knows that its franchisees will contribute many of the groundbreaking ideas that will propel the system forward.

Franchising comes with no guarantees. It takes hard work, long hours, good decision making, and, ultimately, the ability to assemble a strong team. And along the way there will be dozens of people who will tell you that you are crazy—that your dream is unachievable and that you should go out and get a job.

Foreword by John Leonesio

Franchising, like entrepreneurship itself, is not for the faint of heart. But if you have a sound concept and the "fire in the belly" that is so common among true entrepreneurs, this book can put you on the right path to building a successful franchise.

—John Leonesio, founder of Massage Envy

Preface

Over the course of my 30-plus years in franchising, I have had the privilege of working with some of the world's premier franchisors. In the past ten years alone, the iFranchise Group has received more than 50,000 inquiries from prospective franchisors. Of those, we have met with fewer than 2,000 companies. And of that number, we have worked with about 250 companies that chose to franchise. Franchising is not an appropriate strategy for every business, and I hope that is one of the lessons this book conveys to its readers.

During my career, I have worked with many of the best and brightest in the franchise world, some of whom I have had the honor of calling my friends and colleagues at the iFranchise Group. Currently, our 27 consultants have more than 500 years of experience in franchising—much of which has come in senior roles with major brand-name franchise companies.

My partner at iFranchise Group, Dave Hood, is the former president of Auntie Anne's Soft Pretzels, which he helped grow from the ground up to more than 650 units. Our collective partner at Franchise Dynamics, Robert Stidham, has personally sold more than 1,700 franchises, making him one of the most successful franchise salespeople of all time. One of our senior advisors, Leonard Swartz, has led six different franchise brands in senior level positions—starting as the COO of Dunkin' Donuts, and later holding senior management positions at Dunhill Staffing Systems, Snelling Staffing Services, Adia Services (now Adecco), PIP Printing, and a franchise division of ITT. Another senior consultant, Scott Jewett, grew Line-X from its entry into franchising to its sale to a private equity firm after opening more than 700 franchise units. And our collective partner at TopFire Media, Matthew Jonas, has helped me transition into the digital world of modern franchise marketing.

Some of the other brands in which my consultants have held senior leadership positions include Aloette Cosmetics, Armstrong World Industries, Chem-Dry, Famous Famiglia, Management Recruiters International, McDonald's, Nutrisystem, Pearle Vision Centers, Rocky Rococo Pizza and Pasta, Roy Rogers, Saladworks, Snap-on Tools, and Taco Bell. Between them, our consultants have provided consulting services to more than 40 Fortune 500 companies and to 98 of the world's top 200 franchisors as rated by *Franchise Times* magazine.

Judy Janusz, the COO at the iFranchise Group, has been with me from the beginning—and without her steadfast leadership and unwavering commitment to quality, I could never have built this company, let alone found the time to write this book.

It has been my distinct privilege and honor to learn from these people, and from the many others—clients, consultants, and lawyers alike—who have shared their franchise insight and experience with me over the years. It is my sincere hope that I will be able to impart some small part of the lessons that they have taught me in this book.

Notes for the Reader

In the interest of readability, this book is written to address a general audience of potential franchisors. Some of the discussions will have less relevance to you than they might have to others. The book will also focus on common practices in franchising, although new and innovative approaches should always be taken into consideration and may even be the key to your ultimate success.

Throughout this book, all references are primarily to the laws of franchising in the United States. Franchise law varies from country to country, as do laws that touch on franchising, such as trademark and intellectual property laws.

I have attempted to provide a businessperson's perspective on a significant number of legal issues. In doing so, I have simplified language in an effort to make this text more readable and promote better understanding. I have thus eliminated a certain precision that lawyers might find more attractive. This book is not meant to provide you with anything approaching legal advice.

It is also important to point out that franchising can be found in literally hundreds of different industries. With this in mind, there will be some substantial differences when discussing restaurants, retail operations, B2B service businesses, consumer service businesses, hotels, medical practices, and some of the more esoteric franchises that are arising in today's market. Some of these businesses will find real estate and site selection to be very important, some will find it less important, and some will be home-based businesses with no real estate needs. Some will call for sophisticated supply channels and inventory management, while others will carry little or no inventory. The metrics for measuring each business will be different. And the support needed to help a franchisee succeed will be very different as well.

Likewise, this book will often speak in generalities. Royalties, for example, are usually a percentage of revenue, but they can be flat fees, a percentage of gross margins, or any of a number of different configurations. The franchisee is responsible for the entire initial investment in most cases, but there are franchise companies in which the franchisor shoulders much of this investment. The fact is that there are few absolutes in franchising, as a franchise ultimately is a reflection of the business decisions made by the franchisor.

Some franchises are home-based businesses that operate largely in a customer's location, and others have physical locations. Regardless, I will, on occasion, refer to a "franchisee's facilities" or "operation," again in a concession to readability.

Please forgive these literary shortcuts.

Introduction

Franchising:
A David Becomes
Goliath Story

*"Franchising has been the savior of free enterprise in this country.
It has given the small businessman a way to survive."*

—Art Bartlett, Founder, Century 21 Real Estate

In 1954, Ray Kroc was a little down on his luck. At the age of 52, Kroc had sold just about everything in his life and was now selling Multi-mixers—a five-spindle milkshake machine that was losing market share fast to lower-priced competitors. So when he received an order for eight Multi-mixers, he had to find out what was going on.

After a trip to San Bernardino, California, to meet Dick and Mac McDonald and seeing the efficiency of their operation, he knew he was on to something. With visions of selling multi-mixers to every McDonald's that would open, Kroc pitched his expansion plan to the brothers and began franchising. Shortly thereafter, Kroc was forced to file for bankruptcy, but even that would not slow him down. He focused on his vision and on franchising.

The McDonald brothers, who were doing quite well with their business, did not share the same vision for a national chain. And so when Kroc made them an offer to buy the rights to the franchise for $2.7 million (so that each would have $1 million after taxes), they jumped at it. And I am fairly sure they danced a little jig when the checks arrived.

Fast-forward a decade.

In 1965, a 17-year-old named Fred DeLuca needed money to fund his education and talked to his family friend, Dr. Peter Buck, at a picnic—perhaps hoping the nuclear physicist might give him a loan. Buck, instead, suggested that DeLuca open a sandwich shop and agreed to invest $1,000 in the venture—which would be called Pete's Super Submarines. They started by setting a goal: they would get to 34 stores in ten years—a number they chose because it was the size of a competitor after which they had, in part, patterned their store.

Sales started strong but then started falling until February 1966, when during their weekly meeting, DeLuca told Buck they had sold only seven sandwiches for the entire day. Buck began to sketch out their alternatives. The first alternative he listed was abbreviated simply "LTDATATK." When DeLuca asked him what it stood for, Buck replied, "Lock the door and throw away the key." Instead of doing that, however, they decided, perhaps against all reason, to open a second location to show the community how well they were doing. Eventually, they began to make money, and within eight years, they had 16 stores. And while 16 stores certainly made them a successful chain, they realized they weren't going to get to their goal of 34 stores in ten years. Rather than lowering their sights, they decided to try to franchise their business, which by now had been rebranded to the name it carries today: Subway.

Fast-forward to the turn of the century.

I first met John Leonesio shortly after a handful of fanatical terrorists had killed nearly 3,000 innocent people, throwing the nation and the economy into shock. Flags were flying in the streets. But on Wall Street—and on Main Street—the economy was flying at half-mast, as the one-two punch that had started with the dotcom bubble bursting was now overshadowed by the fear that these maniacs would strike again. In the immediate aftermath, the Dow Jones Industrial Average plummeted 14.3 percent in a week—then a record number—on top of the losses already sustained from the end of the dotcom bubble. Unemployment jumped from 3.9 percent to 6 percent in a matter of months. And fear was everywhere. The sale of gas masks in some quarters jumped 500 percent overnight as anthrax was found in the postal system. Would our malls be next? A sporting event?

In the face of this market, Leonesio had developed a therapeutic massage concept that was different from those around the country. And despite their economic woes, people loved it. In fact, the economic times may have contributed to his success. At the time, fewer than 15 percent of Americans had ever experienced a therapeutic massage, and Leonesio knew a tremendous opportunity existed in the marketplace.

Using his decades of experience in the health club industry, he had created a new, membership-based model for marketing spa and therapeutic massage services. He first opened the new concept in a strip mall in suburban Phoenix, and now the business was so successful that he was actually turning away new members.

But Leonesio had a dilemma, the same dilemma I have seen dozens of times over the years. People were walking through his newly opened operation with notepads and cameras. And while he tried to keep them out, he knew it wouldn't be long before the competition jumped into his market.

He knew what would happen next. People would begin knocking off his concept, and if he didn't move fast, someone else would get the financial rewards for the concept he had developed.

Leonesio was sitting on a gold mine. His concept, he was sure, could be expanded throughout the country and even internationally.

The problem was capital.

To take advantage of the market, Leonesio needed tens of millions of dollars. Bankers weren't going to lend him the money. He only had a single unit, his concept was too new, and he had limited collateral. He was too small to consider an IPO, of course. Likewise, venture capitalists and private equity investors had no interest in a company his size and would need to see more of a track record. And even if they wanted to invest, Leonesio was unwilling to give up control of the company.

In short, Leonesio found himself in precisely the same dilemma that thousands of entrepreneurs are facing today: How do you expand a great business quickly and with minimal capital? His answer: franchising.

Fast-forward four years.

Leonesio's company had sold more than 720 franchises, of which some 300 were open. And while he now had a half-dozen competitors, he had rapidly dominated the market by moving quickly into franchising. More important, Leonesio was able to do this without bringing in outside capital. He estimates his total cost of expansion at $300,000—about the cost of opening two more company locations.

In May 2008, Leonesio sold Massage Envy for close to $100 million—a feat that would never have been achievable without the leverage of franchising.

Today, Massage Envy has more than 1,000 locations nationwide that collectively provide more than 1.5 million massages every year. It was recently acquired once again by Roark Capital, a private equity firm with investments in 22 different franchise brands (seven of which I have had the privilege of helping during my career). And Leonesio? He moved on to franchise The Joint—a chiropractic company that as of this writing has 160 locations with another 100 scheduled to open this year. More recently, he began working with Amazing Lash (another iFranchise Group client), which has sold 300 locations in less than two years.

And while not every company that turns to franchising will experience this level of success, every year, like clockwork, brand-new franchisor success stories emerge to illustrate the power of franchising.

These stories show just how fast a company can grow using franchising. Today, more and more entrepreneurs are finding that franchising has a number of advantages that makes it worth considering. More and more are asking, "Is franchising the answer?"

If you are a business owner who is thinking about franchising, this book will help you answer that question and, in the process, gain a better understanding of franchising as an expansion strategy.

Franchising is not the right choice for everyone. But for those companies for whom franchising is a good match, the explosive growth potential franchising affords is unparalleled in the world of business.

It is worth pointing out that in each of the franchise success stories above, persistence and belief in their vision of what the company could become played a significant role in their ultimate success. I am sure there were plenty of doubters and naysayers along the way. But each of these entrepreneurs persisted in the face of adversity.

Another story serves to illustrate that point. When Harlan Sanders began selling franchises at the age of 65, it was said he spent two years driving around the U.S., often sleeping in the back seat of his beat-up old car, going from restaurant to restaurant trying to sell his recipe for a better fried chicken. On the 1,009th visit, he persuaded Pete Harman in Salt Lake City to open the first Kentucky Fried Chicken in 1952.

I sometimes wonder what the world would look like today if Colonel Sanders had said, "I'll try this 1,000 times, but if nobody buys it, I will need to move on."

PART ONE

Exploring
Franchising

CHAPTER 1

What Is
Franchising?

"Do ... or do not. There is no try."

—YODA

Everyone knows what a franchise is, right?

It's McDonald's and Jiffy Lube and Century 21. It's Subway and Massage Envy and Holiday Inn.

But many people would be surprised to hear that some of the biggest companies in janitorial services are also franchises. The same holds true for carpet cleaning, wood restoration, lawn care, and dozens of other industries. The largest providers of in-home, nonmedical care for senior citizens are franchises. And so are many of the world's largest hotel brands. There are franchises that specialize in cleaning bathrooms and franchises that specialize in removing pet waste. You name it, and chances are it has been franchised.

How It Works

Generally speaking, a franchisee is someone who pays a franchisor an initial franchise fee, averaging close to $30,000 in today's market, for the right to operate a business under the franchisor's name using the franchisor's business model. The franchisee furnishes all the capital required for opening the business and assumes full financial and operational responsibility for running the business. The franchisee generally will also pay a continuing royalty (usually between 4 and 10 percent of gross sales, or even higher) to the franchisor, and often the franchisee will buy products from the franchisor.

The franchisor, for its part, will allow the franchisee to use its trademark. The franchisor trains the franchisee to run the business according to its standards. The franchisor will generally assist the franchisee during the startup period, and provide ongoing support and assistance to the franchisee. The level, type, and quality of this ongoing support will often differ, but for many franchisors, it will take the form of advertising assistance, purchasing power, brand maintenance, financial guidance, and ongoing operational support.

Generalities aside, it is important to understand exactly what constitutes a franchise. Most people probably have a good idea of what a franchise is— at least we think we know one when we see one, even if we cannot define it. That said, the term "franchise" has a very specific legal definition within the U.S. and in other countries in which they are regulated.

The Federal Definition

In the U.S., the Federal Trade Commission in FTC Rule 436 (which was amended effective July 1, 2008) defines a franchise as a business relationship that has three definitional elements:

1. The use of a common name or trademark
2. The presence of "significant operating control" or "significant operating assistance"
3. A required payment of more than $500 in the first six months of operation by the franchisee (including initial fees, royalties, advertising fees, training fees, or fees for equipment)

The first element of this definition is self-explanatory. It is triggered by the *right* (not the obligation) to use the name. If a contract is silent on this issue, that alone may be enough to trigger the law. A good rule of thumb is that if you are hoping to avoid franchise laws by eliminating the trademark element of the definition, you should specify in the contract that your licensee is *prohibited from* using your name.

The "significant control" or "assistance" element of the definition can be triggered by any of at least 18 operational elements. The commentary to the original rule goes into detail here. It states:

> *Among the significant types of controls over the franchisee's method of operation are those involving a) site approval for an unestablished business, b) site design or appearance requirements, c) hours of operation, d) production techniques, e) accounting practices, f) personnel policies and practices, g) promotional campaigns requiring franchisee participation or financial contribution, h) restrictions on customers, and i) locations or sales area restrictions.*

> *Among the significant types of promises of assistance to the franchisee's method of operation are a) formal sales, repair, or business training programs, b) establishing accounting programs, c) furnishing management, marketing, or personnel advice, d) selecting site locations, and e) furnishing a detailed Operations Manual.*

> *In addition to the above listed elements—**the presence of any of which would suggest the existence of "significant control or assistance"**— the following additional elements will, to a lesser extent, be considered when determining whether "significant" control or assistance is present in a relationship: a) a requirement that a franchisee service or repair a product (except warranty work), b) inventory controls, c) required displays of goods, and d) on-the-job assistance in sales or repairs. (Emphasis added by author.)*

The important point to remember is that just *one* of these elements could trigger the "significant control and assistance" element of the definition.

The FTC makes few exceptions. It does not include trademark controls designed to protect trademark ownership rights. It does not include health or safety restrictions. It does not include product-specific controls that do not extend to the entire business. But for the most part, the commission intends for this law to be interpreted broadly, and franchise lawyers will tell you that this particular element of the definition is probably the easiest to trigger.

The required payment element is interpreted in the same broad light. It is intended to capture any payment of at least $500 during the first six months of the franchisee's operations. Quoting from the same commentary to the rule:

> *The Commission's objective in interpreting the term "required payments" is to capture all sources of revenue which the franchisee must pay to the franchisor or its affiliate for the right to associate with the franchisor and market its goods or services. Often, required payments are not limited to a simple franchise fee, but entail other payments which the franchisee is required to pay to the franchisor or an affiliate, either by contract or by practical necessity. Among the forms of required payments are initial franchise fees as well as those for rent, advertising assistance, required equipment or supplies—including those from third parties where the franchisor or its affiliate receives payment as a result of such purchases—training, security deposits, escrows, deposits, nonrefundable bookkeeping charges, promotional literature, payments for services of persons to be established in business, equipment rental, and continuing royalties on sales.*

The one exclusion from the rule involves the sale of inventory at a bona fide wholesale price. Again, quoting from this commentary:

> *In order to minimize ambiguity in this respect, but consistent with the Commission's objective that "required payment" capture all sources of hidden franchise fees, the Commission will not construe as required payments any payments made by a person at a bona fide wholesale price for reasonable amounts of merchandise to be **used for resale**. (Emphasis added by author.)*

Thus, if you sell someone goods for resale at a genuine wholesale price and do not take any other fees in the process, you will not trigger this element of the definition. But exercise caution: If you sell them products that are not intended for resale—for example, display merchandise, displays, point-of-purchase material, and other items they would not sell to customers—you may trigger this rule if the price exceeds $500.

In looking at this exclusion, one should note that nowhere in the commentary is there any mention that the franchisor must make a profit on these items to trigger the rule. For many, this element seems an oversight. After all, if they are not making a profit, how can they possibly be a franchisor? But those people would be well-advised to remember that the FTC's intent in drafting these laws was to protect the person buying a franchise—not the franchisor. And if someone spends money, they are at risk.

What It Means to Be a Franchisor

If a business relationship has the definitional elements of a franchise under the FTC rule, the franchisor must provide the prospective franchisee with a Franchise Disclosure Document (FDD), which makes certain disclosures to the franchisees prior to the sale of a franchise. Along with these disclosure obligations, the franchisor's sales process is also regulated by this rule.

An FDD must contain 23 specific items of disclosure in a specific format. In addition, the FDD must include all contracts the prospective franchisee must sign (including the franchise agreement and other ancillary legal documents, such as any financing agreement or an area development agreement, for example) and a copy of the franchisor's audited financial statements. (If you do not have audited financial statements, don't worry. Almost all new franchisors will create a new corporation and simply disclose the newly audited balance sheet of that corporation to satisfy the requirement.)

You must then follow a fairly simple set of rules governing the sale of franchises, including:

- ➤ You must present the FDD to the prospective franchisee at least 14 days prior to the sale of the franchise (not counting the day you present the FDD or the day on which the contract is signed), or within a reasonable time upon request of the prospective franchisee.
- ➤ You must provide the prospective franchisee with a fully completed franchise agreement at least seven days prior to the sale of a franchise. (This time can run concurrently with the 14 days discussed above if the agreement is filled out.)
- ➤ You must limit what you say on certain matters (financial performance representations, etc.) to only what you have included in your

FDD. If you choose not to do a financial performance representation (previously called an earnings claim), you cannot provide the prospect with any information on sales or earnings. And while you can provide them with information on expenses, you cannot do so in a format that would allow them to calculate sales or earnings—so percentages of revenues are not allowed.

- ⌐ You must treat all similarly situated prospects in the same way—so the material terms of the agreement cannot be negotiated unless you are willing to enter into those same negotiations with all similarly situated franchisees and fully disclose both your willingness to negotiate and the range within which you will negotiate (which, of course, is negotiating suicide).

While there are other compliance and documentation issues you will need to be aware of, the process is fairly simple.

We will deal more with the legal aspects of franchising and pre-sale disclosure in Chapter 7.

Further Complications: State Definitions

This is all made more fun by the fact that, at present, 30 states currently regulate either franchises or business opportunities. These state laws come in a variety of flavors.

- ⌐ There are franchise registration laws, in which you must go through a formal registration and review process with various state agencies to sell franchises in that state. These states are apt to require changes to your FDD based on their specific concerns. And, of course, those changes must be disclosed to any prospective franchisee in that state (usually through a state-specific addendum to the contract).
- ⌐ There are business opportunity laws that require any business opportunity (including but not limited to franchises) to file its legal documents with the state to be approved to sell franchises in that state.
- ⌐ And there are relationship laws governing what can and cannot be done in a franchise relationship within a particular state.

To complicate things even further, there are a slew of various exemptions to these state laws as well. For example, in certain states, franchisors are exempt from business opportunity laws if they will grant the right to operate under a registered trademark. In some states, there are exemptions for large franchisors, based on net worth and number of operating franchises.

Of course, many of these states have their own definition of just what constitutes a franchise under their laws.

For many, the legal definition involves: a) the use of the trademark, b) a community of interest or a common marketing plan, and c) the payment of a fee. But in some states (like New York), you can trigger franchise laws even without allowing someone to use your trademark. In others, like Illinois, the triggering element for the required payment is not $500 in the first six months of operation, but $500 throughout the lifetime of the relationship. Moreover, the disclosure exemptions that are recognized at the federal level may not be recognized at the state level as exemptions to registration or filing.

The list of complexities goes on and on. Eight of these states require you to submit your franchise advertising for approval before you use it. While most of these states have similar language regarding timing of disclosures (having adopted the new 14-day waiting period between disclosure and signing a franchise contract), others continue to operate under the old 10-business-day waiting rule that was originally promulgated under the 1979 version of FTC Rule 436. Likewise, while most no longer require broker registration, again adopting the standards of the new federal rule, some continue to hold on to this cumbersome requirement. Some states, in fact, require franchisors to disclose their prospective franchisees at the first personal meeting—another holdover from the previous version of the FTC rule.

Moreover, the situations that trigger the need to register or file your documents will vary from state to state. These include:

- If the franchisor is physically located in that state
- If the franchisor is incorporated in that state
- If the franchisee is a resident of that state

⟵ If the franchisee's territory will include territory in that state

⟵ If the discussion of the sale of the franchise takes place in that state

And, of course, it is worth mentioning that these laws are constantly changing; by the time you read this, the definitions or exemptions above may already be out of date. If you are exploring franchising as an expansion vehicle, it is important to retain an experienced franchise attorney who deals with these issues on a daily basis. Your franchise attorney will help keep you on the right track and make navigating the franchise laws seem much less complex. But before you find an attorney, understand the business issues to be sure that franchising is right for you.

The key point to take away from this section is that in these states, you must comply with *both* the state and federal laws.

We will go into the state and federal franchise laws in more detail in Chapter 7. But for now, we will focus on the federal definition, which we will use throughout this book.

THE BOTTOM LINE

If It Looks Like a Duck . . .

Differentiating between a franchise and any other form of third-party distribution is relatively easy. Look for the three definitional elements:

1. The franchisee uses your name.
2. The franchisee uses your systems of operations.
3. The franchisee pays you fees.

If all three are present, it probably is a franchise. If they are not, you probably are not.

CHAPTER 2

Advantages and Disadvantages of Franchising

"I think a dream is just a suggestion to start something out, do something."

—COLONEL HARLAN SANDERS, FOUNDER, KENTUCKY FRIED CHICKEN

The primary advantages for most companies entering the realm of franchising are capital, speed of growth, motivated management, and risk reduction—but there are many others as well. We often see companies that choose to franchise for a variety of other reasons.

Some business owners choose to franchise because they want to create opportunities for their heirs. Some want to provide additional opportunities to their employees. Some want to build a legacy that will last beyond their lifetime. Some do it purely out of opportunism, because someone has come to them asking to buy a franchise (while it does not happen often, it does happen). And some simply enjoy the challenge of building a business.

Of course, none of those reasons are wrong. Ultimately, your business should be designed to do one thing: to meet your goals (and the goals of your shareholders, if you have them).

And yes, there are disadvantages as well. We'll discuss those later in the chapter.

So ultimately, any decision you make on franchising your business should start with your goals and take both advantages and disadvantages into account.

The Advantages of Franchising

Capital

The most common barrier to expansion faced by today's small businesses is lack of access to capital. Even before the credit-tightening of 2008-2009 and the "new normal" that ensued, entrepreneurs often found that their growth goals outstripped their ability to fund them.

When thinking about financing the growth of company-owned locations, entrepreneurs have typical choices for capital formation: debt or equity. Debt can come from a variety of sources, ranging from banks, leasing companies, friends, relatives, and angels. Even credit cards have provided nervy entrepreneurs the capital they have needed to grow their business—at substantial cost, I hasten to add.

Anyone who has been to a bank recently knows how difficult it is to secure a loan for a new business venture. Unlike the "go-go" days of the 1980s, when banks would often lend a company several times its net worth on little more than a cursory review, banks today are often reluctant to lend even in situations in which they are fully secured. It is tougher than ever for most entrepreneurs to obtain the expansion capital they need from a bank.

Even if an entrepreneur could get the needed capital, one needs only to look over the effects of the Great Recession to fully understand the risks associated with heavy borrowing. Many otherwise profitable companies went under because they could not withstand the debt load they were carrying in a down market. When sales and profits decline, debt service that was once manageable can quickly become impossible to meet.

As an alternative to borrowing, expansion-minded businesses can look to equity markets for growth capital. Equity financing at its simplest involves selling a portion of your company to investors. The influx of capital can go to you personally or can be invested back in the growth of the company. In either case, if you choose to go the equity route, you will lose absolute control of your company.

Again, the first problem is availability. Entrepreneurs usually start by turning to the most obvious sources of equity capital—friends, relatives, and sometimes suppliers. But these sources of funds are quickly exhausted and the process can cause stress in personal relationships.

At this point, some entrepreneurs will turn to the professional investment community to raise capital. Here, too, the first problem they are likely to face is that of availability. Venture capitalists may fund only one business plan out of every 100 or more that they receive. The issues of cost and control are important as well, because while venture capitalists generally do not collect interest, they usually value your company in such a way that provides them a minimum 35 percent annualized ROI. And while most venture capitalists want you to run the company, that will quickly change if you do not make your projections.

Franchising, as an alternative form of capital acquisition, offers some advantages. The primary reason most entrepreneurs turn to franchising is that it allows them to expand without the risk of debt or the cost of equity. First, since the franchisee provides all the capital required to open and operate a unit, it allows companies to grow using the resources of others. By using other people's money, the franchisor can grow largely unfettered by debt.

Moreover, since the franchisee—not the franchisor—signs the lease and commits to various contracts, franchising allows for expansion with virtually no contingent liability, thus greatly reducing the risk to the franchisor. This means that as a franchisor, not only do you need far less capital with which to expand, your risk is largely limited to the capital you invest in developing your franchise company—an amount that is often less than the cost of opening one additional company-owned location.

Motivated Management

Another stumbling block facing many entrepreneurs wanting to expand is finding and retaining good unit managers. All too often, a business owner spends months looking for and training a new manager, only to see them leave or, worse yet, get hired away by a competitor. And hired managers are only employees who may or may not have a genuine commitment to their jobs, which makes supervising their work from a distance a challenge.

But franchising allows the business owner to overcome these problems by substituting an owner for the manager. No one is more motivated than someone who is materially invested in the success of the operation. Your franchisee will be an owner—often with his life's savings invested in the business. And his compensation will come largely in the form of profits.

The combination of these factors can have several positive effects on unit level performance.

- 🦃 *Long-term commitment.* Since the franchisee is invested, she will find it difficult to walk away from her business. If their franchise is going through a rough patch that might cause you to close a company-owned unit, chances are the franchisee will tighten her belt (by working more hours, by using family members as a workforce, by taking a lower salary, etc.) or reinvest in the business, allowing units to stay open through tough times.

- 🦃 *Better-quality management.* As a long-term "manager," your franchisee will continue to learn about the business. When a manager walks out the door, you find yourself needing to replace that knowledge. But a franchisee is less likely to walk and more likely to gain institutional knowledge of your business that will make him a better operator as he spends years, maybe decades, of his life in the business. In fact, some franchisors are seeing second- and even third-generation franchisees as a franchise is passed down from parent to child. Moreover, the average franchisee (who may be a displaced senior executive) tends to be a cut above the average manager (who may be a younger worker looking to learn on the job).

- 🦃 *Improved operational quality.* While there are no specific studies that measure this variable, franchise operators typically take the pride of ownership very seriously. They will keep their locations cleaner and train their employees better. This was driven home to me some years ago when I worked on a study on the impact of franchising for Texaco in the United Kingdom. The company wanted to test the impact of franchising on financial performance and operational quality. So they identified ten locations and ten directly comparable

"sister sites" to act as a control group. They then sold the ten locations as franchises and compared their before-and-after performance
to these sister sites. As expected, we saw an improvement in sales in
the franchise stores—both at the gasoline pump and in the convenience
store itself. But equally interesting, consumer surveys showed a dra-
matic improvement in terms of overall unit operations, including
unit cleanliness, helpfulness of staff, and overall service levels.

◥ *Innovation.* Franchisees, because they have a stake in the success of
their business, are always looking for opportunities to improve their
business—a trait most managers do not share. While franchisees are
not allowed to experiment on product introductions without the
approval of the franchisor, their ideas can help drive the business
forward. For example, at McDonald's, franchisees invented the
Filet-O-Fish, the Big Mac, the Egg McMuffin, the Happy Meal,
the McChicken sandwich, and even Ronald McDonald.

◥ *Franchisees typically out-manage managers.* Franchisees will also keep a
sharper eye on the expense side of the equation. If it is a slow day,
a manager might play cards (or, today, a game on their phone) with
an employee to kill time. A franchisee, on the other hand, will send
that same employee home. In fact, labor costs are generally managed much better in a franchise. Franchisees keep a closer eye on
theft (by both employees and customers), so shrinkage is generally
reduced. And depending on the nature of the business, other line
item expenses may also be reduced.

◥ *Franchisees typically outperform managers.* Over the years, both studies
and anecdotal information have confirmed that franchisees will
outperform managers when it comes to revenue generation. Based
on our experience, this performance improvement can be significant—*often in the range of 10 to 30 percent.* Franchisees are very intent
on running their operation professionally—especially on the sales
side. They always focus on the add-on sale. While a manager may
be reluctant to fire a friend who is not selling up to standards (after
all, it is not his money), a franchisee has no such hesitation. And a
franchisee, who lives and breathes this business, constantly promotes
it in the local community.

Decades ago, I was involved in the transition of Sterling Optical into franchising. The company had recently undergone a leveraged buyout and planned to pay down the debt they had accumulated by selling off some of their 200 operating units as franchises. In the planning process, we realized the easiest way to sell the units off would be to sell them to existing store managers—in fact, we devised a very aggressive internal financing vehicle to accomplish that by letting managers buy units for only 5 percent down. (We later bundled these notes together after we had "aged" the paper for about six months and sold them off to Sanwa Business Credit.)

After selling about 66 locations to franchisees, we had the basis for a wonderful experiment. We had the exact same stores: same locations, traffic, parking, signage, layout, inventory, décor, and staff. Nothing had changed. The only difference was that one day the manager was a manager, and the next day the manager was a franchisee. You can probably guess what happened. While sales at the corporate stores remained relatively flat, sales at these stores increased 32 percent! *That is the power of motivated management.*

Speed of Growth

Every entrepreneur I have ever met who has developed something truly innovative has the same recurring nightmare: that someone else will beat them to the market with their own concept. And often these fears are based on reality. On occasion, we hear stories of people with cameras and notepads sitting in stores blatantly preparing to copy the hard work and ingenuity that went into making that business a success. These entrepreneurs realize that even if they had all the capital they needed to expand, they would probably be unable to do so as fast as they needed to in order to get ahead of their competitors.

The problem is that opening a single unit takes time. Depending on the nature of the business, you may need to hunt for appropriate sites, negotiate leases, arrange for the design and build-out, secure financing, hire and train staff, research local competitors, set pricing, arrange supply channels, purchase equipment and inventory, advertise, and then pray a little. Even if capital was not an issue, the number of units you can open in any given time is limited.

For entrepreneurs, franchising may be the only way to ensure that they capture a market leadership position before competitors encroach on their space, because the franchisee performs most of these tasks. The franchisor provides the guidance, of course, but the franchisee does the legwork. Franchising not only allows the franchisor financial leverage, but also allows it to leverage human resources as well. Franchising allows companies to compete with much larger businesses so they can saturate markets before these companies can respond.

Staffing Leverage

Moreover, franchising allows the franchisor to function effectively with a much leaner organization. Since franchisees will assume many of the responsibilities otherwise shouldered by the corporate home office, franchisors can leverage these efforts to reduce overall staffing. While franchisors will typically have a marketing department, for example, the franchisees will generally coordinate all local advertising. The same holds true for human resources—since the franchisee does all the unit-level hiring, this department is typically far smaller in a franchise organization. For the most part, you can go right down the line of administrative functions—finance, accounting, legal, real estate, etc.—and pretty much assume they would either be more lightly staffed or their functionality would be outsourced within a franchisor organization.

Even areas like field support tend to offer the franchisor staffing advantages. In a corporate environment, the field support function will have responsibility for managerial-level hiring and training, and it will be more deeply involved in daily operations. An area manager might typically be responsible for overseeing five or six corporate locations. In a franchise organization, because the franchisee is usually in place for the long term, these functions are replaced with more of an emphasis on business planning, financial analysis, and key performance indicators. While this will differ from industry to industry, a field support person in a franchise organization might service up to five times as many operating units. And if the field staff is dealing with multi-unit operators (who will have their own field staff), a single field support person for the franchisor might be responsible for a much larger number of operating units.

The combined result is that the overall staffing in a franchise organization will allow the franchisor significant leverage. And again, while these numbers will vary substantially—based on the industry, the type of franchisee targeted, the franchisor's philosophy, the age of the franchisor, etc.—a top-performing franchise organization may have one person on staff for every 11 operating units or so. So a franchisor with 100 units in operation might have only nine people on staff.

Ease of Supervision

From a managerial point of view, franchising provides other advantages as well. For one, the franchisor is not responsible for the day-to-day management of the individual franchise units. Moreover, since a franchisor's income is typically based on franchisees' gross sales, not profitability, monitoring unit-level expenses becomes much less cumbersome.

At a micro level, this means that if a shift leader or crew member calls in sick in the middle of the night, they are calling your franchisee—not you—to let them know. And it is the franchisee's responsibility to find a replacement or cover their shift. Again, from your perspective, if they choose to pay salaries that are not in line with the marketplace, employ their friends and relatives, or spend money on unnecessary or frivolous purchases, it will not impact your financial returns.

Of course, the best franchisors will want to focus on the brand and on franchisee performance. If any of the franchisees' actions impact the brand, you will need to deal with it swiftly and sternly. Likewise, if a franchisee's financial performance is leading to a degradation of potential unit financial performance, that should also be a concern—both from the standpoint of royalty generation and franchisee longevity.

As I will emphasize repeatedly throughout this book, franchisee satisfaction and success are the key to your long-term success as a franchisor. That said, your responsibility is to protect the brand and provide your franchisee with effective coaching on how to improve his financial performance. It is not your job to implement any necessary changes, and, aside from those changes impacting the brand, it is not your responsibility.

By eliminating this responsibility, franchising allows you to direct your efforts toward improving the big picture. Instead of focusing on mundane day-to-day activities, your job as a franchisor is to focus on strategy—both at the micro level (improving unit-level performance) and at the franchisor level.

Increased Profitability

This staffing leverage and ease of supervision allows franchise organizations to run in a highly profitable manner. Since franchisors can depend on their franchisees to undertake site selection, lease negotiation, local marketing, hiring, training, accounting, payroll, and other human resources functions (just to name a few), the franchisor's organization is typically much leaner and often leverages off the organization that is already in place to support company operations. So the net result is that a franchise organization can be much more profitable.

Unfortunately, it is difficult to quantify or prove this contention. Since most franchise companies are privately held, they often choose to minimize the bottom line and minimize their tax burden. Since they often do not maintain their income statements using a consistent chart of accounts, it is difficult to aggregate data across different franchise networks. And since their non-franchise small-business brethren have the same issues *and* do not need to make their financials public, a direct comparison is impossible.

This much we do know: a 2002 Financial Benchmarking Study (published in 2004) prepared by Business Resource Services for the International Franchise Association (IFA) Educational Foundation and a study of 2000 data (prepared by Profit Planning Group and published in 2001) for the IFA showed top quartile franchisors put an average of 40 and 45.6 percent to the bottom line in 2001 and 2002 respectively. I would be the first to note that there was limited statistical validity to these numbers at the time they were produced, and they are now more than a decade old. But that said, how many industries can you think of where net incomes in this range are even possible?

Improved Valuations

The combination of faster growth, increased profitability, and increased organizational leverage helps account for the fact that franchisors are often valued at a higher multiple than other businesses. So when it comes time to sell your business, the fact that you are a successful franchisor that has established a scalable growth model could certainly be an advantage.

Since franchisors can be found in dozens of different industries, it is difficult to conduct this analysis across the spectrum of private industry. But one relatively easy method is to compare publicly traded franchisors to publicly traded companies.

When the iFranchise Group compared the valuation of the S&P 500 versus the franchisors tracked in *Franchise Times* magazine in 2012, for example, the average price/earnings ratio of franchise companies was 26.5, while the average P/E ratio of the S&P 500 was 16.7. This represents a staggering 59 percent premium to the S&P. Moreover, more than two-thirds of the franchisors surveyed beat the S&P ratio.

These numbers are even more astounding when you track the performance of franchise companies over time. The Rosenberg International Franchise Center, for example, has compiled an index of 50 publicly traded franchise companies that they have tracked historically. When comparing the Rosenberg Center Franchise 50 Index to the S&P 500 Index, they found that between 2000 and 2011, the Franchise Index *more than doubled* the performance of the S&P.

From an investor's point of view, it is relatively easy to understand this premium. Franchising allows for much faster growth without an influx of additional capital. Franchise companies can thus grow without incurring cumbersome debt—providing leverage without the associated risk.

When it comes to strategic sales, this leverage is even more important. In a strategic sale, the buyer typically gains an additional advantage from the sale because the franchise channel also provides the buyer with a distribution channel for their products. In the franchise world, not only can the strategic buyer acquire a distribution channel, but each time they sell a franchise, they can also get an otherwise independent business in which they have no investment to commit to a supply relationship that can, in essence, last decades.

Penetration of Secondary and Tertiary Markets

This ability for franchisees to improve unit-level financial performance has some weighty implications. Remember, a typical franchisee will not only be able to generate higher revenues than a manager in a similar location, but will also keep a closer eye on expenses. Moreover, since the franchisee will likely have a different cost structure than you do as a franchisor (she may pay lower salaries, may not provide the same benefits packages, etc.), she can often operate a unit more profitably even after accounting for the royalties she must pay you.

As a franchisor, this can give you the flexibility to consider markets in which corporate returns might be marginal. Of course, you never want to consider a market you do not feel provides the franchisee with a strong likelihood of success. But if your strategy involves developing corporate units in addition to franchising, you will likely find your limited capital development budget will not allow you to open as many locations as you would like. Franchisees, on the other hand, could open and operate successfully in markets that are not high on your priority list for development.

Reduced Risk

Finally, by its very nature, franchising also reduces risk for the franchisor. Unless you choose to structure it differently (and few do), the franchisee has all the responsibility for the investment in the franchise operation. He pays for any build-out, purchases any inventory, hires any employees, and takes responsibility for any working capital needed to establish the business.

Not only is the franchisee responsible for these investments, but generally it is also the franchisee who executes leases for equipment, autos, and the physical location. The franchisee has the liability for what happens within the unit itself, so you are largely out from under any liability for employee litigation (e.g., sexual harassment, age discrimination, EEOC), consumer litigation (the hot coffee spilled in your customer's lap), or accidents that occur in your franchise (slip-and-fall, workers' comp, etc.). The issue of vicarious liability will be discussed in more detail in Chapter 7, a well-constructed franchise should largely allow you to avoid these risks.

Moreover, it is very likely that your attorney and other advisors will suggest you create a new legal entity to act as the franchisor. This will further limit your exposure. And since the cost of becoming a franchisor is often less than the cost of opening one more location (or entering one more market), your startup risk is greatly reduced.

The combination of these factors provides you with substantially reduced risk. Franchisors can grow to hundreds or even thousands of units with limited investment and without spending any of their own capital on unit expansion.

The bankruptcy of Bennigan's in 2008 makes an interesting case. At the time of its bankruptcy, Bennigan's boasted 150 corporate restaurants and 138 franchise locations. When consumers began tightening their belts early in the Great Recession, the losses Bennigan's was incurring in the company locations were simply too great to cover the overhead necessary to support the company. And while Bennigan's had to close their 150 corporate restaurants during the bankruptcy, their franchisees hunkered down. While some of these franchisees failed, most continued to operate—sending royalties to the franchisor. Within months, a new parent company bought the franchise and began repositioning it for growth, with plans to open 50 to 60 new franchises in locations that were previously company-owned. While no one can say for certain, one can speculate that had the majority of units been owned by franchisees, a leaner franchise organization that generated royalties from these franchisees might have stood a much better chance of survival.

The Disadvantages of Franchising

Of course, franchising is not without its drawbacks. Like any other form of business expansion, it comes with certain disadvantages that should be considered when deciding on a growth strategy.

Per-Unit Contribution

As a franchisor, you will not profit from every dollar that goes to the franchisee's bottom line. The revenue you generate from each franchisee will be a fraction of what you might otherwise achieve if you owned and operated the franchise unit yourself.

If you were to open a company-owned location, you would be entitled to 100 percent of the profits from that unit (and, of course, would be responsible for 100 percent of the losses). As a franchisor, your revenues instead come from some combination of royalties, product sales, rebates, advertising assessments, and other fees.

As a franchisor, you might need to sell four to five franchises or more to realize the same financial gain as you would with just one company-owned operation—assuming, of course, that it was profitable. And while your ROI will be immeasurably higher through franchising, you will have the potential for higher total dollar returns if you grow through a company-owned-and-operated channel if you can achieve market saturation without significantly taxing your resources.

The Specter of Litigation

At least once a month, someone tells me they are worried about franchising not for business reasons, but because they are afraid of litigation.

They have all heard the horror stories: McDonald's hit with a multimillion-dollar lawsuit because its coffee was too hot. Franchisees suing franchisors. The Big Bad Wolf is outside the door, in the form of a franchisee attorney, huffing and puffing and threatening to blow your house down.

And it can be scary. Litigation is a fact of life in America, and ignoring that is the business equivalent of building a straw house—good shelter, but not in the long run.

That said, litigation is much less of an issue in franchising than most people imagine it is. A franchisor's contractual liability is largely limited to the commitments you make in your franchise agreement. And if you know what you are doing, your franchise agreement will be written by an attorney who is an expert at limiting that liability. The fact of the matter is that most franchise agreements are decidedly one-sided in favor of the franchisor, making successful litigation very difficult for franchisees.

Let me tell you another story. My business partner at the iFranchise Group, Dave Hood, is the former president of Auntie Anne's. Over a decade or so, he helped grow that company from six to more than 650 locations in the U.S. and another 100 locations internationally. In that time, Auntie Anne's had just one franchise lawsuit—initiated when a franchisee opened a competing location in the Mall of America.

In 2000, Dave moved on and became my partner at the iFranchise Group. Auntie Anne's continued to grow under new leadership. When it was sold to Roark Capital in 2009, they had grown to more than 1,200 locations. And at that time (and I expect this is still true today), they benefited from excellent franchisee relations and have avoided franchisee-initiated litigation for almost two decades at the time of this writing.

The risks of litigation are, in fact, much lower than one would expect, but the headlines make it seem much more prevalent than it is. In fact, the 2004 Litigation Report, a study of franchise disclosure documents by FRANdata, a franchise industry data company, indicated that only 26 percent of franchisors reported *any* litigation. And since some of these franchisors were required to report minor legal problems or litigation that had nothing to do with their franchise contracts, it is fair to say that the threat of litigation from franchisees may be much lower than perceived.

In making the decision to franchise, you should understand that there are legal risks. And while these risks can be minimized, they can never be entirely avoided. In America, anyone can sue anyone for virtually anything. That is just the nature of our legal system. And the more contractual relationships you enter, the more exposure you will have. Period.

> ### ▼ Best Figures Available
>
> While the 2004 Litigation Report is admittedly out of date, it is the only definitive study on the subject we know of, and we expect an analysis conducted today would show similar findings.

At the same time, you also need to understand that there are increased risks of litigation associated with whatever form of business expansion you choose. So by avoiding franchising, you are not avoiding litigation risk; you are simply shifting it elsewhere—unless, of course, you choose not to expand at all.

Compare the risk of litigation with the risks posed by company-owned expansion, for example. If, instead of franchising, you were to open an equal number of company operations, you would avoid the contractual liability associated with franchising. But that would be replaced by different litigation exposure:

➤ As a franchisor, you largely avoid the "slip and fall" liability associated with accidents that happen in a franchisee's place of business. If you open another company-owned facility, that responsibility rests with the business owner—you.

➤ As a franchisor, you will avoid most of the potential "employment liability" associated with company-owned operations (sexual harassment, wrongful termination, etc.). Of course, if you open another company location, that liability falls on you.

➤ As a franchisor, you are not responsible for on-the-job injuries. The responsibility for proper conduct and workplace safety is shifted to your franchisee. Open a company location, and that responsibility is yours.

➤ As a franchisor, you also avoid several areas of peripheral contractual liability. Your franchisee signs the leases for their property and equipment. Your franchisee signs their loans and contracts. Your franchisee is responsible for their tax liability. Again, if you open corporate operations, those potential areas of liability fall to you.

The bottom line is that as long as you are careful that your franchise relationship qualifies as an independent contractor and you have not created an "agency" role or been negligent as a franchisor, your franchisee has the responsibility for virtually everything that happens at her location.

Finally, there are things you can do to minimize (and insure) that risk that we will discuss in Chapter 7.

The Issue of Control

Another possible issue with franchising is the notion that you do not have the necessary level of control over operations to maintain high levels of quality.

As a franchisor, it is fair to point out that you will not have the same level of control over day-to-day operations as you would in a company-owned facility. You are not responsible for hiring, training, disciplining, scheduling, compensating, monitoring, or terminating employees. In virtually every franchise, the franchisee makes the final decision on where to locate the business and which contractors to use for build-out. The franchisee enters into contracts, and although you may specify some suppliers, many suppliers are likely local and discretionary. The franchisee typically makes most decisions in regard to pricing their services.

So with the franchisee making the day-to-day decisions, you may naturally have some fear associated with this loss of control.

Moreover, with company operations, you can hire and fire at your own discretion. In most states and with most employees, you can terminate at will, allowing you to make changes swiftly. But when it comes to terminating a franchisee, you will not have that same level of discretion.

That is not to say that you cannot terminate a franchisee. You can.

So let's talk a little about "the hammer."

When it comes to terminating a franchisee, you will need to show cause, which will amount to some type of violation of the franchise agreement. Moreover, many of the causes that could trigger a franchisee's termination may need to provide the franchisee with an opportunity to "cure" the contract default. So, for example, if you were to walk into a dirty company store, you could fire the manager. If that same store was owned by a franchisee, you might need to send a default letter that would allow them a certain period of time to cure the default (in this case, clean up the store). Of course, some more serious violations of your contract are not curable and can lead to immediate termination.

Generally speaking, any violation of the franchise agreement will be deemed a curable default unless it is specifically listed as noncurable. And the time the franchisee will have to cure the default will vary based on the nature of the violation.

Some examples of noncurable contract default provisions might include (this is not necessarily a comprehensive list):

- Misrepresentations made by the franchisee in the application process
- Falsification of financial data or reporting
- Failure to open a location within a required time frame
- Improper use or disclosure of your confidential information or trademark
- Violations of health or safety standards
- Insolvency
- Felony convictions

- ➤ Failure to cure any default (within a specified period of time) that reflects poorly on the trademark of the franchisor
- ➤ Multiple defaults of contract provisions within the franchise agreement
- ➤ Repeated failing scores (defined by you) on compliance checklists

So, for example, if a franchisee needed a business license to operate, any franchisee who did not have the appropriate license would be in default. They might be given 14 days to cure that violation; failing to obtain the license would be a noncurable default that could subject them to termination.

If a franchisee were to receive a failing score on your compliance checklist, you would send her a default letter that would spell out the problem and give her a period of time to cure the default. If she passed your compliance checklist in your subsequent compliance visit, but failed to pass at a later time, she would go through that same process again—even if the issues that caused the problem were different. But this time, your default letter might specify that a third failure of the compliance audit within a certain period of time would lead to termination.

So, as a franchisor, you will not have the same rights to terminate that you would in a company-owned-and-operated scenario. If you want to terminate a franchisee who is a consistent challenge to work with, you will not have that ability as long as he is in compliance with his contract. But you can control quality.

Remember too, that while the process for terminating a franchisee is more cumbersome, the threat of termination is much more meaningful to a franchisee (who might lose her life's savings) than it would be to a manager, who may have been planning to leave in any event.

And it is once again important to remember that your main tool in controlling a franchisee is his motivation to succeed. Franchisees are highly motivated and take pride in ownership that is difficult to instill in someone without a deep investment. Often, franchisees will run a tighter ship and serve their customers better than their nonfranchisee counterparts. Franchisees are often lifers—staying with their franchisors sometimes for generations. So instead of having to constantly train and retrain employees and hope for the best, franchisees develop a depth of knowledge and experience that is virtually impossible to replicate in a company-owned operation.

The bottom line is that consumers vote with their dollars. And the fact that franchise units generally outperform company operations is a strong indicator that quality levels in franchise locations generally exceed those of their company-owned counterparts.

The Investment in Franchising

Finally, let's not forget that while franchising is often a lower-cost means of expanding a business, it is not a no-cost means of expansion. Starting a new franchise company will require the prospective franchisor to invest in several areas.

As a new franchisor, you may need to anticipate costs (in terms of time and capital) in a number of areas:

- Creating your business plan and financial analysis
- Developing appropriate legal documents
- Developing a franchise operations manual and other quality control documents, systems, and processes
- Creating marketing plans and collateral materials
- Adding a franchise opportunity section to your current website
- Training your people on the franchise process
- Creating a new franchisor legal entity
- Printing brochures, letterhead, and other marketing materials
- Marketing for new franchisees
- Refining your local store marketing materials for use by franchisees
- Negotiating third-party vendor agreements on your franchisees' behalf
- Accounting for franchise sales expenses (which might initially be your time) and perhaps longer-term personnel expenses

For most companies, the costs of developing a franchise business are significantly lower than opening just one more company-owned facility—and the returns can be substantially higher. While the amount of capital needed will be directly related to your goals and your desired rate of growth, you should never go into franchising undercapitalized.

THE BOTTOM LINE

Franchising Is Not Right for Everyone

Franchising embodies the basic philosophy that you are worth more for what you carry in your head than what you can carry on your back. It is about leveraging your intellectual property—your accumulated knowledge—in a way that allows you to get compensated when other people are successful in capitalizing on your knowledge. Franchisees are willing to pay you both for your past successes and failures—their goal is to learn what you have learned without making many of the mistakes you have made along the way.

In the process, franchising allows you to grow at a rate that would be otherwise unachievable. It allows you to benefit from not only the capital of your franchisees, but also their highly motivated nature. And while it is not right for everyone, franchising is, without a doubt, the most dynamic growth vehicle ever invented.

CHAPTER 3

Is Your Business Franchisable?

"There are two ways to get to the top of an oak tree. One way is to sit on an acorn and wait; the other way is to climb it."

—KEMMONS WILSON, FOUNDER, HOLIDAY INN

Now that we know something about what franchising is and how it is regulated, let's take a look at your business and see if it is franchisable—that is, does it have the characteristics of other successfully franchised businesses?

In theory, any established business that can be expanded can also be franchised. But to be successful as a franchise, a concept requires additional qualities. So what are the criteria that set a franchisable business apart? Here are the most important:

- In almost every instance, it needs to have at least one viable *prototype* to show that the concept works.
- It must be *marketable* as a business opportunity. It must appeal to prospective investors who can readily see its potential for themselves. A franchisable business is adequately differentiated from its competitors so that it has a genuine competitive advantage.

⬇ It needs to be *"cloneable."* Could someone of average competence learn to operate the business in three months or less? Are systems in place that can accommodate rapid growth? Are all operating procedures documented? It won't work if the business requires the technical brilliance or artistry of the founder.

⬇ It needs to provide an *adequate return on investment.* In today's demanding marketplace, if a business cannot generate a 15 to 20 percent ROI after deducting a royalty (which typically runs between 4 and 8 percent), it is going to have difficulty keeping franchisees happy and motivated.

⬇ It needs to be *supported.* It is one thing to sell franchises; it's quite another to train and support them over the long haul. Is the management team experienced, knowledgeable, and committed to franchisee success?

If your business meets these criteria, it may be a good candidate for franchising.

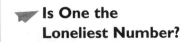

> ⬇ **Is One the Loneliest Number?**
>
> I occasionally get the question, "How many locations do I need before I franchise?" And while having two units of operation is more credible than having one, and three units are more credible than two, there are numerous examples, dating back to McDonald's, that started with a single operation. More recently, when we started working with Massage Envy, they had only one unit in operation, and today they have more than a thousand.

Is Your Business Marketable?

Clearly, you must start by creating a business that people will want to buy, own, and operate.

Called a variety of things—"marketability," "sex appeal," "sizzle"—a franchise should have some quality that makes it appealing to the potential buyer, a "value proposition." Sometimes the value proposition is created by a marketing campaign, sometimes by the look of an operation, and sometimes because it is in a rapidly growing market. It can be created based on the nature of the work involved (like the flexibility offered by a homebased business), the taste of a recipe at a restaurant, or by pure return on investment (ROI).

In scanning the franchise universe, one can readily find franchises that, on their surface, do not seem particularly attractive to potential franchisees. One need look no further than DoodyCalls (yes, they specialize in "pet waste" removal) to realize that not every franchise opportunity is glamorous, sexy, and fun. In the case of DoodyCalls, the combination of a low-investment, home-based business with a service that is in high demand has helped grow the business to *Entrepreneur's* Franchise 500 status. But regardless of the point of differentiation, every business must have something that sets it apart from its competitors—a unique recipe, proprietary products, an innovative marketing approach, or support services for their franchisees—if it hopes to have success in franchising.

Often, the value proposition is created by the nature of the prospective franchisee—like the appeal an optical franchise has to an optician, a sales franchise to a salesperson, or even a pet waste removal franchise to a pet lover. Regardless of how you create your value proposition, as a future franchisor you *must* develop a business that people want to purchase. One great indicator that you have a salable business comes from the unsolicited franchise inquiries you may receive—even if you only get two or three a year. While many successful franchisors never receive these unsolicited leads, for those who do, they are a great indicator of potential franchise sales success.

Moreover, to be salable, a business must have credibility in the eyes of its franchise prospects. That credibility can come from strength of management, a track record of success, publicity, or a number of other places. Remember, franchisees may be investing their life's savings, so without some credibility, franchise sales are impossible.

A business must also be unique—or at least differentiated from its major franchise competitors. This can come in the form of a unique product or service, a reduced investment cost, an exclusive marketing strategy, a different franchise structure or target markets, or any of a number of other factors. However differentiation is achieved, it is imperative that your franchise stands out from its competitors, or it will be difficult to succeed in today's franchise marketplace.

The key is the development of a *unique selling proposition (USP)*—the one thing that will set you apart from every other franchise in the industry. By some counts, there are more than 3,000 active franchisors in the U.S. With that many franchisors to choose from, how do you stand out from the crowd? How does a new franchisor create a USP that will allow them to compete against their better-established brethren?

In the restaurant industry, there are literally hundreds of franchisors offering similar products at similar price points. Virtually all of these restaurants claim some unique recipe that differentiates them from their competitors. Beyond recipes, though, look at how some of these companies position themselves in the market.

For years, people thought no one could succeed in the hypercompetitive burger market (the same thing they said to Dave Thomas when he launched Wendy's, of course). But we have seen restaurants such as Rally's and Checkers thrive by offering their product in a double drive-thru format, reducing their startup and operating costs. We have seen others like Five Guys succeed by focusing on the gourmet burger segment—raising their prices in a highly competitive marketplace to draw customers looking for the best, even if they have to pay more. In the pizza arena, Little Caesars grew to prominence on their two-for-the-price-of-one marketing strategy. Franchisors such as Domino's, Jimmy John's, and a handful of others have differentiated themselves by focusing on delivery services, where their primary competitors focused on dine-in or pickup options.

These strategies have worked well for them. So where are the Mexican and Asian delivery franchises? Uniqueness is usually not about finding a new idea. Often it is about filling an empty niche or using successful old ideas in new combinations.

Finally, in order to be salable, the franchise has to offer the prospective franchisee something of value. In some cases, this can be as simple as the brand name and the systems of operation. But the best franchisors will find additional ways to provide their franchisees with ongoing value. Whether it is advertising support; initial training; negotiated purchasing discounts; proprietary software, products, or recipes; or any of a variety of backroom services the franchisor can provide on behalf of its franchisees, the stronger the value proposition, the easier a franchise will be to sell.

Will They Buy Without Knowing What They Can Make?

As we will see later in this book, the Federal Trade Commission (FTC) rule on franchising does not permit companies to discuss sales or earnings with prospective franchisees unless they have disclosed the numbers in Item 19 of the Franchise Disclosure Documents (FDD). And, in fact, these financial performance representations (FPRs) can be relatively simple to develop and do not have to follow a standard accounting format. For example, hotels will often discuss occupancy rates, restaurants may limit their disclosure to food and labor costs, or service businesses might discuss the "average ticket." So you can choose to disclose whatever you want as long as it is true and not misleading.

That said, there are some companies that choose not to disclose past performance—perhaps because it would not be representative of franchisee performance or because they do not want to make that information publicly available. And, of course, it seems obvious (and in fact is true) that most franchisees will ask how much they can earn early in the buying process.

While we will deal with overcoming these questions in Chapter 11: Selling Franchises, rest assured that you can franchise your business whether or not you do an FPR. As recently as several years ago, only about 30 percent of franchisors provided FPRs. And while that number is on the rise,

the iFranchise Group surveyed the Fast 55 a few years ago, publishing the results in *Franchise Times*; we found no statistically significant correlation between inclusion on this list of the fastest-growing new concepts and the use of an FPR.

 FPRs Widely Used

By some estimates, about 60 percent of franchisors now do FPRs. And in some industry segments, that number is even higher.

But I Am Not Really Unique

The other question that is often asked in the context of salability is the question of uniqueness. And while we will address the question of creating a USP in Chapter 9, it is worth pointing out here that few of the major successful franchising brands are actually unique.

Consider the following:

- All the top real estate franchises—Century 21, ERA Real Estate, Coldwell Banker—employ licensed professionals doing exactly the same job, so what really differentiates them at the consumer level?
- All the top brands in janitorial services—each of which has thousands of locations—are franchised: Jani-King, Jan-Pro, and ServiceMaster Clean.
- All the top carpet cleaning brands are franchised: Chem-Dry, Rainbow International, COIT, and more—all with thousands of franchises.
- All the top lawn care companies are franchised: Scotts, TruGreen, U.S. Lawns, Weed Man, and more.

You get the idea. While many of these companies have big names now, they did not when they started. And yet, through good marketing and franchise support networks, they sold thousands and thousands of franchises, despite offering a service that is far from unique. So while it is great to have a unique concept, few of us really do.

Is Your Business "Cloneable"?

Franchising starts with a successful concept. But not every successful concept can be duplicated. Some businesses are too complex. Some are too regional. Some are too regulated.

Of course, as a franchisor, you will not be offering your franchisees any guarantees or assurances of success. Nonetheless, nothing is more important to your success as a franchisor than the success and happiness of your franchisees. So the ability to duplicate your success is vital to a franchisor with aspirations of rapid growth.

First and foremost, a business must be readily teachable. In order to franchise, a franchisor must be able to thoroughly educate a prospective franchisee in a relatively short period of time. If your business is so complex that it cannot be taught to a franchisee in three months, you may have difficulty franchising—although there are occasional examples of franchisors with lengthier training programs. Franchisees want to be taught the business quickly, as they will be burning through their working capital while waiting for their doors to open.

Never was the "keep it simple" principle more important than in the franchise environment—especially if your franchise profile is focused on individuals with little or no prior business ownership experience. Your franchisees will come to you from very different backgrounds. Many will not have the requisite skills or experience to run a business when they first start with you. In fact, it is just this lack of experience that will bring them to your door in the first place.

If, for example, your concept requires a Le Cordon Bleu chef who makes different specialties every day based on the availability of local produce, it is unlikely that you can maintain consistency across the brand. And that consistency of consumer experience is the lifeblood of franchising.

That said, some well-known franchisors have overcome this obstacle by targeting only franchise prospects who are already educated in their business area. Medical and dental franchises, for example, target doctors and dentists, focusing their training only on the business systems. Similarly, law firms, insurance companies, real estate firms, and others have franchised by targeting already-licensed professionals. More complex restaurants will often target only experienced restaurateurs to ensure quality control. The downside of this strategy, of course, is that the franchisor's prospect pool is greatly reduced—but for these franchisors, this is the only approach that does not sacrifice quality.

Another alternative would be for the franchisor to consider simplifying the business: a restaurateur might reduce the menu or arrange for third-party production of spice packets and sauces that make food preparation and quality more reliably uniform. The franchisor might divide the business into different components or segments, with the franchisee responsible for certain aspects (for example, sales) and the franchisor responsible for others (for example, service fulfillment).

A second measure of concept duplicability is the degree to which a concept can be adapted from one market to the next. Some concepts, for example, are successful only after years of perseverance and relationship building. Some work only because of the unique abilities or talents of the individual behind the concept. Still others work only because they have found a unique location—such as an Elvis memorabilia store near Graceland, a waterfront dining concept, or a business that succeeds because of an once-in-a-lifetime lease.

Some concepts will have significant regional variations in demand due to taste or geography. For example, a lawn care or pool cleaning franchise will have a shorter season in the North than in the South. Some concepts such as medical practices, child care, teaching facilities, and liquor stores will be constrained by varying state laws that can impact a business model.

Some restaurant concepts are constrained by regional tastes. Barbecue, for example, tends to be prepared very differently from region to region. In South Carolina, barbecue means pulled pork with a mustard-based sauce. Try to sell that in Texas, where barbecue means beef, and you might be hanged from the nearest mesquite tree.

In Cincinnati, Skyline Chili and Gold Star Chili have made their reputations based on a "five-way" chili—a concoction of spaghetti, chili, beans, onions, and cheese—that wouldn't even be recognized as chili in some parts of the country. Unique? Certainly. But does it have mass appeal? In the case of Gold Star and Skyline, both have franchised successfully but limited their growth to those markets in which their regional brands are most likely to succeed.

Concepts with these types of adaptability constraints can still be expanded through franchising as long as the business model (or an adaptation of the business model) can be made to work from a financial perspective. There are numerous lawn care franchises with locations in colder climates (Spring-Green, TruGreen, etc.) despite the shorter lawn-care season. There are medical franchises operating in multiple state venues (AFC/Doctors Express). There are child-care and education franchises (Sylvan Learning, The Goddard School, and Kumon) throughout the country, and barbecue chains (Sonny's BBQ, Famous Dave's) that have expanded despite the regionalism of their core product. So while these regional differences do not prevent concepts from franchising, they should certainly be taken into account when a franchise strategy is being developed.

If a franchisor has a concept that does not travel well, it must evaluate the nature of the business, determine exactly what has made it successful, and identify and consider any factors that might constrain its replication before determining its franchise expansion strategy.

Another important factor in cloneability is the degree to which the business has developed systems to help ensure the franchisee's success. All successful businesses have systems. But the question is not whether these systems exist, but *where* they exist. Are they simply in the owner's head? Or have they been properly and thoroughly written down?

In order to be franchisable, the systems integral to the operation of a business must be documented in a way that communicates these systems effectively to franchisees. This form of documentation should minimally come in the form of a user-friendly operations manual that includes policies, procedures, forms, performance standards, compliance checklists, and business best practices. And, for franchisors looking to grow more aggressively, this documentation will often include formal training programs, training videos, train-the-trainer programs, and online training programs (often referred to as learning management systems).

The documentation of these systems is essential for several reasons. First, without documented systems, it will be impossible to train your franchisees consistently. Moreover, as employee turnover occurs, the lack of documented systems will create variations in unit-level performance that will only increase over time. But most important, without these documented systems, you, as a franchisor, will be unable to enforce any of your standards from a legal perspective.

Note: Many new franchisors do not have this documentation in place, nor do they have the time or expertise necessary to develop it. Because of the various liability issues that are intertwined with this documentation, we always recommend that all such documentation is either prepared or reviewed by a professional. (Read more on developing quality control documentation and the various liability issues in Chapter 8.)

The Acid Test: Return on Investment

The acid test of franchising, however, is return on investment. A franchise business must, of course, be profitable. But a profitable prototype is not enough. A franchise business must allow enough profit *after* a royalty (or any other fees or incremental product markups) for the franchisees to earn an acceptable return on their investment of time and money. So a business that offers an acceptable return to you as an entrepreneur may not provide adequate returns to your franchisee once you have assessed your fees as a franchisor.

Profitability, of course, is relative. A franchisee's profitability—either as a stand-alone dollar amount or a percentage of sales—is not the relevant number. There are, for example, grocery store franchises where the franchisee's potential return can be as low as 4 percent, yet the franchisee is making a good return on their investment.

Profitability must be measured against the capital invested to provide a meaningful number. A franchisee who invested tens of millions in opening a hotel franchise might be very upset if he or she made a return of $200,000 a year, while a franchisee who invested $100,000 to open a service-based business would be thrilled. In this way, the franchise investment can be measured against other investments of comparable risk that compete for the franchisee's dollar. To be competitive in today's franchise marketplace, the iFranchise Group generally looks for the franchisee to achieve an ROI of at least 15 percent by the second to third year of operation. And, if the franchisor is targeting area-development or multi-unit operators, it will need to provide a higher return at the unit level to offset the incremental overhead associated with multiple unit management.

It is important to note that these returns must be calculated after deducting a market-rate salary for the owner-operator franchisee, since the franchisee's alternative to buying your franchise is to invest his money *and* get a job. So he is entitled to a return on both his money and his time.

It is also important to remember that in calculating the ROI, adjustments must be made to capture the different financial considerations a franchisee will have when running the business.

To assess the potential return of a franchise business, we recommend the franchisor look at franchisee ROI from a cash-on-cash perspective. Thus, the franchisor would assume that the franchisee is not financing any of the initial investment, but instead plunking down cash for all the startup expenses—including the franchise fee and working capital. While this is generally not the way a franchise is purchased, this method has the advantage of taking the franchisee's various financing options out of consideration, as well as other non-cash factors such as depreciation and amortization.

Likewise, if land and building are involved in a franchise opportunity, we generally recommend the calculation be based on a leased facility— and that the costs of land and construction are excluded. While there are some exceptions, the rationale for this recommendation is that the franchisee's decision to buy land and build is a separate investment. He is purchasing the land and building presumably because he feels he can obtain a separate return on that investment in the long term—not because he has to do so.

Finally, our shorthand version of this calculation does not account for the terminal value of the assets being developed by the franchisee, but instead looks only at the cash-on-cash ROI in any given year (usually year two or three) at "maturity." The reasoning is that a profitable business will be sold as a going concern and will generally command a multiple of earnings. Just as an investment in a stock or a bond eventually anticipates the recapture of the initial investment, a franchisee anticipates that she will someday sell her business for more than she initially invested in it. And if the franchisee achieves a 15-percent rate of return on the business, she would need to achieve an earnings multiple of only 6.7 to recoup her initial investment. Since this is not unreasonable (and a higher multiple would provide a less conservative approach), this shorthand version of the ROI analysis is both simpler and more conservative.

That said, our version of franchisee ROI is calculated as the adjusted cash flow of a particular investment in a franchise, expressed as a percentage of that investment. To get to that percentage, one would divide the adjusted return by the estimated investment:

Adjusted Cash Flow ÷ Total Cost of Investment = ROI

At the iFranchise Group, we conduct this analysis with virtually all of our prospective franchisors prior to accepting an engagement because we feel it will be such a major factor in their success. Remember,

Calculating ROI

Technically, the formula for ROI is defined as (Gain From Investment-Total Investment)/ Total Investment. As such, a true ROI cannot be calculated until the hypothetical franchisee sells the franchise at some point in the future. ROI, as I have used the term in this book, assumes that the hypothetical franchisee will sell the business at some point in the future for the exact amount of the initial investment and that the profits generated by the franchise remain relatively constant over the years. So the ROI represents the annualized cash-on-cash returns a franchisee could realize from his investment in the business. Likewise, as a part of this calculation, we do not include the cost of land or buildings (if either will be purchased by the franchisee), as the purchase of either is a separate investment decision made on the assumption that these investments will increase in value over time. The actual finance formula I use for ROI is more akin to the formula for dividend yield.

though, that it will be up to the individual franchisee to work out these finances on their own, as disclosure laws prohibit projections of profitability unless presented properly in Item 19 in the FDD.

The first thing we need to determine is what a franchisee will have to invest to obtain a particular franchise. This yields the total number required by Item 7 of an FDD and is a good reality check for the new franchisor. The number should include all the costs incurred in starting an operation from the ground up, including any equipment, build-out, or inventory costs. You will also want to include an estimate of any initial franchise fee you will charge and any cash flow expenses the new franchisee will incur for initial advertising, personnel recruiting, training expenses, and the initial salaries and rent the franchisee will need to pay prior to achieving break-even.

It is important to project costs in current dollars to make them relevant. A founding entrepreneur may have bootstrapped his own growth by buying used equipment, acting as his own general contractor, starting with an unsuitable office space, etc. However, as a franchisor, you will expect your franchisee to enter your business based on your current standards of operation—not based on the costs you incurred when you got started. The result will serve as your denominator to the equation above.

Once you have calculated your franchisee's projected initial investment, you will need to make some adjustments to your current income statement to calculate a franchisee's projected return. If you have multiple units in operation, start by looking at the unit or units you feel are the most representative of franchisee performance. You do not want to look at a best-case scenario that franchisees are not likely to achieve consistently. Likewise, you do not want to be overly conservative, as this will adversely affect your ultimate fee and royalty structure. The goal is to start with your best estimate of annual franchisee financial performance once a unit is mature, with the caveat that the franchisee will need to make their requisite return by year three or sooner.

You will then need to make some adjustments for franchising. The primary adjustments you should consider are:

- *Normalize the manager's salary.* If you as an owner-operator are taking a larger salary than you might pay a hired manager (or are paying longtime employees a higher-than-average salary and/or benefits), you would adjust that salary downward. Conversely, if you are not yet taking a salary (or taking a below-market salary), you would adjust it upward.
- *Adjust expense items.* Look at each and every expense line item on your income statement to see if a franchisee's expenses will vary from yours. For example, if the franchisee will own a single location, but your income statement shows the cost of a vehicle to move inventory between multiple locations, you should eliminate that line item.
- *If your franchisee will be buying equipment or goods from you at a markup,* you need to increase their "anticipated cost of goods sold" line. If the franchisee will be paying more (or less) for rent, for example, you would need to take that into account.
- *Eliminate any expenses a franchisee will not incur.* Franchisees will not, for example, have costs associated with a separate administrative office or field support team, if you have those expenses allocated in your income statement. They will not incur certain legal expenses,

such as trademark work, but you will want to include the expenses of incorporation or any locally required licensing or bonding.

- *Eliminate any one-time-only or investment expenses* that show up as an expense item on your income statement.

- *Eliminate any financing expenses such as interest.* Since you will be conducting this analysis on a cash-on-cash basis, it's assumed that the franchisee will not need to finance anything.

- *Eliminate any non-cash expenses such as depreciation and amortization.* These expenses help reduce taxes but do not alter the franchisee's cash flow.

- *Eliminate any allocations for income taxes*, as these taxes would need to be paid on any alternative ROI.

- *Confine expenses added to those pertaining to business operations.* Do not include extraneous tax minimization strategies you may have employed for your personal benefit (automobiles, entertainment, insurance above an industry norm, etc.).

- *Add to your expense line an approximation* of royalties, contributions to a system marketing fund, or other fees you will assess your franchisees.

Once you have made these adjustments, you will have an approximation of your franchisee's adjusted return that can be used in the numerator when calculating ROI. With revenue and investment figured, you can now calculate the projected ROI. As stated above, the iFranchise Group typically looks for the franchisee to achieve an ROI of at least 15 percent by the second (or at a minimum, by the third) year of operations—and franchisees with multiple units will need a somewhat higher return at the unit level to cover the overhead associated with multiple-unit operation.

The return offered by a franchise opportunity should be commensurate with the franchisee's associated risk. If, for example, you could anticipate a 25 percent ROI with a lower risk, a logical investor would take the low-risk investment every time. As perceived risk increases, so must anticipated return.

The implication is thus that franchisors with long and successful track records do not need to offer the same anticipated return as would a newly established franchisor. Thus, all other things being equal (which, by the way, they never are), a pure return-oriented franchise prospect would only buy a startup franchise in which they perceive the potential for a greater return.

There are, of course, additional returns available to the franchisee. There is the "psychic" return a franchisee gets by being her own boss and building a substantial business. And there may be similar psychic returns associated with the nature of the work. So there are occasional opportunities where the financial rewards may fall short yet still provide the franchisee with an adequate "return."

But in the vast majority of cases, if your business does not meet these return criteria, don't franchise. Period.

Other Factors Affecting Success

Of course, just because a business is franchisable does not mean the franchisor will succeed. Like any other business, there are literally hundreds of things that can impact the franchisor's likelihood of success. Of those hundreds, most fall into one of three major categories: market trends, capital, and management.

Market Trends and Conditions

Market trends and conditions, of course, play a key role in the success or failure of any company. Is the market growing or consolidating? How will that affect your business in the future? Who are your competitors? How are they positioned? Is your offer unique (in which case, you will want to move quickly), or are you generally undifferentiated from larger, better-established competitors with more resources? Who will be your competitors in the future? How will you differentiate yourself at the franchise level and the consumer level? How will trends in the market and the competitive environment affect your franchisee's likelihood of long-term success?

Many new franchisors succeed by answering market questions at a local level before moving on to national expansion. By focusing on the competition in their immediate vicinity, they can bring all their forces to bear in a single market. So even if there are national competitors present, the resources the local player is devoting to expansion may—in that one market—be greater than those of the national players. And by starting a franchise program locally or regionally, you can increase your size, resources, and competitive strength, allowing your business to compete more effectively as it expands outside your current area.

As a new franchisor with national aspirations, however, these questions become much more complex. Instead of competing with every similar concept within an hour's drive, you could be competing with every similar concept in the world's most competitive franchise marketplace.

Capital

While franchising is a relatively low-cost means of expanding a business, it is not a no-cost means of expansion. A franchisor needs the capital and resources to implement a franchise program and support the franchisees operating under the brand. Again, the savvy franchisor would be well-advised to remember that it is essentially starting a new business.

The resources required to initially implement a franchise program will vary depending on the scope of the expansion plan. If a company is looking to grow slowly and locally, the necessary legal documentation may be completed relatively inexpensively. Add to that the costs of developing an operations manual and some modest franchise marketing expenses, and a company could conceivably start franchising—with first-class legal and operations documentation—for less than $50,000.

For franchisors targeting aggressive expansion, however, startup costs can easily run $100,000 or more. And once the costs of printing, audits, marketing, and personnel are added to the mix, a franchisor may require a much more substantial budget. (For more on the costs of franchising, see Chapter 13.)

Whatever you do, make sure you have a sound budget and adequate resources when you get started. The worst possible strategy involves counting on franchise sales (and their associated fees) to fund your growth, as this often leads to selling franchises to underqualified candidates, which can result in the failure of the system. (See "The Importance of Franchisee Success" in Chapter 12.)

Management

Finally, the single most important aspect contributing to the success of any franchise program is the strength of its management team.

Good management will modify businesses to better meet the criteria of franchisability. It will develop and enhance the franchise value proposition. It will recruit a strong support team—using internal or external resources—to develop and implement a franchise program. It will adapt to market conditions, raise the necessary capital, and candidly recognize its shortcomings and organizational gaps. It will retain outside experts and recruit knowledgeable internal staff who can help get their company to the next level.

In the context of franchising, good management also means that the owner(s) and management team understand the core principles of franchising and are capable of and committed to the development of strong and long-lasting relationships with the franchisees they recruit. Over the years, we've seen many highly educated and capable management teams that, on paper, would impress any prospective franchisees. However, some of these teams performed very poorly in terms of the leadership they have provided to the franchisee community. As a result, their franchise programs floundered (or even worse, failed), due to the franchisor and franchisees not being aligned in their mission and values.

There is no cure for bad management. The rule of thumb is that great management can make a mediocre concept succeed, but bad management is certain to destroy even the best concept. Behind most successful franchise systems is a qualified management team that provides strong leadership to the franchisee community.

Erecting Barriers to Entry and Planning for Change

The successful franchisor must anticipate and adapt to changes in the competitive landscape over time.

The more successful your company is, the more certain you can be that knockoffs will follow you into the consumer and franchise marketplace. Smart franchisors will anticipate these newcomers and do everything they can early in the process to erect barriers to entry, adapt to the new marketplace, and stay one step ahead of the competition.

Establishing barriers to entry can be as simple as being first to the market and establishing a dominant brand position. Or it can be as complex as obtaining a business process patent. It can be a recipe, a product, or an attitude. But if you have an undifferentiated product or service with low barriers to entry, your business will quickly become commoditized. And if this happens, you will have a difficult time maintaining a leadership position—let alone the kind of growth that will help you achieve industry prominence.

The aspiring mega-franchisor must remember that even McDonald's did not become McDonald's overnight. When the company first started franchising, it had a much more limited menu. It did not have Big Macs, Filet-O-Fish sandwiches, or salads. It did not have Ronald McDonald. It did not have drive-thru windows, and it did not serve breakfast. But it continued to adapt and thrive and overcome the competition day after day, year after year, and it is still evolving to meet the changing consumer—and franchise—marketplace.

Of course, there are a thousand hurdles to overcome on the road to success, but with the right planning and enough time, your company could be the business that everyone emulates years from now.

THE BOTTOM LINE

Franchisee Success Dictates Your Success

A franchisor's first and most important responsibility is to provide a concept, brand, and support structure that will allow its franchisees to succeed. If your franchisees succeed, you will likely succeed as a franchisor.

Unfortunately, the converse is also true. While no business is failure-proof, you will want to be sure you have provided your franchisees with the tools they need to succeed.

If there is a single axiom in franchising, it is this: If your franchisees fail, you will fail as a franchisor.

Failing franchisees require more support (and thus cost more). They pay less money in the way of royalties (if they pay them at all) and purchase fewer products from you. They will drain your staff resources. And they will provide poor validation when they are contacted by your prospects in the sales process.

The corollary is also true. Successful franchisees are, perhaps more than anything else, responsible for your long-term success as a franchisor.

They will become your best sales tool. They will expand into additional locations, and they will refer others in their network to become franchisees in your system. As a result, they can dramatically reduce your overall cost of candidate lead generation.

Ultimately, a franchise must operate as a "win–win–win" environment if it is to be successful. First, the customer must get value for his or her money and have a positive experience with your brand. Then the franchisee must make an attractive return and respect you as the franchisor. And, finally, the franchisor must prosper. This is the equation that makes for a successful franchise network.

CHAPTER 4

Is Franchising Right for You?

"The two most important requirements for major success are: first, being in the right place at the right time, and second, doing something about it."

—RAY KROC, FOUNDER, MCDONALD'S

Just because a particular business *can* be franchised doesn't mean it *should* be franchised.

As a business strategy, franchising is a tool designed to help business owners reach more aggressive expansion goals. If your goals exceed your current grasp, you need to find a way to leverage your business to meet those goals—or you need to redefine your goals. And often, when aggressive growth goals are involved, franchising is the best answer.

Defining Personal Goals

Whenever I meet with an entrepreneur interested in franchising, I ask, "Where do you want to be in five years?" Perhaps unsurprisingly, most entrepreneurs have never given any thought to the question before. But to determine which growth strategy is best, I need to understand three things:

their personal goals of ownership, the assets (both human and capital) they can devote to achieving those goals, and the time frame within which they hope to accomplish them. Armed with that knowledge, the strategy you will choose is often just a matter of plugging in the numbers.

In determining goals, business owners often tell me they "want to grow as fast as possible without sacrificing quality." But such "goals" are not really goals at all, but statements of ownership philosophy. In order to use goals as a foundation for your decision making, they must be concrete, measurable, and tied to a specific time frame.

So start by asking yourself where you want to be in five years. You need to be specific, and you should ideally have a reason. For example, people will often answer my question by saying, "I want to open 100 locations in the next five years." And while this is the type of specific goal that will help in the planning process, it raises the question: "Why?"

Do you remember the line from *Cool Hand Luke*? George Kennedy's character turned to Paul Newman's Luke after he bet he could eat 50 eggs and asked, "Why you got to go and say 50 eggs for? Why not 35 or 39?" To which Luke replied, "I thought it was a nice round number." When planning for your business, however, I would urge you not to take the Cool Hand Luke approach.

Instead, I encourage my clients to start by asking "lifestyle" questions. Do you still want to be working in the business in five years? Do you want to sell the business? Are you looking to pass this company on to your heirs? If you are looking to cash out, how much money is "enough"—not only for the time and effort you will have devoted to developing the business, but for you to move on with the next phase of your life? And if you want to hold on to your business, how much would you like to be earning at a certain point in the future?

When you ask yourself how much you want for your business when you sell, it is important that you *do not* ask how much you think it will be worth. Valuation should not enter this process until later. Instead, ask yourself where you want to be personally. Do you want to retire? If so, do you want to be living on your private island collecting shells? Or would you be happy on a golf course somewhere? Or do you want to open a new business and move on?

Once you have painted the picture in your mind of where you want to be, you should ask yourself how much money it will take for you to achieve that goal. Add up the house, the private island, the cars, the retirement fund, and whatever other personal goals that require money, and you will have your number. Whether your number is a selling price for the business or a desired level of future earnings is irrelevant.

Once you have your number, the next step is to determine where the business is now. How well-defined is the concept? How much money is it currently making, and what is the current value of the business? What are its financial and human resources? How strong is the management team? Is it ready for expansion?

Once you have answers to these two variables, you can measure the distance between your current reality and the goal you have set. And that distance, combined with an understanding of your goals, capabilities, and time frame, will dictate your strategy.

Deciding on Direction: An Example

Let's say you have a small business generating $600,000 in sales and bringing about $100,000 to the bottom line after paying yourself a market-rate salary of $50,000 for your role as manager. Over the years, you have managed to save $150,000 (at a rate of about $10,000 a year) that you are willing to invest. Let's further say you could start a second unit for an initial investment of about $200,000, and you are confident you can borrow the balance of $50,000 from your banker. You are also confident you can duplicate the performance of your first unit if you open another company location. On the other hand, you could invest $100,000 or so in the development of a franchise company and have some working capital left over to fund your franchise marketing and startup expenses. In either event, you have the capital and are prepared to invest. Both management and concept are in place and ready for expansion. The market appears to be ripe.

Should you franchise now or open a second company-owned operation?

The simple truth is you are not yet in a position to answer this question—not until you have established where you want to be five years from now.

Let's add some information and see how it changes our perspective. Let's say you are 55 years old and want to retire at age 65. You own the business with your wife, who does not work in the business. With your house paid off, you figure you will need $150,000 per year to live comfortably in retirement. You and your wife have decided that at 65, you will sell the business and focus on your golf game. Looking at your assets, you have estimated that your Social Security and other investments will yield around $80,000 per year in retirement, so the gap between your goal and your current position is about $70,000—and that will need to come from the business.

The next step is to research the selling price for the average small business in your market. For this example, we will assume it would sell for between five and seven times earnings. You could then estimate that the current value of your business is between $500,000 and $700,000. And if you continued your current savings plan of $10,000 a year, you could add $100,000 to your existing $150,000 nest egg, and with interest, you might have additional savings of $350,000 or more. If you were to sell the business for $500,000 (a conservative estimate) and made 5 percent on your total assets of $700,000 (after the tax man took his piece), you could close the gap by $35,000—but you would still be $35,000 short of your goal.

But if you invested the $150,000 in a second unit and took on $50,000 in debt to do so, that might earn an additional $100,000 per year. After debt service and taxes, you might be able to save an additional $50,000 per year—perhaps a little over $600,000 with interest over the next ten years. And with the debt service paid off and two units earning a combined $200,000, you could sell the business for between $1 million and $1.4 million in ten years. After taxes, your combined assets might total $1.5 million to $1.6 million. So if you could earn 5 percent on that money, you could swing the retirement of your dreams.

So should you open one more company-owned location, or just continue to run your existing business and scale down your retirement plans?

Actually, we still do not have enough information—although we are getting close.

What we have not yet addressed is risk. Investing your life's savings and borrowing another $50,000 could completely derail your retirement plans if the second location were to fail. So while you have now narrowed your options, the final call will boil down to risk. If you are risk-averse, you can continue on your current path and reduce your goals. Or you can stretch out the timetable on those goals a little farther into the future and postpone your retirement. Or, if you have a great level of confidence in the second unit or a higher tolerance for risk, you can invest in a second company location—and you would not even need to consider franchising as a growth strategy.

As a counterpoint, let's say you have a business, assets, and capabilities that are identical to this first example, but you are a hard charger. Based on your personal goals, you want to sell your business for $10 million in five years instead of ten—and you will settle for nothing less. Using the same rules of thumb on business valuation, you know you will need earnings of between $1.4 million and $2 million in year five to achieve that goal.

Maintaining the status quo will not get it done.

Moreover, aggressively investing in company-owned growth will fall far short as well. Based on the availability of bank financing, it is unlikely you could leverage your growth enough to open the 10 to 15 company-owned locations (after accounting for incremental overhead) it would take to achieve your goal. If you were willing to take on an equity partner, you would have to find someone who was willing to invest $3 million or more (after accounting for reinvestment) to grow the chain to 25 to 30 locations (after accounting for the dilution of your equity) in return for 50 percent of a business that is worth $600,000 in today's market. That's a lot of "blue sky" to sell—and frankly, you would be very unlikely to raise it.

In this instance, franchising (or a combination of franchising plus company-owned growth) would likely be the *only* strategy that will allow you to achieve your financial goals.

The business economics of becoming a franchisor, of course, would be quite different. If you were a franchisor, you might receive a 5 percent royalty on revenues, generating $30,000 in revenue per franchise—so the contribution per operating unit will be much lower.

A variety of factors will need to be considered before finalizing a franchise growth plan that will achieve the same goal, including the time it takes for franchisees to open units, average unit volume (remember that franchisees typically outperform managed units), royalty rates, franchise fees, support structure, rebates, product sales to franchisees and the associated margin on that product, structure of the franchise (area development, sub-franchise, etc.), organizational gaps, and organizational growth and staffing plans. It is also important to consider that franchisors generally receive considerably higher business valuations based on their faster growth. But it could well be that the franchisor might need to sell 100 to 150 franchises to achieve the same valuation.

While this rate of growth is aggressive for a new franchisor, it can be achieved given the right concept, a capable management team, and a well-executed franchise plan. And if you do not want to put more capital at risk or have decided you do not want to expand outside your current markets, the franchise-only strategy would be the one you would likely choose to take.

If your top priority is maximizing company valuation (as opposed to reaping the fruits of your hard work as you grow), you may also want to examine franchising your business first and then reinvesting your profits from franchising in a combination of more aggressive franchise growth *and* opening additional company-owned locations. While nothing will beat the pure ROI of franchising, opening additional company units can give you an opportunity to develop prime markets, seed new markets with corporate locations (helping your franchise efforts), and test new prototypes or new types of locations—all while growing your balance sheet. And as long as your corporate growth does not adversely impact the speed of your franchise expansion, the combination of franchising plus corporate growth can provide you with the highest valuations.

And of course, a big part of developing your franchise plan will be answering all of these questions and deriving an appropriate growth plan.

Evaluating Risk

Of course, there is more to making the decision than simply an assessment that other alternatives will not work. You should also have a reasonable belief that franchising offers you a good chance of success. Business success does not occur in a vacuum. So before making a decision to move ahead, you would be well-advised to examine what your competition is doing in the marketplace.

Essentially, what we are doing here is measuring risk. In the scenario above, franchising may be the only strategy that will allow you to sell your business for $10 million. But if your chances of success are one in ten, you may want to rethink your growth goals rather than embarking on such a high-risk strategy.

Quantifying risk involves an analysis of those factors most likely to be responsible for franchise failure. The big three are market, money, and management. Thus, before finalizing your decision, you should be sure you understand the factors that will influence your success or failure.

Market

When examining the market into which you are expanding, you should look at the sustainability of demand, differentiation of your concept, and existing and potential competitors. If you are going to go head-to-head with entrenched competitors in a mature industry, you will need to get your franchise concept as close to perfect as possible before entering the franchise marketplace. Operations procedures and management techniques should be tight. Store design and marketing materials should be first-rate. Furthermore, before you consider franchising, you need a strong track record of successful operation. In short, you must be able to offer potential franchisees advantages at least comparable to, if not better than, those offered by your competitors.

No franchise industry is more mature than fast food hamburgers: it includes Burger King, Wendy's, and the granddaddy of them all, McDonald's. If you want to compete with these industry giants, the concept will need to be extremely innovative and appealing. This is not an industry in which a five-unit hamburger chain can easily compete for franchises. Yet every market is always big enough for a competitor that carves a unique niche.

When Five Guys Burgers and Fries began franchising in 2002, they were going up against these giants. And while they had a 16-year track record behind them, they only had five units in operation. In order to succeed, Five Guys took the time to refine their concept and differentiate themselves in the marketplace. While the Big Three fought the Burger Wars with $1 burgers, Five Guys served fresh (never frozen) made-to-order burgers with generous portions of hand-cut fries to command a premium price. And in the process, they developed an unassailable position. They knew, perhaps instinctively, that McDonald's, Burger King, and Wendy's could never afford to abandon their existing systems. Thirteen years later, with 1,000 stores and $1 billion in revenues, they have not yet reached king of the hill status, but their reasoned approach to timing their franchise decision has turned them into one of the most successful franchise companies in America.

Today, this gourmet burger segment is being plowed by others, as it is increasingly viewed as a separate category by consumers. Companies that are less than a decade old are now vying to be part of this distinct market. Elevation Burger is on track for more than 100 locations, and Smashburger has more than 300. And while others like The Counter, BGR, and BurgerFi are entering the fray, the iconic brand In-N-Out Burger, which has owned this segment since 1948 and now boasts 300 units, remains steadfastly on the franchise sidelines—just as White Castle did when McDonald's decided to franchise years ago.

The examples of how fast a mature market can be redeveloped through niche marketing are everywhere—especially when a concept has low barriers to entry. Another recent example that comes to mind is the market for tart frozen yogurt. For years, the market had been dominated by TCBY and was seeing little in the way of growth. But when a new tart yogurt concept was introduced, the market exploded. Today, there are more than a dozen concepts in this space, many with more than 100 locations, including Pinkberry, Red Mango, Menchie's, sweetFrog, Orange Leaf, and Yogurtland.

Once a market is beset by a substantial number of competitors, your ability to catch the market leader will, of course, be reduced. But this does not mean you cannot succeed as a franchisor. You can develop local or regional franchise marketing strategies (something we call a "fortress strategy") that can be quite successful. Or you can find ways to differentiate the offer or the franchise or both, based on factors such as product offering, service offering, investment, marketing strategy, franchise structure, or a variety of other factors. (For more on competitive differentiation in franchising, see Chapter 9.)

And tart frozen yogurt is not the only example of this trend—even within the frozen treats category. Years ago, if you wanted a frozen treat, you would go to Baskin-Robbins for a premium product or Dairy Queen for soft serve. But over the years, new niche markets have emerged in gourmet (super-premium) frozen ice cream (Häagen-Dazs, Ben & Jerry's, etc.), frozen custard (Culver's, Andy's, etc.), mixed frozen treats (Cold Stone Creamery, MaggieMoo's, Marble Slab Creamery), water ice (Rita's), and even some categories that are still emerging (Tasti D-Lite, which offers a soft-serve, nonfat ice milk).

On the other hand, if you have a concept that really is new to the market or has a unique niche, you will need to move quickly if you want to capitalize on it. Given the availability of information in the internet age, your points of difference will rapidly find their way online. So if you play it conservative and wait until everything's just right to franchise, you may find that instead of being first to franchise the concept, you're third or fourth—or worse! Lots of people with money and business know-how are looking for bright new ideas that someone else has taken the time and effort to test in the marketplace. So while you're meticulously developing that last new recipe, product, or service that will perfect your business, your competitor may be quickly developing a franchise concept based on yours that will leave you standing in their dust.

Years ago, I spoke with an entrepreneur who built a small chain of double drive-thru burger locations. He told me the story of how he saw several guys sitting on the hood of their car across the street, watching his business. When he walked over to ask what they were doing, they told him they were admiring his business—and he proceeded to sit down with them and tell them his life story. Years later, when he finally decided to franchise, he found he was going head-to-head with a more established competitor with hundreds of locations. And it was run by those same guys.

Over the years, I have heard similar stories from companies that started a concept first, only to have someone else run with it. In some cases, like the one above, the purported originator of the idea (I cannot confirm this story, after all) has long since gone out of business. In others (I am thinking about a six-unit burger chain that claims to have invented the gourmet burger, only to have another major player run with the idea), they are still in business. And while they have grown since they were founded decades ago, I cannot imagine how I would feel if others had run with my idea and I was, at best, an asterisk in the marketplace.

In making a decision about market risk, the essential lesson is that there are two kinds of risk. The first, which we call concept risk, reflects the risk associated with franchising before you have perfected the concept. The longer the concept runs and the longer your track record, the more you reduce this risk. The more company-owned locations you run, the more you reduce this risk—both by obtaining more information on what works and by improving cash flows that may be needed to support your early franchise efforts.

This risk, however, is offset by the risk we call competitive threat. The longer you wait to expand aggressively (whether through franchising or another means), the longer you leave an opportunity for a competitor to run with your concept. As entrepreneurs observe your success, some will think to copy you. They may be better capitalized, or they may simply choose to franchise sooner. But whichever it is, the sooner they get to the franchise market before you, the more likely it is that they will be perceived as the market leader.

From a purely economic perspective, you can think of the competing risks posed by market factors as a graph as in Figure 4.1 on page 61.

Ultimately, it is up to the entrepreneur to determine the slope of these lines and how much risk he is incurring. If the technology is patented or truly proprietary, or there are other high barriers to entry, you may be subject to less competitive threat than other businesses. The easier it is for your business to be duplicated by others (who may have a lot more money than you do, allowing them to reverse engineer your concept), the greater the risk.

So from a purely economic standpoint, when concept risk is greater than competitive threat, you should wait before you franchise. And when the reverse is true, you should franchise before you spend time and

Figure 4.1: **Market Risks When Timing Your Decision to Franchise**

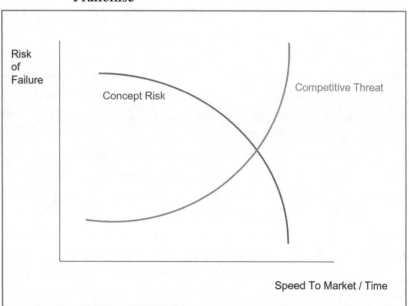

resources on growth or model refinement. In other words, the time to initiate your franchise efforts is when these two lines intersect—or even a few months prior to that point, as it will generally take four to six months once the decision is made to prepare your organization to sell franchises.

Capital

Another component of the risk equation is capital. While franchising is certainly a low-cost means of expansion, it is not a no-cost means of expansion. So the amount of capital you can devote to your franchise expansion efforts will impact your risk—not only from the standpoint of the total amount you are risking, but in terms of the riskiness of the decision itself.

If you go into a business undercapitalized, you run the risk of taking a nine-foot leap across a ten-foot ditch. In addition to the costs of developing appropriate strategies, manuals, marketing materials, and legal documents, you will have costs associated with franchise marketing and franchise sales.

If you don't have the capital needed to properly support your franchisees, you increase your risk of franchisee failure, difficult franchisee relationships, and litigation.

In franchising, there are three ways you can capitalize your initial development efforts. You can have the capital (or access to the capital through lenders or investors) when you begin franchising. You can use the cash flow from your company-owned operations to fund your entry into franchising. Or you can try to finance your franchise efforts out of your initial fees and/or product sales.

This last method is considered a "worst practice" in franchising. This practice, occasionally used successfully by undercapitalized franchisors, often encourages franchise sales to unqualified candidates. And even if used with constraint, relying on fees to fund cash flow is always dangerous.

The costs of becoming a franchisor, of course, can vary considerably based on a number of factors. A more aggressive growth plan, for example, will increase the costs associated with your initial franchise marketing efforts and may require additional training documentation to deal with the influx of franchisees. On the other hand, if you have internal resources who can assist with the development of operations manuals, legal documents, brochure design, and the other tools you will need to franchise, you can use these resources to reduce your costs.

Since every situation is different, the best strategy is always to get the advice of experts on the costs you may incur and be sure you are adequately capitalized before jumping into franchising.

Is Franchising Right for You?

Perhaps just as important as understanding goals and risks is to evaluate your temperament as a potential franchisor. To the neophyte, franchising sounds tremendously exciting. And if you are successful, there is no business that affords the enthusiasm and growth that franchising does. But, like any new business, franchising requires hard work, motivation, and dedication.

And not everyone is well-suited for franchising. Some business owners find it difficult to deal with franchisees; as independent business owners, they require a different management style than you might use with corporate employees. If, for example, you tend to have an autocratic management style, you may find franchisees difficult to manage. Franchisees are not employees, and if you treat them as if they are, conflict is sure to follow. Successful franchisors know how to motivate and lead their franchisees, and they enjoy the day-to-day interactions with them. This leadership requires that franchisors establish a high degree of credibility with their franchisees. That does not come easily, and not every successful entrepreneur is capable of or willing to devote the energy toward this important task.

One of the most important things to remember when making the decision to franchise is that you are creating a *new business*—not simply an extension of your existing business. Regardless of the business you first founded, you need to understand that franchising is the business of selling and servicing franchisees. And your first and most important priority in that business must be to make your franchisees successful.

Are you a cowboy? We firmly believe that entrepreneurs make the world go round. That said, some entrepreneurs change direction faster (and more frequently) than a cowboy draws his six-shooter. But franchisees need a good sense of direction—not several. So if you are the type of entrepreneur who likes to turn frequently on a dime, your capricious nature may not be appreciated by your franchisees. Today's franchisees are looking for a collaborative relationship that requires the franchisor to provide strong leadership. And to do that, the franchisor must truly listen to what its franchisees have to say and provide for open and frequent communication.

This is not to say the franchisor cannot enforce standards or lead the company in the direction it sees fit. In fact, it is the franchisor's duty as brand ambassador to assume this role. That said, the best franchisors are often those with exceptional communications skills. Good franchisors need to be good salespeople: They need to sell the franchisee on why things need to be done a certain way, not simply declare that that's how things will be done. Appealing to a franchisee's best interests brings about all sorts of cooperation, and this kind of leadership takes a certain knack. If your management style is to say, "It's my way or the highway," you are likely heading for a wreck.

The new franchisor must also have sound management skills. Because of the potential for unfettered growth through the use of the franchisee's capital, one of the most important of these skills is discipline. Franchisors must have the discipline to say no to growth if it cannot be supported properly, if a franchisee is unqualified or a bad fit for your network, or if you are not ready to expand in a particular market.

Finally, keep in mind that new franchisors will have many demands on their time, and if they meet that demand by taking time away from their existing operations, they may find they are robbing Peter to pay Paul. If the core business suffers, the cash flow supporting the franchise program may be reduced—causing your new business to suffer as well.

So even if franchising meets your financial goals, you need to ask yourself if you will love your new career as much as your current one. The founders of more than one franchise company have found they left their passion behind when they started franchising. In at least one case, they sold the franchise company to return to their passion—by owning and operating an individual franchise of the system they once founded.

The Value of Opening a Second Operating Unit

One thing you may hear from time to time as you evaluate franchising is that you cannot franchise unless you have at least two operating units. In fact, nothing could be farther from the truth.

An interesting case in this regard was Massage Envy, which started franchising when it had only a single unit in operation and today has more than 1,000 locations. (For more on this story, see Leonesio's video endorsement of the iFranchise Group at www.ifranchisegroup.com/testimonials.)

Of course, opening a second location has a number of advantages. It will allow you to test different aspects of the business, demographics, and types of sites. It will improve cash flow. It will increase credibility.

Two units are almost always better than one. And three are almost always better than two. Five are better than three. And ten are better than five.

But again, you cannot answer this question in a vacuum. And saying that opening more company-owned units is empirically the better decision fails to account for issues of competition, timing, and focus. While having more operating locations may increase your credibility, the impact on your close rates will likely be relatively small. If the average close rate on franchise leads is about 2 percent (more on this in Chapter 10), this increase in credibility might bump the close rate up to 2.2 percent.

When you consider that a franchisor looking to sell 12 franchises a year needs to generate about 600 leads to achieve that goal, that incremental increase would be responsible for about one additional franchise sale in the first year. Alternatively, it would allow you to decrease your franchise marketing budget by about 10 percent—saving about $9,600 in today's market.

Measure that savings against the cost of starting your franchise efforts a year sooner, and the financial choice quickly swings in favor of franchising sooner. This is especially true when considering where each of these choices would take the entrepreneur in year two.

The entrepreneur who spent a year opening his second location would have two operating locations and could now offer franchises with the expectations of a 2.2 percent close rate. In contrast, the entrepreneur who spent a year franchising with a lower 2 percent close rate would have one corporate location but perhaps 10 to 12 franchise locations—allowing her an even higher close rate, more publicity, and a faster jump on competitors.

And this does not even account for the possibility that the second unit could end up being a distraction, underperform, or allow a competitor to gain a "first mover" advantage in your industry or in the market(s) you wish to develop.

We have often seen people delay the decision to franchise because they have an opportunity to capitalize on a particular site or for some other reason of convenience. But again, the question they should ask is whether the resources spent on a second operating location are going to ultimately provide the best incremental returns or allow them to pursue their best alternative strategy.

That said, there are certainly times when opening a second or third unit is the best strategy. In some instances, an entrepreneur might need to test different types of locations or refine different aspects of the business. This is particularly true if the first location is not considered a reasonable prototype for the business format or location that would ultimately be offered to franchisees. If the first unit is not providing adequate returns to franchise, a company should not use it as the model for franchise operations and must refine it first.

But when looking at the question objectively, if franchising is your chosen expansion strategy, starting sooner will often have incremental long-term benefits.

Franchise or Corporate—Should You Do Both?

For the company trying to choose a growth strategy, it is important to point out that it does not have to be a matter of choosing one or the other. The vast majority of franchisors use both company-owned and franchise strategies in combination. McDonald's, for example, currently owns and operates about 15 percent of its 31,000-plus worldwide units and, in some international markets, is involved in joint ventures.

Some franchisors will choose to own and operate the best locations or markets while franchising secondary and tertiary markets. Others will choose to develop a company-owned presence in their core marketplace and franchise in more distant markets. And some treat company growth and franchise growth opportunistically and end up with many markets that have both franchise and company-owned locations.

Regardless of the strategy taken to integrate these two growth models, for many companies, the combination of franchising and company-owned growth provides the best of both worlds. From a pure financial standpoint, it is almost impossible to beat. The excess cash produced by your successful franchise operations can fuel increased franchise growth, but at a certain point, the cash used for franchise lead generation will outstrip your opportunities to spend it wisely on franchise marketing. Reinvesting in corporate locations can improve your cash flow and build your balance sheet.

Moreover, opening corporate locations in unpenetrated geographic markets can help build the brand and spur franchise sales interest in advance of your franchise marketing efforts. And if you are thinking of selling franchises that would differ from your current model (e.g., offering franchises in malls, strip centers, different demographic markets, etc., when you have not done so in the past), you do not want your franchisees to act as your guinea pig.

As discussed above, when taking a multichannel approach to franchise expansion, the most effective way to do so is to focus your initial efforts exclusively on developing the corporate prototype or prototypes. Once the business system is in place, most companies will find the best strategy is to focus exclusively on franchising until the franchise program is throwing off enough excess cash flow to support opening more company-owned locations.

The reasoning is simple. For almost every company, the cost of marketing, selling, training, and supporting a new franchisee will be far, far less than the cost of opening a single corporate location. So it is generally best to focus on franchising until you have the staff to support this dual distribution strategy.

Again, it is important to understand that franchising—or any strategy for business expansion—is simply a means to an end. It should be, first and foremost, a way for the owners of a company to reach their personal goals.

"What's the Magic Number?"

One question I field frequently is whether there is a certain "magic number" of franchises you have to sell to make franchising a worthwhile investment.

And while there is no magic number, my usual answer is "One."

The reason for this is leverage. While no one adopts a franchise strategy to sell a single franchise, imagine that is all you sold and ask yourself:

- ☛ Would you go out and rent additional office space?
- ☛ Would you hire a franchise sales team?
- ☛ Would you hire a full-time field support staff?
- ☛ Would you continue to work with lawyers to keep your legal documents current (despite the fact that you would not need to)?
- ☛ Would you continue to hire consultants to help you grow?
- ☛ In fact, would you commit to any incremental costs?

Chances are you answered "no" to all of the above. Why? Because you could service your single franchisee very simply using your existing time, effort, and staff.

You can see that if a franchisor keeps its expenses in check, it can be profitable and recapture its initial investment by selling a single franchise. Its only incremental expense will be the sweat equity it invests in the franchise program.

The key to maintaining your profitability as a franchisor thus becomes the development of a franchise plan that allows you to leverage your existing resources as you sell new franchises, so the need for hiring is eliminated or minimized until franchise royalties provide enough coverage to begin hiring.

THE BOTTOM LINE

The Answer Is Not in the Stars

To paraphrase Shakespeare, the answer to whether franchising is the right strategy lies not in the stars, but in ourselves.

It's a big decision. While you can create the documents you will need to legally franchise for less than $50,000, for most franchisors, a budget of $100,000 or more is more realistic. And if you are looking for an aggressive franchise launch, you can plan on spending $200,000 or more. (These costs are examined in more detail in Chapter 13.) So this is not a decision you will make overnight.

If you are seriously thinking of franchising, ask yourself the following questions first:

- Is my business franchisable?
- Do I need to franchise to achieve my personal goals?
- What is happening in my marketplace?
- Will I be committed to the success of my franchisees?
- Do I have adequate resources?
- Do I have the intestinal fortitude to do franchising right—even if it means not selling a franchise to someone I believe will fail or will not meet brand standards?
- Do I have the fire in the belly to make this happen?

The ultimate answer to whether or when you should franchise cannot be found in any book, nor can it be provided by a consultant, an accountant, or an attorney. The answer to that question can only be found within yourself. Is the market ready? Is the concept ready? But mostly, are *you* ready?

CHAPTER 5

Alternatives to the Franchise Structure

*"Don't waste time on reasons why something can't be done.
Find a way to do it instead."*

—BILL ROSENBERG, FOUNDER, DUNKIN' DONUTS

When making a decision to franchise, a prospective franchisor should determine not only if the company is franchisable, but also if franchising is the best expansion strategy to pursue. No examination of franchising is complete without an understanding of the alternatives available to the business owner intent on growth using the resources of others.

Company-Owned Operations

The most obvious expansion method for many companies is the development of additional company-owned outlets using internal or personally borrowed funds or capital raised publicly or privately.

This strategy offers several advantages over franchising. Perhaps most important, company-owned growth allows owners to keep 100 percent of each unit's profits rather than sharing those profits with franchisees. At the same time, it offers increased control over unit management, as owners can hire and fire management largely at will. This control allows for increased flexibility and the ability to react to market changes more quickly. For the company contemplating first-time franchise expansion, it also represents a more predictable method of growth, as there is no need to learn the new business of franchising. Finally, the addition of company-owned locations allows the business owner the opportunity to build tangible assets in the business, which can have a very positive impact on the company's valuation when the owner begins to consider exiting the business.

Of course, along with the advantages, there are some disadvantages. First and foremost is risk. While you get to keep 100 percent of the profits, you are also responsible for 100 percent of the losses. And the more money you invest in corporate operations, the more you have at risk.

Increased control also comes with increased responsibility. Sexual harassment, EEOC violations, ADA violations, slip-and-fall, workers' compensation, and other worker or customer liability issues will all be directed at you. A franchisee, by contrast, is an independent contractor, and assuming you direct them appropriately, the ultimate responsibility for all these issues will likely remain with them. And while a corporate-owned-and-operated chain can institute concept changes more quickly, the costs for these changes (new décor package, new equipment, etc.) will be yours as well.

Business Opportunities or Licensing—The "No Name" Options

We often see companies expanding with what they call a license program—sometimes something they dreamed up and sometimes the creation of their attorneys. But simply calling something a license or a business opportunity does not make it so. Going back to the three-part definition of a franchise (name, support or control, and a fee), an entrepreneur will need to remove one of those elements for the relationship to be something other than a franchise. It becomes a license, or more technically, a business opportunities license (also called a biz opp), when you remove the name, or trademark, element of the franchise definition. (*Note*: this still may not exempt you from franchise laws in New York.)

The advantage to the biz opp route is that in many cases the licensor does not have to comply with the FTC's franchise disclosure regulations, which saves money and makes the sales process less complex. That said, a biz opp may still have to comply with franchise disclosure laws in some states and will need to comply with the patchwork quilt of biz opp laws that exist in more than two dozen states. So while the biz opp licensor may avoid some legal costs if a company plans to roll out the offering on a *local* level, a national rollout may require them to pay *more* in the way of legal fees and make it only marginally easier to sell.

At the same time, avoiding a common brand identity often puts the licensor at a long-term disadvantage over its franchising brethren. First and foremost, the use of a common brand and identity can benefit both the franchisor and franchisees. Even a one-unit chain looking to expand through franchising will be likely to double their advertising exposure with the sale of their first franchise, whereas the licensor who sells 100 biz opps will get little, if any, in the way of brand recognition—because their operators will do business under their own names. From the unit owner's perspective, trading under a common name associated with a larger, multilocation system can increase their valuation as a result of increased name recognition by consumers who support the brand.

Moreover, because each biz opp will operate under a different name, the licensor cannot legally control *how* the licensee operates. The legal principle here is simple: If someone is operating under your name, you can control their operations because it affects how people perceive *your* name. But when they operate under their own names, you no longer have a vested interest in their performance, as it is not your name that is getting dragged through the mud.

For this reason, the fees charged by an unbranded biz opp tend to be substantially lower and often have no long-term component or royalty— unless it involves ongoing purchases from the licensor. Again, without a common name, you cannot exercise control, and without control, it is difficult to provide the value of a franchisor that is developing common advertising campaigns, marketing initiatives, merchandising schemes, and other ways of enhancing value and performance at the unit level.

Finally, biz opps will often find themselves competing with one another in ways that franchises generally do not. Because biz opps do not share a common name, consumers may shop the different locations to see which offers the better price—encouraging price competition and decreasing each operator's margins. Franchises, on the other hand, rarely get shopped against each other at the consumer level because the consumer views the franchise chain as a unified whole with a single price structure.

On balance, biz opps do not substantially reduce the burden of legal compliance and, at the same time, offer far less quality control than franchising. And since fees are generally lower and there is no ability to create a national brand, this expansion method is often not a satisfactory alternative to franchising.

Trademark Licenses—The "No Support and No Control" Option

The second option available to those looking to expand through third parties is the use of a trademark license. A ready example of such a license would be Michael Jordan allowing Nike to use his image in their advertising or on their shoes. After all, who doesn't still want to be like Mike?

But for those of us with less prominent names, trademark licenses are exceptionally difficult to market—especially if we are branding a business instead of a product. After all, if someone is going into a business, it is the system of operation—the recipes, the advertising, the operating procedures, and the knowledge of how to succeed—that the prospective buyer is looking to obtain, not simply the name.

More important, it is extremely easy to step over the line of providing "significant operating control or significant operating assistance." As you will recall from the definition in Chapter 1, some of the elements cited by the FTC as being significant are controls over site approval, design specifications, production techniques, promotional campaigns requiring franchisee participation, and territory restrictions. And the FTC has stated that training programs, management and personnel advice, site selection assistance, and operations manuals are all forms of "significant assistance." Again, you do not need to provide all these elements to trip the support and control element. One slip in the wrong place, and, oops . . . you are an inadvertent (and illegal) franchisor.

Even if one were to remain pristine on this issue—not providing any support or exercising any control—wise trademark owners should be asking themselves, "Do I really want to allow someone to use my name on a business *without* the ability to control how my name is used?" These are not T-shirts here. The damage done by a single rogue operator could harm a brand that took years to build.

The line between trademark licensing and franchising is very thin. Walking that line can often result in a business owner making decisions not based on what is best from a business standpoint, but only on the need to avoid imposing so much control or uniformity that the license falls over the line into the definition of a franchise. For that reason alone, developing a system of related businesses through trademark licensing is usually not a viable alternative.

The "No Fee" Options

The last alternative to franchising, of course, involves removing the fee element from the equation. Since the federal definition of franchising specifies that a fee is "$500 or more in the first six months," one way of avoiding this is simply to wait more than six months to collect any fees from your "nonfranchisee." But while this may work in some cases, variations in state laws make this a treacherous path indeed. Remember the case of *To-Am Equipment v. Mitsubishi Caterpillar Forklift America*. Mitsubishi granted a distributorship to To-Am, assuming that since it was not charging To-Am a fee, it was not subject to franchise laws. But over the course of an eight-year relationship, as To-Am purchased $1,600 worth of manuals from Mitsubishi, they triggered Illinois franchise laws, which ultimately cost Mitsubishi $1.525 million in damages.

Even if you are operating in a state without franchise laws, the question that should be asked is why anyone would want to go the fee-deferral route. The nonfranchisor will undoubtedly incur major marketing and selling costs as well as additional support and training costs, all without compensation for six months—simply to avoid the minor inconvenience of complying with franchise disclosure laws. And, of course, if the nonfranchisee runs out of money, you are left holding the bag—having provided support at significant cost in the process. And there is the precedent of waiting those six months—rest assured that when your nonfranchisees are required to start paying fees, they will be very difficult to collect.

Aside from fee deferral, other no-fee options are more rational and often appropriate for certain companies. These include dealerships, distributorships, agencies, independent sales representatives, and joint ventures.

Dealerships and Distributorships

Like the Mitsubishi example above, dealerships and distributorships involve the provision of products to a third party at a bona fide wholesale price for resale. This is certainly a tried-and-true means of establishing a distribution channel. Of course, these alternatives are only appropriate for manufacturers and wholesalers. And again, caution must be the byword. Selling equipment, displays, and other items that are not intended for resale—*even if not sold at a profit*—will trigger the fee element of the franchise definition and potentially create problems similar to those cited in the Mitsubishi example.

Moreover, many manufacturers these days are finding that the traditional dealer model is much less efficient and much less profitable than franchising. Because the dealer relationship lacks a fee, support must be provided for free—essentially eating into the manufacturer's wholesale margin. And while dealers will clamor for more and more support as their competition increases, they will often have little loyalty to the manufacturer's brand when a competitor comes calling with a product that offers increased sales and/or improved margins, or is perhaps just the flavor of the month—turning the manufacturer into a red-headed stepchild overnight. In a franchise, of course, the franchisee commits to your product line long-term and generally pays fees on top of the wholesale margin you would otherwise receive—allowing manufacturers that choose to franchise to benefit from service components that are often not part of the wholesaler's revenue stream—as well as the product margins more typically associated with these relationships.

Agency Relationships

Similar issues can be found in agency relationships. In an agency structure, an independent salesperson sells a service on your behalf—so, this form of relationship is only appropriate for companies for which fulfillment of the contract is provided by the corporation, and not by the agent. The easy distinction here (much like that of an independent sales representative) is that all money flows downward (from corporate to the agent) and not upward (from the franchisee to the franchisor). If your agent is taking money and sending you any, the relationship has likely triggered the fee element of the franchise laws. Minimal brand loyalty, high turnover, and support-specific margin erosion typify these types of relationships.

Joint Venture

This is the last type of no-fee option. A joint venture partnership is characterized not by fees, but by sharing both equity and profits. So, for example, your joint venture partner might put up 70 percent of the money and work at a salary that is below market for one year. You might put up 30 percent of the capital, sign personally on a bank note, and provide your intellectual property. Based on your negotiations, you might end up in a 60/40 split of the ownership of the company. Your 40 percent would entitle you to 40 percent of any profits that are distributed—but only if profits are distributed.

You would also be required to pay taxes on 40 percent of the reported profits of that company—even if no profits are distributed. So if, for example, the controlling partner chooses to make a capital expenditure in the company (which is not tax-deductible) instead of making a distribution, you could be on the hook for the taxes, even though you did not see any of the money.

While there are measures you can take to make sure you control the joint venture or at least have no unplanned tax liability, joint ventures are notoriously difficult to make work.

One major issue encountered by those who use a joint venture structure is defining and tracking profits. How should the operating partner get compensated for her time? When does an expense become a perk? What constitutes overhead, and how does that get allocated? How does the non-operating partner get compensated for her time? Does the operating partner have the latitude to hire friends and family, and if so, how is this controlled? What kinds of controls need to be established to ensure all profits are, in fact, reported?

Even in relationships in which the operator is honest and well-meaning, the process of tracking profitability for a single unit can be cumbersome;

across a hundred units or more, the accounting involved quickly becomes daunting. And one more cautionary note: any joint venture that pays fees to the owner of the intellectual property will be deemed both a joint venture *and* a franchise, even if the intellectual property owner is one of the joint venture partners.

Finally, the joint venture relationship itself is extremely difficult to manage. Unlike a franchisee who is obligated to follow the rules by contract, the joint venture partner is, in fact, a partner, and will often attempt to take greater latitude with the system of operations than would a franchisee. We often liken a joint venture partnership to a marriage. It is an individually negotiated, occasionally contentious partnership of equals that often ends in divorce. A franchise relationship, by contrast, is much more like a parent-child relationship. The franchisee starts as a highly dependent infant and will evolve into an increasingly independent, occasionally rebellious adolescent, who will (assuming you are good at parenting) still follow the rules—despite occasional protestations—and in many cases, will remain your child forever (or until they leave the nest).

Franchise Exemptions—The Nonfranchise Franchise

Of course, the government would not be at its bureaucratic best if it did not create exceptions to the rule. So the FTC definition has incorporated a number of exceptions as to when a company that otherwise meets the legal definition of a franchise does not need to behave like one. Some of the exemptions include:

- ▼ *Fractional franchise exemption.* When a prospective "franchise" is sold to an existing business owner who has two years of experience in the same type of business and the sales arising from the relationship itself will not exceed 20 percent of the franchisee's total dollar volume. Essentially, this exemption focuses on "store within a store" types of operations. A related exemption is in place for leased departments.
- ▼ *PMPA exemption.* Relationships that are separately covered under the Petroleum Marketing Practices Act.
- ▼ *Large investment exemption.* For investments of more than $1 million (excluding financing from the franchisor and excluding unimproved

land) in which the franchisee signs an acknowledgment verifying the grounds for the investment. The assumption here is that larger investments of this nature require a more sophisticated investor who does not need the protection afforded by pre-sale disclosure.

➤ *Sophisticated buyer exemption.* For franchisees who have been in business for at least five years and have a net worth of at least $5 million.

➤ *Management sales exemptions.* For franchisees in which one or more purchasers of 50 percent of the equity in the franchise has been an officer or an owner of at least 25 percent of the franchisor organization.

➤ *Verbal agreements.*

More Than One Size Can Fit All—Combination Structures

One last point is worth noting here. Just because you create a business relationship that qualifies as something other than a franchise, that doesn't mean it's not a franchise too. For example, you can create a dealership or distributorship, and if you provide for branding and support and charge a fee, you have also created a franchise. If you structure a branded joint venture that pays a license fee for the use of the name, you have likely created a joint venture that is also a franchise. You can charge an upfront fee using an agency structure and create an agency that is also a franchise.

And, of course, you can also combine nonfranchise options. You can, for example, create a branded dealership that is also a joint venture. You can create a business opportunities license that sells your products as a nonbranded dealership.

So regardless of whether you are trying to create something other than a franchise, remember the simple three-prong test to see if you have created more than you bargained for.

Combining Growth Strategies

Although some franchisors choose to grow exclusively through franchising, many will combine growth strategies. Most often this involves franchising coupled with continuing to build company-owned operations, but other combinations are occasionally used as well. Manufacturers, for example, may simultaneously promote a dealer and a franchise channel if the two can be adequately differentiated.

We often recommend that our clients grow through a combination of corporate and franchise growth (or dealer plus franchise growth, when warranted), as these combined growth strategies often build shareholder value faster than any other option. Developing company operations can, for example, help the franchisor build asset values and cash flow by reinvesting money that might otherwise be taken in the form of dividends or distributions. Corporate stores in distant markets can also act as training centers for remote franchisees and even serve a marketing goal by furthering the exposure of the brand. Moreover, a franchisor's commitment to the development of additional company stores helps reinforce its belief in the concept while keeping it current (in a very meaningful way) with what is happening at the unit level. Company operations can also provide a career path for top-performing employees who may eventually fill training, field support, or other roles within the franchisor company.

That said, the existence of company stores also raises the issue of potential conflicts with franchisees, especially when the franchisees and the corporate locations are competing for customers or resources. Conflict can arise due to geographical proximity and issues of encroachment, relative contributions to advertising and marketing funds, access to products or services, and varying standards imposed relative to adherence to operating hours, staffing, and other operational standards.

If a multichannel approach is the strategy of choice, it is generally best to implement the franchise channel as a separate initiative that does not conflict with continued corporate development. Since franchising is, in many respects, a new and separate business endeavor, we recommend that when you are ready to launch your franchise program you should do so with your full attention and focus. Thus, smaller companies entering franchising for the first time would be well-advised to put corporate growth on the back burner for a year or two while establishing their capabilities as a franchisor. Larger companies that already have a substantial base of company-owned locations simply need to ensure that adequate resources are devoted to the franchise program to ensure its growth and success.

Never Decide to Franchise

I have one simple piece of advice for anyone thinking of expanding through a third-party channel of distribution: Don't decide to franchise.

The last thing you want to do is try to jerry-rig your growth strategy to fit a particular definition because you are afraid of triggering franchise laws or because your lawyer said it was easier. Decide on the best growth strategy for you and *then* let a good lawyer determine how to comply with appropriate laws.

Remember, your job is to drive strategy. The lawyer's job is to document your strategy and keep you out of trouble—not tell you how to best run your business.

All this explanation of the various alternatives is, in some respects, putting the cart before the horse. In deciding how to expand, the savvy business owner will put labels out of his head and instead focus on the elements of his business strategy that are best-suited to meet his goals.

Begin your examination by asking several very basic strategic questions. Start with the end in mind. Where do you want to be five years from now? Do you want to be building your business to pass it on to your heirs? Creating a personal legacy? Or do you want to build something of value to sell so you can move on to the next adventure? If you are building it, how much profitability should it be producing for you? If you want to sell it, what is the lowest price you would accept?

Remember, these are personal questions, NOT projections. Do not ask yourself what you think the business will be worth. That is allowing the business to drive you. Ask instead what you want out of the business—then you will need to craft a decision based on what it will take to reach those goals.

Once you have determined where you want to be in five years, figure out where you are currently. The distance between these two measures is the gap you have to close to achieve your goal.

Ask yourself first if you can reach your goal by continuing down your current path. Perhaps you open a few more locations or markets. If so, ask yourself if you have enough capital and management bandwidth to grow in this manner. If you do not, ask yourself if you can realistically raise the capital needed without giving up more than you are willing to. If you have the resources and this strategy will achieve your growth and personal goals, read no further. You do not need to franchise.

If you cannot reach your goals in this manner, you have several choices:

- 🤍 You can stretch out the time frame.
- 🤍 You can reduce your goals.
- 🤍 You can change your strategy.

A good friend of mine who is a senior executive at a major franchise company is fond of the quote (which has been attributed at various times to Ben Franklin, Mark Twain, Albert Einstein, and others): "The definition of insanity is doing the same thing over and over again and expecting a different result."

If you choose to change your strategy to one that involves third parties, you next need to ask yourself the following questions.

NAME—Do You Want to Build a Common Brand?

For most, this is a fairly easy question. Brand recognition allows businesses to compete more effectively. It starts with advertising, of course. Even when you first start franchising, your franchisee will benefit from any advertising and name recognition that you have built, along with your track record. For example, let's say I have a 10-year-old company and a track record of success serving Fortune 500 clients in Houston. Even if no one has ever heard my name in Chicago, it would be easier to sell my services if I were to say, "Hello, I am Mark Siebert. I represent XYZ Company. We have been in business for more than a decade, have served dozens of Fortune 500 companies, have references dating back a decade, and have a track record of success. We are opening a new office in Chicago, and I would like to know if I could talk to you about how we might help . . ."

For most companies, brand recognition is a huge value in addressing national accounts as well. If you can say you have 50 XYZ offices around the U.S., the bigger players are going to be more interested in talking to you than if you say you have an affiliation of 50 licenses all operating under different names with different standards.

And if you have a consumer-oriented product or service, a brand will clearly be a major factor in determining preference.

In some cases, though, a brand is not vital to a business. If, for example, you are providing backroom services to a particular group, you may have no need for branding. For example, karate schools, doctors, dentists, and others have, for years, farmed out much of their billing to billing companies, allowing these businesses to continue to run under their own names. (There are, of course, franchise companies in the martial arts, medicine, and dentistry, which provide a more complete branded alternative as well.)

SYSTEM (Part 1)—If So, Do You Want to Control the Way that Brand Is Represented?

If you are going to allow someone to use your name, this is really a no-brainer. A rogue operator could destroy decades of brand building and goodwill by deciding to do things their own way. If you are a retailer, an uncontrolled licensee might sell pornography. If you are a restaurateur, they might decide to create new recipes, change your interior décor, or fail to live up to your standards of quality.

Moreover, under the Lanham Act (the federal trademark protection act), you could actually lose your trademark for failing to enforce quality standards.

SYSTEM (Part 2)—Is It Important to Provide Support and Assistance to Those Operating Under Your Brand?

Frankly, your knowledge of how to run the business is what your franchisees are paying for. Moreover, if you want to control the operations of anyone who will be using your brand, you will need to train people on your standards and systems of operations. Again, this is a no-brainer.

FEE—And Finally, How Do You Want to Be Compensated for that Support?

If you want to take any kind of franchise fee, training fee, materials fee, royalty, advertising fee, bookkeeping fee, or any of the other fees mentioned previously, you will trigger the fee element of the definition. In fact, if your third party sends you more than $500 for anything other than a distribution of profits (joint venture) or a payment for goods to be resold (dealer or distributor), you will trigger the franchise laws.

So at the end of the day, if you want your third-party relationship to use your name, you want to control or support them in the process, and you want to receive a fee of any kind, you will be a franchise—no matter how hard you try to avoid it.

For many businesses, there is no "right" answer to selecting the right growth strategy. And sometimes, multiple strategies can be combined to optimize profitability and shareholder value. But ultimately, the decision about what you are building will have to come from you—not from your lawyers.

THE BOTTOM LINE

Let Your Goals (Not the Law) Drive Your Strategy

Success in business does NOT happen by accident.

That bears repeating.

Success in business does NOT happen by accident.

It happens because businesspeople execute against a good plan. Don't start with the law in mind. Use lawyers to help you execute your plan—not create it.

Start with the end in mind. Make good business decisions.

We routinely help businesses decide on issues surrounding business growth strategies. And while franchising is not right for everyone, it offers a dynamic growth vehicle unrivaled in the history of business.

PART TWO

Developing Your Franchise Company

CHAPTER 6

Strategy for
"Growth on Steroids"

"No matter how good an idea sounds, test it first."

—HENRY BLOCH, COFOUNDER, H&R BLOCK

Every month at the iFranchise Group, we receive several hundred inquiries from companies that think they have the next McDonald's. And while most of these companies are, in fact, running successful businesses, only a handful have what it takes to become a successful franchisor.

In Chapter 3, we talked about what it takes to have a franchisable business. But there is a long road between franchisability and achieving success as a franchisor—especially the kind of overwhelming success that is often associated with franchising.

In the 1950s and 1960s, companies could succeed in the franchise marketplace with a good concept and a well-honed sales pitch. But the days of fast money franchising are long gone. With more than 3,000 active franchise companies in the U.S. alone, today's competitive marketplace is far more complex than in decades past. To compete with the best, franchisors need to be armed with the best.

And the decisions that franchisors make early in the process will impact their ability to succeed. Because franchisors are able to grow while leveraging the time and money their franchisees invest, growth can be extremely rapid. But this "growth on steroids" has its disadvantages too. Any mistakes you make are replicated over and over—like a rogue gene— and if you do not realize it quickly enough, it may be too late for a cure by the time the diagnosis is made.

The Tools You Will Need to Compete

When you become a franchisor, you are entering a new business, and you will need to incorporate several new skill sets into your business arsenal. The primary skills you will need to develop are learning to market and sell franchises, as well as creating the infrastructure and leadership to properly support a franchise network. And as you're learning these skills, of course, the demands of your existing business will remain—so that may tax your management skills as well.

If you are like many entrepreneurs, you may find yourself prone to adopt the "Ready . . . fire . . . aim" strategy many of us used when we started out. But given the complexities of this competitive market, successful franchisors focus on several key issues before launching into this new endeavor:

- A sound business strategy
- Well-written legal documents to support the franchise strategy
- Quality control systems and processes
- Franchise marketing strategies and materials
- A plan for developing a capable franchise sales and support organization

Developing Your Franchise Plan

To paraphrase Lewis Carroll, "If you don't know where you are going, any road will get you there." And never were truer words spoken than in franchising.

The first and most important rule of franchising is this: Success in franchising does not happen by accident. Success is achieved because companies follow a sound and well-defined plan.

The best plans start with a specific goal and develop objectives and tactics that allow you to reach this goal. In franchising, you will need to address a number of franchise-specific topics in your plan: program structure, fees, territorial rights, and other key business decisions that will lay the foundation for a long-lasting relationship with your franchisees.

The best planning processes will also account for the long-term nature of the franchise relationship and the contract under which the franchisee will operate. Many franchise relationships span 20 years or more, and many times, franchises are passed down from generation to generation.

Think back 20 years ago. Were you living in the same house? Driving the same car? Using the same computer? Or even using a computer at all? As I write this in 2015, I'm amazed at the pace at which business strategy, technology, and franchising have evolved.

So in planning your franchise, you need to structure something that will not just work today, but give you enough flexibility to work 20, 30, 40, or more years into the future.

Note: Many of the most important elements of your plan will involve the services you provide to your franchisees, as these services will translate into costs to you as a franchisor, generally in the form of the people you will hire (or outsource) to provide certain services. Since you will need to understand the support you will provide to determine your cost structure, and you will need to understand that cost structure to figure out what fees to charge your franchisees, writing about one without an appreciation of the other is a fool's errand. This chapter will deal with some of the core planning issues and decisions you will need to make. Some of the cost elements you will need to understand to make these decisions are addressed in Chapter 13.

Reverse Engineering Your Future

Every good plan starts with an understanding of your goals and objectives. And while we talked about the use of shareholder (or personal) goals in determining your strategy, when you begin the planning process, you will need to get even more granular with your analysis.

Our team at the iFranchise Group encourages every new franchisor to begin the planning process by gaining an understanding of the specific goals they are hoping to accomplish through franchising. Step back and ask yourself:

- ⟶ Where exactly do you want to be in five years?
- ⟶ Do you want to sell the business? If so, for how much?
- ⟶ If you want to hold on to it, what are your specific financial goals?

When you are conducting this analysis, it is important you try to answer these questions based on the goals you are looking to achieve—NOT based on what you think the business will be worth. Start with the desired end in mind, and then figure out what you will need to do to achieve it. That is the essence of good strategic planning.

As an example, let's say you want to sell your company in five years for a price of $10 million. Start by subtracting an estimate of the current value of your existing business from your desired selling price, and this will tell you the growth in valuation you need to achieve over the next five years to reach your goal. Armed with this information, you can work backwards into a game plan.

You would then divide your required incremental valuation by an assumed multiple of earnings (based on the selling price of comparable businesses) to learn the earnings your business will need to generate to achieve your goal. Since you are projecting your earnings multiples some time into the future, you will want to use a hypothetical earnings multiple that is realistic but conservative.

For example, if your business has a current value of $1 million, you would subtract that from your goal of $10 million and know you needed to build $9 million in incremental value. If midsize franchise businesses in your industry typically sell for nine times earnings, you could then estimate that your year five Earnings Before Interest and Tax (EBIT) would need to be around $1 million to reach your goal (this is the figure typically used when calculating valuations).

You would then build a financial model that would allow you to achieve that level of earnings to determine how many franchises you would need to sell and open during that time to achieve your target earnings. The development of this model, of course, is a relatively complex process. It requires you to understand the fees you will charge, the average revenues achieved by your franchisees, the staff organization you will need to develop, and the overall costs you will incur in selling and supporting these franchisees.

As a vastly oversimplified shortcut, you might start by estimating average levels of franchisee financial performance. Based on that performance, you might then estimate the ongoing revenue you will realize from each franchisee based on royalties and estimated product sales or vendor rebates (if any). After deducting an appropriate cost of goods from your product sales revenue, you would then multiply the combined number by an approximation of your net margin to give you an estimate of net contribution per franchisee.

▼ Net Margin Estimates Unreliable

FYI, there are no reliable figures to use when estimating net margin. The studies by Business Resource Services and Profit Planning Group cited in Chapter 2 showed top quartile franchisors put an average of 40 and 45.6 percent to the bottom line in 2001 and 2002 respectively, but the same sample on which it was based was not statistically significant, and even if it were, the study is more than a decade old. No similar studies have been completed since then, although the International Franchise Association (IFA) has an online tool that some franchisors are beginning to use for that purpose. At the time of this writing, though, the tool does not seem to be collecting enough data to be useful.

To carry this example a little further, if you were to estimate you would achieve a 6 percent royalty (with no product sales) on average franchisee revenues of $500,000, you might expect revenues of $30,000 per franchisee per year. If you were to further assume you could carry about a third of this number to the bottom line, you might anticipate an annual contribution per franchisee of about $10,000.

You would then divide the amount of your target earnings ($1 million) by your contribution per franchisee ($10,000) to get an estimate of how many franchises you would need to open to achieve your goal. In this case, you would need to open about 100 franchises over five years.

Once you have determined what you need to do to achieve your goal, you would then develop a tactical game plan based on staging that number of franchise sales over your five-year planning horizon. Generally, you will start with fewer franchise sales and openings in the early years as you build your staff and your competence as a franchisor and continue to refine and validate your operating systems. This also has the impact of creating a "hockey stick" growth curve for your franchise revenues, which will help you achieve a higher valuation when you sell. But the end result of this exercise should be a specific target number of franchises to sell and open for each year of your plan.

At this point, everything will fall into place from a tactical perspective. Once you know how many franchises you need to sell each year, you can set your marketing budget based on an assumed marketing cost per franchise sale (see Chapter 10). You can develop a hiring plan based on staffing ratios relative to franchise salesperson effectiveness, field support ratios, and other measures of an efficiently run franchise organization. In fact, this process will tell you virtually everything you need to know to create a successful franchise development program. You then simply need to execute against that plan.

Of course, the process outlined above has been vastly oversimplified. We have not accounted for franchise fees, product sales, and other sources of revenue. And we have not discussed the complexities of properly establishing an earnings multiple or estimating franchisor profitability. The truth is that this process requires a substantial amount of forethought, planning, and financial analysis—often in numerous iterations—before a reasonable game plan can be established. But in every instance, it starts with goals and ends with the strategy and tactics needed to support the growth plan.

⬦ Suggested Reading

To better understand the complexities of valuing a franchisor company, I suggest you read "Why Valuing Franchise Companies Is Different From Valuing Other Businesses" by Bruce S. Schaeffer and Susan Ogulnick in *Business Appraisal Practice*, published by the Institute of Business Appraisers in 2008.

Note: Please bear in mind that a sound plan for expansion requires that sound decisions be made upfront: structure, fees, territory, franchisee support, and staffing, to name several of the most important. In addition, larger companies need to address more complex issues such as channel conflict, antitrust, and resource allocation. And obviously, the entire plan needs to be subjected to rigorous financial analysis to fine-tune the strategy. But once you have completed this exercise, you will have a good understanding of just what you need to do to achieve your goals.

Planning Around Your Exit

As part of the planning process, it is also a wise idea to consider your end game. For example, if you are planning on selling your company, you may want to consider who might be a likely buyer. If, for example, your franchisees will be large buyers of products from one or more of your large suppliers, you may want to consider a strategic buyer as part of your ultimate exit strategy. In situations such as this, selling your company to one of your vendors would provide you with a higher earnings multiple. This is because your buyer will assess you both for your value as a going concern (what most other buyers would pay) and for the value you represent to them as a secure channel of distribution for their products (providing them with a second source of profit).

Alternatively, you may also want to consider selling to one of your larger competitors. If there is a multibrand franchisor in your space or a franchisor that may attempt to consolidate brands, they may ultimately value your company at a greater multiple knowing they will realize certain economies of scale (by further consolidating overheads in areas such as franchise sales, marketing, and support; human resources; and administration).

In each of these situations (and others), it is important to anticipate your exit strategy from day one. If, for example, you plan to sell to a strategic buyer, you will need the right to dictate the suppliers your franchisees will use—and you will need the right to change suppliers. You will not want your current suppliers to be a major stakeholder in your company, and you will not want to enter into any long-term supply relationships.

Ultimately, your goal will be to get multiple vendors to compete to acquire your business. In the best-case scenario, you will tell your existing vendors, "Mr. Vendor, we have been very pleased with our relationship and hope our franchise company can continue to work with you, but we have decided to sell the company and feel we owe it to our shareholders to explore all our strategic sales opportunities—including a sale to your major competitor."

Likewise, if you plan to sell to a competing franchisor, you must carefully draft your territory provisions. If they do not allow for the competing franchisor to operate in your franchisees' territory, you may find yourself unable to sell your company to them because of the rights you have granted to your franchisees.

In keeping with our concept of reverse engineering your success, these "reservations of rights" clauses are best crafted from day one of your strategic planning to ensure you do not encounter any stumbling blocks when it comes time to realize your ultimate goal.

How Fast Should You Grow?

At the iFranchise Group, we have had a number of clients who have achieved meteoric growth. But despite these success stories, our advice for the vast majority of our new clients remains the same: *Grow slowly at first!*

◥ Quick vs. Slick

There are, of course, times when faster growth is called for. For example, if you are worried about an influx of competitors, you will need to incorporate that concern into your growth planning. In an article I wrote some years ago titled "Quick vs. Slick," I pointed out that if you are going head-to-head with a well-established competitor, you will need to be very buttoned-up (slick), but if you are the first one to a brand-new market, you may need to be quick instead. A good example of this is John Leonesio and Massage Envy—which had dozens of competitors within a couple of years of their launch. Of course, a more aggressive launch requires more resources, as we will see later in this book.

One of the biggest advantages of franchising is the relatively unfettered nature of the franchise sales process. To a large extent, a franchisor can sell franchises almost as fast as it can generate franchise sales leads. Spend more money on franchise marketing, get more leads, and sell more franchises. But this unfettered growth can also be one of franchising's biggest potential problems. Without constraint, this can lead to franchisees who fail, franchisees who never open, or franchisees who feel dissatisfied.

Bottom line? Don't grow faster than your ability to support your franchisees.

Entrepreneurs looking for very rapid growth early in their lives as franchisors also see much more substantial risks for themselves. This is because franchisors attempting to grow quickly need to hire staff to sell and service franchisees just as quickly. They need to spend more money on franchise marketing. And they need to focus more heavily on the business of franchising—sometimes to the detriment of the core business they have established.

When a franchisor gears up for super-fast growth, it can become a balancing act between the resources devoted to franchising and the revenues it generates. And while this balancing act is manageable if you have a good plan, a sound concept, adequate capital, and a strong management team, you should be very careful about growing fast in the early years. Many of the companies we meet with are very successful, thanks to the owner's hard work. But they do not have the proper operational systems in place (e.g., inventory procedures, staffing models, accounting systems, local marketing programs, etc.) to successfully replicate their success across a large number of independent franchises. Without the right systems in place, an aggressive franchise program will replicate the flaws in the concept, rather than the successes.

A corollary to not growing too quickly is to stay as close to home as possible, at least at first. We typically advocate initially limiting franchise growth to within three hours' drive of the franchisor's home office. That way, if a franchisee needs assistance, the franchisor (or his staff) can respond quickly and personally. They do not need to book a flight and a hotel room and spend days away from the office. Support will be easier and more economical to provide—not only from a transportation perspective, but from a staffing perspective as well. Clustered support allows fewer field support staff to handle more units—thus reducing cost and allowing increased face time with your franchisees.

This local approach will also mean that franchise marketing can be more targeted and likely more affordable. Rather than relying on national publications or media that may be too expensive, the franchisor can focus on less costly local media as well as capitalize on the reputation its brand has already achieved in the market.

Staying close to home will also allow your consumer advertising to be more concentrated and will provide you with a bigger brand presence. A franchisor with 25 units spread across the U.S. is unlikely to realize brand dominance, whereas a franchisor with 25 units in a single region can have a major footprint and achieve economies of scale in purchasing and advertising. And with a good reputation already built locally, its franchisees will likely be more successful and become stronger validators for the franchise program.

Ultimately, however, all decisions relative to a best practices growth plan link back to your goals and your marketplace. Conservative growth carries its own risk—the risk that perhaps while you are growing slow and steady, you are losing the race to a more aggressive competitor.

So while the easiest and most reliable growth plans will be conservative and local, risk tolerance and an assessment of your market's direction must also play a role in your selection of the most appropriate growth strategy. That said, to the extent a new franchisor can minimize the number of moving parts in its early-stage franchise strategy (e.g., supporting franchisees at a distance, opening franchise locations in sites that are very different from its prototype units, etc.), the more likely it is to be successful.

The Franchise Sales-Quality Cycle

While we will discuss the elements of franchise marketing, franchise sales, franchisee support, and quality control in later chapters, this is perhaps the opportune time to introduce the concept of the Franchise Sales-Quality Cycle.

In essence, the Franchise Sales-Quality Cycle is a paradigm developed by the iFranchise Group that shows the interrelated nature of franchise sales and franchisee support. The basic premise of the cycle is that you need to start with a strong concept and a competitive franchise structure if you are to succeed as a franchisor. From there, franchise sales becomes a process in which the combination of a sound marketing plan, well-designed creative materials, and a well-executed sales process will yield a predictable number of franchise sales. And the more money you spend on franchise marketing, the more franchise sales you will achieve.

But franchise sales are only half the battle. The franchisor must be selective in the sales process and must then provide the franchisee with the tools and support she will need to succeed in this new business. This process, along with effective communication and leadership from the franchisor, leads to strong franchisee validation (franchise jargon for franchisees who say great things about you)—which, in turn, leads to the ongoing perception that you have a great concept. This cycle is visually illustrated in Figure 6.1.

The most important aspect of this illustration is that franchise sales— and thus your viability as a franchisor—can be derailed at any point of the

Figure 6.1: **The Franchise Sales-Quality Cycle**

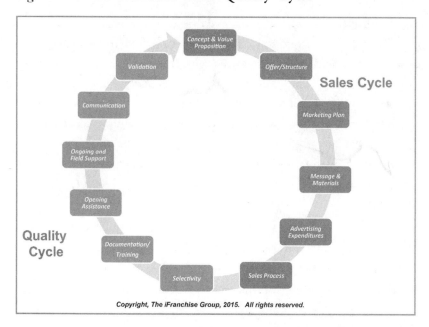

cycle. And ultimately, the single most important factor in your success as a franchisor is the success of your franchisees.

Remember, with most fast-selling franchisors, successful franchisees are an invaluable asset in the sales process. And virtually every article and book on buying a franchise will urge prospects to contact these franchisees before making a decision. If your franchisees are your biggest cheerleaders, franchise sales will come easily. But if these cheerleaders become detractors, sales will come to a grinding halt.

Over the years, many franchise systems have brought in the iFranchise Group to help them grow more aggressively. In many cases, the brand has recently been sold and the new owners have told the management team that they want to double or triple their sales in the coming year. As we begin such an assignment, one of the first questions we ask the management team is how many of those franchise sales they expect to come from their existing base of franchisees. We're often shocked by the responses, as many franchisors don't expect much of their growth to come from their existing franchisees.

In a high-performing franchise system, the *majority* of growth will often come from the existing franchisee community or from referrals to their friends and business contacts. A few examples of such systems include Auntie Anne's, McDonald's, Massage Envy, Panera Bread, and Wingstop. These and other successful brands have benefited tremendously from growth from within the system. Growth from your existing franchisees or through the people they refer helps a franchisor build and maintain a strong culture around the brand, minimizes its lead generation costs, and strengthens unit-level operations through the ability to expand with proven operators in the system. If a client tells us she doesn't expect any significant growth to come from her existing franchisees, we know there are internal problems that must be addressed for the system to expand at an aggressive pace.

Choosing the Structure of Your Franchise Offer

One of the first things you will need to do in creating your franchise plan will be to choose one or more structures under which you will offer franchises. The choice of franchise structure will impact a number of variables that will further define your franchise organization—targeted franchisee, support requirements, staffing, and cost structure—so you should not enter into it without some forethought and financial modeling.

Understand that when it comes to franchise structure, there is no standard naming convention. What I call an "area representative" structure is referred to in some organizations as an "area developer" strategy and in others as "master franchising." What I refer to as an "area development" strategy, others call a "multi-unit operator strategy." So we have provided my shorthand definitions below for quick reference:

- 🖝 *Single-unit or individual franchising* involves granting a single franchise to a franchisee for just one business operation. While the franchisor may choose to award more than one franchise to some of its franchisees, they are typically sold individually and not as part of a multi-unit territorial grant. Perhaps the most prominent example of a company that grew primarily through single-unit franchising is McDonald's.

- 🖝 *Conversion franchising* is a variation of single-unit franchising that involves granting a franchise to an operator who is already running a similar business. Conversion franchises are generally sold with preferential terms, often involving reduced fees, based on the fact that the franchisee has an established business and clientele and/or requires less training and/or support. Many of the largest real estate franchisors, including Century 21 and RE/MAX, initially had a strong emphasis on conversion franchising.

- 🖝 *Area development franchising* involves the sale of development rights to a territory in which the area developer is given the exclusive right to open and operate a (usually) pre-established number of individual franchises on a (generally) pre-defined opening schedule. While all area developers sign contracts that would make them multi-unit operators, not all multi-unit operators are area developers—some may instead be individual franchisees who acquired additional units without the benefit of an area development contract. Many large franchisors in the food-service arena (like Burger King, Pizza Hut, and KFC) have relied heavily on area development franchising, and some, like Panera Bread, McAlister's Deli, and Buffalo Wild Wings, now focus exclusively on area developers.

- *Subfranchising (also called master franchising)* involves a grant of the right to sell individual franchises in a specified territory along with the obligation to provide some level of support and service to those individual franchises in return for a shared-fee arrangement with the franchisor. In a subfranchise relationship, the master franchisee enters into contracts directly with franchisees. Subfranchising is often reserved for international markets (where it is also referred to as master licensing, just to make things more confusing), where many of the most prominent franchisors use it regardless of their domestic structure—at least in some markets.

- *Area representative franchising* is a variation of the subfranchise arrangement. While the roles of each party are largely identical, in an area representative relationship, the franchisor (not the master franchisee) enters into the franchise agreement with the individual franchisee, allowing them a greater degree of contractual control. Area representative franchising has been used successfully by fast-growing franchisors such as Subway, Quiznos, Jani-King, The UPS Store, and Massage Envy.

Your choice of strategy will be based on a number of factors. There is no right or best strategy for everyone. And again, not only can your strategy involve multiple franchise structures, but it may well evolve from one structure to the next over time. Companies

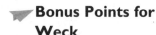

Bonus Points for Weck

When I first worked with McAlister's Deli and Buffalo Wild Wings (which at the time, was called Buffalo Wild Wings & Weck), I advised both to start with individual franchise strategies, as they did not have the resources to attract and support area development franchisees. As they grew, they switched almost entirely to an area development focus. So you can certainly start with one strategy and evolve into another. P.S. Bonus points if you know what "weck" is.

such as Subway and Quiznos began by selling single-unit franchises and later evolved to incorporate the sale of area representative franchises. And numerous franchisors that started by selling individual franchises have evolved to focus on area developers.

For most new franchisors, individual franchising is the safest bet. Individual franchises are generally easier to sell and can often be the best way to gain an understanding of the support you will need to provide your franchisees to help ensure their success. Individual franchising offers the greatest control over your franchise operations, as well as which franchisees you will allow to open additional franchises, as you can predicate it on their performance with their existing location(s).

That said, awarding more individual franchises means you will need to sell more franchises, manage more relationships, and accept higher support costs. And if you are selling multiple franchises in a single market, you may find yourself with more territorial disputes to manage as well.

If you are currently operating in a highly fragmented market, conversion franchising may be worth considering—especially if you can demonstrate true incremental value to your franchise candidate (remember, you will be asking someone who is already operating in your industry to pay you an additional fee). In conversion franchising, prospects are usually easily identified, reducing marketing costs substantially. Prospects generally have established business relationships and thus begin paying their royalties sooner. Conversion franchisees may require less training and initial support than startup franchisees and are also easier to qualify because you can evaluate their existing operations.

However, conversion franchising presents a number of challenges. As entrepreneurs, these franchisees can be more resistant to the controls imposed by the franchise system. Typically, the best operators (those you would most like to convert) are the least likely to see the value of your offering, while the worst operators (who are likely struggling for a reason, and thus should probably be avoided) will be your most eager candidates. Moreover, if a particular conversion franchisee does not work out, the post-termination, noncompetition agreements that might otherwise come into play will be much more difficult to enforce (if they can be enforced at all).

Area development franchising continues to be the favored method of expansion of many brick-and-mortar businesses. As a franchisor, you work with a limited number of more sophisticated franchisees, allowing you to allocate less time and fewer resources to unit inspection and franchisee support. Area development contracts can also minimize territorial disputes. And, of course, each sale of an area development contract will, at least in theory, result in multiple store openings.

But like other strategies, area development has its disadvantages as well. As a franchisor, you will need to recruit franchisees from a much smaller pool of candidates, as area developers must be better capitalized than individual franchisees. And if you look to area developers of other brands, you will find that the competition for these prospects is intense.

If one of the reasons you are turning to franchising is that you feel your business will perform better with an owner-operator, area development franchising may not be the best route, as these area developers will be hiring managers of their own. Likewise, if your business does not provide the incremental returns that will allow the area developer to create the infrastructure to manage multiple units, this strategy is probably not appropriate.

While many tout area development franchising for its speed of growth, it can, in some cases, actually be a slower growth structure than individual franchising—at least in regard to opening units. Consider the area developer who purchases a ten-unit territory with a development schedule that calls for a unit to open every six months. In this case, the franchisor might expect to open ten units within five years—assuming that the area developer meets the schedule. Alternatively, however, that same franchisor could blitz the local market with advertising and subsequently sell and open ten units in a much shorter time frame using individual franchisees, each of whom would be focused on developing a single unit with fewer cash, staffing, and management demands.

It is also worth noting that a substantial percentage of area development contracts go unfulfilled—by some estimates, more than 50 percent—not to mention those contracts that do not get fulfilled according to the agreed-upon development schedule. And if the contract is not fulfilled, the franchisor will often need to get lawyers

Panera Bread— the Exception

There are, of course, exceptions to every rule. As an example, Panera Bread required most of its franchisees to commit to a minimum of 15 locations under their development contracts, and most fulfilled their obligations and are thriving.

involved to regain the rights to sell franchises in that territory. The more locations awarded under an area development contract, the greater the risk for the franchisor. For most of our clients, we recommend that a typical area development agreement provide the rights to open between three and five locations. Whenever we see a press announcement for a franchisor that has, for example, awarded the rights to 50 locations to an area developer, we know it is highly unlikely the area developer will fulfill its obligations.

Subfranchising and area representative franchising are both known for helping franchisors accelerate their growth. Essentially, the franchisor is selling the rights to sell and service franchises—so each sale means the franchisor will have one new franchise salesperson on staff. The area representative will often build and operate a unit of her own, spend her own money on marketing, and begin selling on the franchisor's behalf. And since the area representative will generally have some responsibility for training and supporting franchisees, the franchisor does not need to greatly increase corporate staff along with these sales.

But while subfranchising and area representative franchising provide the fastest growth, they also have some of the most substantial disadvantages. First and foremost is that the area representative is entitled to a portion of the franchise fee and the royalty on an ongoing basis. And while they will be providing services in return for these fees, they will also be entitled

50/50 Split Common

While the split of franchise fees and royalties varies for most franchise systems, it is not uncommon for the franchisor to give up 50 percent or more of such fees to the area representative.

to a return on their investment—thereby decreasing franchisor profitability as a percentage of revenues.

Essentially, the franchisor is trading a substantial portion of its long-term profitability for speed of growth. So again, you will need to be sure there is enough return at the unit level to deliver adequate returns to you, your area representative, and your franchisee while still providing value to your ultimate customer.

And since the franchisor is involving other people in its franchisee selection and training process, it runs a risk that these area representatives will be less discriminating and perhaps less thorough, ultimately reducing franchisee quality. Moreover, the involvement of these third parties in the sales process will not absolve the franchisor from any liability it might incur in the sales process—so the franchisor could find itself in court for misrepresentations made by its area representatives.

Without question, area representative franchising is the most complex form of franchising in the U.S. Not only does the franchisor need to establish support structures for individual franchise operators, but it must also develop detailed operations standards and training programs for its area representatives. For that reason, we rarely recommend this structure for a new franchisor, particularly if the franchisor's management team does not have a strong background in franchising.

In deciding which structure (or structures) to employ, you should take a number of factors into account:

- What speed of growth is required to meet your goals?
- What is your return at the unit level?
- How much support can you provide to your franchisees?
- Does your business lend itself to passive ownership?
- Are you able to cluster units effectively?
- How fragmented is the competitive market?
- What is the degree of competition for your targeted franchisee?
- What is your value position for your targeted franchisee?

Ultimately, your decision will need to account for the best interests of all parties—you, your franchisees, and, of course, your customers. You want to choose a strategy in which you can support your franchise owners effectively and at a reasonable cost. The best strategies will achieve this goal while ensuring that quality remains high, the risk of litigation is minimized, and the chances of franchisee success are optimized.

Fee Determination

The single most important aspect of your business plan are the fees you charge your franchisees. Amazingly, many franchisors spend far less time than they should on these make-or-break decisions. All too often, they will copy their competitor's structure, choose a fee structure that is lower than their competitor's, ask an attorney, or simply pick a number that sounds good.

But carefully consider the following: A mistake of just 1 percent on a royalty can mean the difference between success and failure.

Let's say you set your royalties 1 percent below the optimal number. Let's further assume that your franchisees' average unit volume is $500,000. If that is the case, this 1 percent mistake will cause you to lose $5,000 per franchise each year. This $5,000 has no associated cost, so it comes right off the bottom line. Moreover, your franchise contract will likely be for five, ten, or maybe 20 years—so you are committing to that mistake for a decade or more. With renewal provisions, you could extend it even further. So this $5,000 mistake could turn out to be a $50,000 to $100,000 mistake—or more.

Next, remember you did not get into franchising to sell just one franchise. And you can take it as a given that your franchisees will never complain that your royalties are too low. There is a certain inertia that tends to occur within franchise organizations, making it unlikely that the franchisor will go back and re-examine structural issues after a franchise program gets off the ground. So how long will it take you to realize you have made this 1 percent mistake? Five years? Ten?

If, during that time frame, you sell 100 franchises, you are looking at a cumulative loss of perhaps $5 million to $10 million (depending on your contract term). Again, this comes right out of your pocket. And that assumes you only award 100 franchises before you recognize you should have been charging more.

That still does not capture the full impact of this mistake. At some point, you may want to sell the business, and companies get valued based on how much money they generate in profits—generally in the form of an earnings multiple. If you decide to sell before you correct your 1 percent mistake, your diminished bottom line will impact your valuation. Again, if you only sell 100 franchises, your bottom line would be impacted by $500,000 per year. So if you were to sell your business for 10 times earnings, your selling price would be worth about $5 million less than it would have been had you priced your royalties correctly. And that assumes a sophisticated investor still wants to buy your company and doesn't view it as distressed merchandise that commands a lower multiple.

The bottom line is that the combined impact of this "tiny" mistake could easily range into the tens of millions of dollars. And if you sell more franchises, it could be much more.

Franchising is like growth on steroids. It allows you to grow bigger and faster and stronger. And a high-performing franchise system replicates its success as the system grows. But start out with flaws in the system, and those flaws will get replicated over and over—potentially leading to disastrous results.

In franchising, there are a number of ways you may end up generating revenues from your franchisees, including:

- An initial franchise fee
- An ongoing royalty
- Markups on products sold
- Advertising fees
- Territory-based fees (subfranchising, area development, etc.)
- Contract-based fees (transfer fees, renewal fees, technology fees, etc.)
- Fees for services provided
- Rebates from vendors to the system
- Sharing in national account revenue
- Financing
- Real estate fees or markups

While not every franchisor will take advantage of all the above revenue streams, each of these should at least be considered in developing your franchise structure. Moreover, bear in mind that you are structuring a franchise that should last decades, so you may want to reserve the rights to incorporate these fees in the future, even if you are not planning to implement them at present.

While a full examination of every aspect of the fee determination process is beyond the scope of this book (and, frankly, could easily be a book in itself), some general guidelines on the major components of the fee determination process are discussed below.

DETERMINING THE INITIAL FRANCHISE FEE

At the iFranchise Group, we recommend that the initial franchise fee be treated primarily as a cost-recovery tool rather than as a profit center. Since franchising is, in principle, about creating long-term relationships, the initial fee should be low enough to avoid erecting unintentional barriers to entry. Remember, in franchising, each franchisee (if properly nurtured) represents a virtual annuity to you. A single franchise sale, over the course of the relationship, may generate tens of thousands of dollars in revenues for you each year. So while you may receive a nice fee upfront, the real return comes from this ongoing relationship. The last thing you want to do is price your franchise out of the market and discourage qualified candidates from moving forward.

While the costs a franchisor might incur in selling, starting up, and servicing new franchisees will certainly vary depending on the nature of the franchise, a franchisor might expect that it will incur costs for franchise marketing, sales commissions, legal advice, collateral materials, site selection, initial training, field support, and travel. Of course, a new franchisor may leverage its existing resources and, by avoiding these expenses, may make a nice profit on its initial fee—but in the long run, a franchisor should account for all these expenses in determining its ultimate cost-per-franchise sale.

Once you have estimated your anticipated costs, you should examine the franchise fees being charged by your franchise competitors. In conducting this analysis, the franchisor must determine how directly comparable these competitors are in terms of reputation, market presence, services provided, investment profile, and similar factors. This will ensure that the fees charged by the franchisor are competitive with the other franchises prospective franchisees are most likely considering as alternatives.

Finally, the franchisor should consider the message it is sending to the marketplace about its offer. If the franchisor desires to promote itself as a premium offering, it will want to price itself at the high end of the range, and perhaps even above it. To do this successfully, however, the value proposition perceived by the franchisee candidate must justify the franchisor's premium pricing position.

ROYALTY DETERMINATION

Royalties are the primary source of revenue in most franchise systems. While they are most commonly charged as a percentage of the franchisee's gross sales, franchisors have used a variety of structures to collect these fees. In some systems, franchisors collect a flat-fee monthly royalty. In others, they collect a flat fee or a defined percentage of sales, whichever is greater. And in still others, they collect a percentage of gross margin instead of a percentage of gross sales. In systems where proprietary product sales are at the heart of the franchise concept, markup on the sales of these products to franchisees may entirely eliminate the need for any royalty on their sales to the end user.

We have seen all kinds of royalty structures. We have seen structures in which the percentage charged is graduated upward (increasing with higher levels of franchisee revenues) and ones in which it is graduated downward (decreasing as franchisee revenues increase). We have occasionally seen even more esoteric royalty structures, some of which require an advanced mathematics degree to decipher. And while we generally do not advocate these less traditional approaches for a variety of reasons, from a structural standpoint, the franchisor has a great deal of flexibility.

Regardless of the structure chosen, as we pointed out above, the royalty you charge will be one of the most critical financial decisions you will ever make as a franchisor. It is such an important decision that at the iFranchise Group, determining that number often takes weeks, encompassing six different steps:

1. The process starts with an *analysis of comparable franchisor fee structures*. This analysis must go beyond simply looking at what the franchisor

charges. It must also account for what the franchisee receives. To do this, you must thoroughly examine the FDD of each competitor to determine what each comparable franchisor is offering in return for these royalties. This examination must account for the entirety of the fee structure, so if other fees are being charged or products sold at a markup, these fees should be included in the analysis.

2. The second step is determining how you want to *position your offering* in the marketplace. While this is somewhat subjective, it must be taken into account. Do you want to be viewed as a low-cost, low-support franchise? A premium offering? Your fees will, at least in part, help solidify that perception in the franchise prospect's mind.

3. Of course, *financial modeling* of various royalty approaches is essential to a proper analysis. Our typical process involves a spreadsheet that may be 16 pages or more in length, including line-by-line cost estimates, hiring plans, projected salaries, franchisee support requirements, structural decisions, month-by-month development schedules, franchisee cash-flow models, and month-by-month franchisor cash-flow models. The modeling process needs to account for specific support requirements, target markets, speed of growth, targeted franchisees, franchisor philosophy, organizational structure, and many other factors.

4. Once the core financial model is developed, we conduct a *financial sensitivity analysis*. Essentially, this involves testing financial models under a variety of altered, generally more conservative assumptions. For example, you might want to test the model under different assumptions for your average franchisee revenues. You might want to determine what would happen if your franchisees' costs were impacted by an increase in the pricing of one of your major goods. And, of course, you will want to test your model on a variety of different fee assumptions. Since no one can predict the future with any certainty, this what-if modeling allows you to understand what might happen under a variety of circumstances.

5. Next we attempt to *quantify the value proposition* perceived by your franchisees and compare that to what they will be paying you.

While some of this value proposition will be composed of intangibles (e.g., your ability to help them minimize risk), it always helps to understand that there is a cost/value element at the heart of every franchise relationship. So you will want to ask yourself how much money franchisees can save through your purchasing power. How will they benefit from your national accounts program? How will your existing marketing help them improve sales? How much would they have to spend to develop your brochures, ad slicks, radio spots, or collateral materials? What is the value of your existing relationships, brand, client list, and track record? What about the value of the many lessons you've learned that will save them time, money, and mistakes?

6. Finally, at the end of this process, you will want to *reverse engineer your royalty* by looking at both the value proposition you are delivering and your franchisee's ROI.

Ultimately, the best royalty and fee structure will be optimized around providing a reasonable return for both the franchisor and the franchisee while allowing you to offer a level of support to the franchisee that will ensure quality and give them the best chance of success.

PRODUCT SALES AND/OR MARKUPS

As a starting point, understand that you, the franchisor, have the right to control anything a franchisee purchases from any supplier, as long as that purchase impacts the ultimate quality of the franchise operation. So if you want your franchisees to purchase a certain type of equipment, a certain item of inventory, a certain chemical, a certain spice—as long as that will affect the way the consumer views your brand, you can mandate that purchase exclusively. And your ability to dictate this purchasing behavior can extend both to third-party suppliers and, should you choose to go that route, to you as a supplier.

Some franchisors derive a major source of revenue and income from equipment, products, or other supplies that they, or an affiliated entity, sell to their franchisees. There are essentially two ways in which you can sell products to your franchisees—either as an approved or a designated supplier.

An approved supplier is, in essence, any supplier that you as a franchisor will *allow* to sell products to your franchisees. In this case, a franchisee is not required to purchase from a single vendor, but instead authorized to purchase from any of a group of approved vendors. If you, as the franchisor, want to sell products to your franchisees as an approved supplier, you will always have the right to do so. And if you offer your franchisees a choice of vendors, you will also find that in healthy franchise systems, franchisees will often prefer to purchase from their franchisor *as long as the pricing is competitive.*

A designated supplier, on the other hand, means you as the franchisor require your franchisees to purchase from a specific vendor. This may again be a third party, or the franchisor may designate itself (or an affiliated entity) to be this exclusive supplier.

While it is not unusual for the franchisor to designate itself as the exclusive supplier for some or all of its franchisees' purchases, there are some limits that fall in the realm of antitrust law. For larger manufacturers, these exclusive supplier arrangements may need to be examined from the standpoint of "tying," which involves the sale of one product on the condition that the purchaser buys a second product (the "tied" product). In these cases, issues such as market power, economic impact, and more esoteric aspects of the law come into play when determining the legality of a designated supplier relationship.

Another issue to take into account, of course, is pricing. While a franchisor typically reserves the right to sell products at market price, if that price is substantially higher than those charged for comparable products, the franchisor may find itself at odds with its franchisees very quickly.

Since this book is intended to provide a businessperson's perspective on these issues and not serve as a legal text (and since these issues are subject to change as courts rule on new cases), I will not spend more time on the underlying legal issues, other than to say that these issues should be examined with the help of an experienced franchise attorney. But the short answer is that in most instances, if you have a proprietary product (or one to which you have exclusive access), you can designate yourself as the exclusive supplier to your franchisees.

Assuming you can legally require your franchisees to purchase some or all of their products from you, you will then need to determine where you will make your money—on the royalties, on product sales, or both. While there are certainly marketing advantages to selling a royalty-free franchise, there are some concerns with substituting product sales for royalties.

Going back to the basic premise that you are structuring a relationship that will last for decades, one concern with using product sales as a substitute for royalties is that your product may be rendered obsolete over time. If a new and better product were to be introduced into the market at some point, would you want your franchisees to sell that product, allowing you to make a royalty on those sales and allowing your franchisees to remain competitive?

A second question along this same vein is whether the franchisees will be generating revenue on services—either now or in the future. If they will, chances are the only way you can participate in those service revenues is to charge a royalty.

Generally, it is advisable to charge separately for each part of the value proposition in which you are participating. As a franchisor, you charge a royalty for adding value through your brand, your intellectual property, and your ongoing support. I believe franchisors should receive this revenue stream for the work they provide and are separately entitled to compensation for the work they do (and the risk they take) in the areas of product development, marketing, and production through a markup on product sales.

INCOME FROM REBATES

Along a similar vein, a number of franchisors generate rebates from those supplying products or services to franchisees. As a franchisor, you are entitled to negotiate these rebates with vendors and use them however you see fit, as long as you disclose them in Item 8 of your FDD.

That said, rebates can create friction between you and your franchisees. Franchisees generally feel they earned the rebates through their purchases, and if you choose to keep them, it can cause some resentment.

There are several ways to resolve this issue. One solution, of course, is to give the rebates back to the franchisees (less some administrative costs for negotiating deals and administering vendor relations) on some type of pro rata basis. Another alternative might be to pass some or all of the rebates you receive into the system marketing fund—benefiting both the franchisees and the franchisor in the process. We generally recommend the latter approach, which benefits all stakeholders in the franchise relationship.

ADVERTISING FEES AND ASSESSMENTS

As a franchisor, you are also entitled to collect and administer advertising fees to promote the brand and the businesses of your franchisees. Often, franchisors split advertising fees into separate components: a system marketing fund and a minimum local advertising requirement.

The system marketing fund is usually structured broadly to allow you, as the franchisor, to spend it as you deem appropriate. For example, a typical fund would allow the franchisor to spend money on national advertising, public relations, regional advertising, or other media, even though it may not benefit each of the franchisees in proportion to their contribution. It would also allow the franchisor to offset the costs of materials development, website maintenance, and even a portion of the salaries for internal staff responsible for developing consumer advertising.

The one area we do not recommend spending these funds on is soliciting franchisees. While there is no legal prohibition on this use, best practices would dictate that this fund is for brand promotion only. Any franchisor that chooses to use the marketing fund to solicit franchisees would certainly need to disclose it, and even then, the franchisor would likely get a significant amount of resistance from its franchisees.

Generally, the system marketing fund ranges between 1 and 2 percent of gross revenues, but depending on the nature of competition in the industry, a larger fund might be called for. The franchisor should closely examine the competitive landscape (and attempt to predict it in the future), with an eye toward understanding how the brand will need to promote itself.

Apart from the system marketing fund, franchisors will often require their franchisees to spend a predetermined minimum amount on local advertising. This number may be a dollar amount (especially relative to grand opening advertising) or a percentage of revenues, but it is not collected by the franchisor. Typically, the franchisees will expend their local advertising requirement on franchisor-approved advertising in their local markets, providing the franchisor with verification of these expenditures.

Designating local advertising expenditures contractually is generally considered a best practice, as it will ensure the franchisee does not neglect marketing in a misguided attempt to increase short-term profitability. In most cases, the appropriate amount for this expenditure can be determined based on the historical advertising expenditures of the franchisor's own units. That said, franchisors with a long operating history that are entering new markets may find a larger amount is necessary.

As part of this process, you may want to consider establishing an advertising cooperative once a certain number of franchisees exist in a region. These provisions should be incorporated into your contracts from the beginning so franchisees in major markets can pool their money and benefit from the economies of scale.

Finally, in setting advertising fees and required expenditures, it is again wise to look to the future. There are a number of ways you can structure flexibility in your advertising clauses to ensure you can properly respond to changes in the competitive landscape.

OTHER FEES

Franchisors often charge a number of fees in addition to the ones described above. These fees include the following:

- *Transfer fees.* When a franchisee sells her business (with your approval, of course) to a new franchisee, the franchisor generally charges a transfer fee to cover the cost of screening and approving the candidate, training the new franchisee, and providing initial support during the transfer phase.
- *Successor agreement fees.* Typically, a franchise contract runs for a predetermined length of time; at the end of this time, the franchisee is often given the right to renew the franchise on the condition that they sign the then-current form of the franchise agreement at renewal. Some franchisors will charge a fee, similar to an initial fee, upon renewal.
- *Territory fees.* For franchisors who are offering master franchises, area representative territories, or area development rights, there

are often fees associated with these territorial rights. These fee structures (along with revenue sharing provisions, in some cases) can be quite complex and will often have associated performance requirements.

➤ *Service fees.* While most services provided by the franchisor are generally covered by the royalty, some franchisors charge separately for specific services, especially if the amount of service provided to each franchisee may vary. For example, some franchisors may assist their franchisees with billing and collection, call center support, advertising design services, and more.

➤ *Technology fees.* As franchise systems evolve, it is common for the franchisor to increase the level of support provided through various technologies such as franchisee intranets, key performance indicator (KPI) dashboards, and other applications that benefit the franchisee community. It is thus common for franchise agreements to include technology fees designed to cover the cost of developing or licensing such technologies.

➤ *Cost recovery fees.* These fees, which typically cover things such as late payments, the evaluation of products or suppliers proposed by franchisees, additional training, operation of the unit in the event of the franchisee's death or disability, audit, and insufficient fund fees (in the franchisee's royalty account) are generally designed to cover the franchisor's costs.

Beyond these fees, franchisors will also want to consider other sources of potential revenue that may be appropriate either now or in the future. These may include fees for your involvement in developing national accounts, fees or profits for your participation in franchisee financing (either directly as a profit center or fees for indirect participation), fees for assistance with real estate, and other fees that may be specific to your particular franchise situation.

As you make these decisions, regardless of the fees being assessed, it is important to remember there is only so much money that can be taken out of the franchisee's pocket before returns will fall below an acceptable level. Ultimately, any fees you charge will need to account for the value you provide as a franchisor while balancing the financial returns for all parties.

Territory Determination

Another important issue relative to the structure of your franchise offer will be the territorial rights you grant your franchisees, along with any performance requirements you may choose to attach to them. Since granting protected territories will ultimately limit the potential size of your franchise system, one of the most important first questions to address will be whether to grant an exclusive territory at all.

While not all franchisors grant territorial protection to their franchisees, for newer franchisors, a protected territory is often a selling point of the franchise value proposition. Franchisees often expect a protected trade area when they buy from a franchisor. And if your competitors offer a protected territory, failure to do so could put you at a substantial disadvantage in the sales process.

But while an exclusive territory can be a great selling point, doing it wrong comes at a major cost. If, for example, you make your territories too small, you run the risk of franchisee failure and alienated franchisees, which can easily lead to your franchise's demise. On the other hand, a territory that is too large may provide an advantage to future competitors, who will develop more units in the same market. Franchisors who make this mistake may find their franchisees operating at a disadvantage relative to competitors who have better saturated the market—providing them with more advertising dollars to spend, better purchasing economies, more market visibility, and more efficient logistics.

Franchisors who make their territories too large also suffer a direct financial impact, even if the franchisees are successful. As an example, if you were to grant territories that are only 10 percent too large, you may forever prevent yourself from fully saturating that market. If a market that should have held 11 franchises was sold out at ten, you could lose a royalty stream of tens of thousands of dollars every year. Multiply that loss by ten territories and again by the decades over which you would lose out on these incremental revenues, and the lost profits could easily amount to millions. And, that is before taking into account the lost enterprise value you will receive when you sell the company.

This decision is made even more complicated because the population required to support a business will likely change over time. Increased name recognition and brand awareness should allow a unit to thrive in smaller demographics. Concept changes, such as new product lines or service offerings, may have a similar effect. And, of course, the emergence of new competitors may have the opposite effect. For these reasons, it is always advisable for you to build as much flexibility as possible into any exclusive territory definitions.

This flexibility will require forethought. For example, you will want to consider exactly what you will include as part of this territorial exclusivity. Will you carve out an ability to sell product through alternative distribution channels? Will you reserve rights to run competing brands in the same territory? Will you award territories based on a radial boundary (easy, but inefficient) or based on a map (more efficient and more difficult)? Will you have different definitions in different types of markets (large urban areas, suburban locations, etc.)? Will you define your territory based on population or based on a more appropriate variable? Will you have demographic carve-outs for certain types of locations (airports, enclosed malls, train stations, etc.)? If you will be granting exclusive territories, should you attach performance requirements (a barrier in the sales process) to maintain exclusivity? If so, should these requirements be sales-based (perhaps posing an even larger barrier) or performance-based?

If your franchise involves outside sales, you will have an entirely new set of considerations as well. Will you allow franchisees to market outside their territory? Will they be allowed to market on the internet? Will they be allowed to sell outside their territory if a buyer wants to work with them, perhaps because of a personal relationship, even though they didn't market outside their territory? How will you handle situations in which the franchisee is selling to a company with offices both inside and outside their territories? What if the franchisee sells something in another franchisee's territory in any of the above circumstances? If there are both sales and fulfillment/service functions, will one franchisee be allowed to sell and another asked to fulfill? If so, how will that work from a compensation standpoint? If you will have a national accounts program, how will you define "national accounts"? Will you allow your franchisees to call on larger accounts, or will you reserve them for yourself? If you sell them, will you involve the franchisee in their territory? Will you provide a financial incentive to the franchisee if they provide a lead to a national account? If you sell a national account, will you require your franchisee to service it? If not, will you have a right to service it? How will you be compensated for these national account sales—just through the royalty, or will you also be entitled to a national accounts fee?

The list of these questions could go on and on, depending on your circumstances, and thus it would be impossible to address all the permutations here. But for virtually every one of the questions above, there are advantages and disadvantages that you should weigh and decide prior to the sale of your first franchise.

Of course, one of the most pressing questions you will need to decide as a franchisor will be how to determine the appropriate size of the territory. In a perfect world, you would have enough operating units to provide a high level of confidence in your ability to predict sales in any given location. And, if you have a number of operating locations, there are firms that specialize in developing multivariate predictive models that can estimate revenues within about 5 percent with a 95 percent level of confidence. But for the vast majority of new franchisors, their data set is simply insufficient for this type of analysis.

While the dearth of customer data will make it more difficult, there are still steps you can take to refine your estimate of territorial parameters. Some of the tools you can use include:

- *Pin-map studies.* These studies plot your existing customers on a map in relation to the location of your site or sites. You then determine the size of the area from which a franchisee could earn an adequate ROI by drawing a hypothetical map around the site and measuring the demographics within that site.
- *Isolated market studies.* If you have a unit in an isolated market, you can study the demographics of that market to determine what it takes to generate a certain level of business. Of course, many times there are no appropriate markets to which you can apply this methodology.
- *Competitive analysis.* It can sometimes be useful to investigate how competitors design their territories or look at the number of franchisees they have placed in various types of markets. Of course,

to use this methodology, you will need to have a relatively similar competitor and some knowledge of how they have defined their territories. The downside to this analysis is that it assumes your competitor made no mistakes in their own analysis—always a risky assumption.

⥤ *Market penetration estimates.* This method starts by looking at an estimate of your current consumer market penetration and extrapolating that number into other markets. If, for example, you were achieving about a 5 percent share of the market in the markets you currently serve, you might assume that same level of market penetration (and similar levels of sales per customer) and use that information to reverse engineer a territory size.

For the well-funded franchisor seeking to grow aggressively, we typically recommend they retain the services of a GIS (geographic information system) analytic firm that can undertake a more comprehensive approach to defining territories using a broad range of metrics. GIS companies have access to many different types of data points, often including data on competitor locations within markets targeted for expansion.

Generally, we advise our clients that if more sophisticated analysis is not an option, they should use some combination of these methodologies to develop a best estimate. That said, the savvy franchisor will develop its territorial structure with the kind of flexibility that will allow it to modify the structure (or at least minimize the impact of initial imperfect estimates) as additional data allows it to more precisely carve up territories.

Other Contract Terms Affecting Your Success

Of course, there are numerous other business decisions that will need to be incorporated into your franchise structure. Some of them include:

⥤ *The term of the agreement and renewal provisions.* On one hand, the longer the term, the more salable the franchise will be, since the franchisees know they can lock in your contract terms for a longer period. But since most contracts require franchisees to execute the then-current form of agreement when they renew (which may have higher fees, for example), a shorter contract term provides you with much more flexibility.

- *Refurbishing requirements.* Your brand is of paramount importance, and while the look and feel of a location may be very modern today, you need to structure your franchise for the long run. Should you mandate that a franchisee must make certain major refurbishments on a specified time frame? Should you create separate requirements for different components of the business (e.g., technology, equipment, and the physical building itself)?

- *Training and support requirements.* Nothing will impact your brand more than the degree to which your franchisees are capable of executing against your brand promise to your customers. And other than franchisee selection, nothing will impact franchisee quality more than the training and support you provide your franchise owners. But this training and support comes at a cost, which must be accounted for in your fee determination.

- *Requirements controlling the use of your intellectual property.* Your franchise agreement should contain appropriate requirements as to how franchisees are to use your logo, display signage, wear uniforms bearing your trademark, or incorporate other aspects of your intellectual property into their daily business operations.

- *Default provisions.* As a franchisor, you need to take into account what will happen in the event your franchisees do not live up to your brand standards. You will need to be sure your contract includes specific provisions that allow you to terminate franchisees or otherwise enforce your brand standards. You will need to be very specific here if you want to enforce these rights.

- *In-term and post-term restrictive covenants.* One of the keys to the long-term success of your franchise system will be your ability to protect your intellectual property. Your contract will need to specify your rights, including noncompetition rights.

- *Reservations of rights.* You will want to spend a good deal of time thinking through the rights you want to reserve for yourself in the franchise contract. For example, many franchisors add language allowing them to operate a competing business in the franchisee's territory. At first blush, that may sound like a very difficult notion to sell to prospective franchisees, but it is included in most contracts to allow the franchisor to sell their business to a competitor (or be acquired by a competitor) in the future without having that sale violate the rights of individual franchisees. Depending on the nature of your franchise business, there are probably half a dozen reservations of rights clauses you should seriously consider.

In essence, virtually every decision you make in the structure of your legal documents will affect your success as a franchisor. With this in mind, it becomes imperative that you make these decisions after fully understanding their business implications. The decisions in your legal documents should blend best practices in franchising with the culture and vision for your own brand.

What to Do When Your Goals Exceed Your Reach

We started this chapter by discussing the importance of using your goals as a guidepost for the development of your strategic plan. By reverse engineering based on specific goals, you will have the greatest chance of achieving those goals.

But you may find yourself in a position where in order to achieve your goals, you would need to use resources you simply do not possess. Perhaps your plan calls for the sale of ten franchises in the first year, and you do not have the necessary capital to fund your advertising efforts, or you do not have the human resources in place to support ten franchisees through the startup process. What then?

Start by realizing that developing a good plan is almost always an iterative process. You may need to modify your plan a dozen times or more before you feel comfortable that it will afford you the greatest chance of success. But this is where the art comes in. If your original plan does not work, you have a number of alternatives:

- 🖝 You can change your franchise structure to a more aggressive structure like area representative franchising (or go to a more aggressive structure earlier in your timetable).
- 🖝 You can alter other elements of your franchise structure (fees, product sales, etc.), if possible.

- ► You can lengthen your timetable for meeting your goals.
- ► You can start sooner (even with a slower growth strategy), as there is a compounding effect of franchising, just as with investing.
- ► You can alter your strategy to incorporate other distribution channels beyond franchising.
- ► You can combine franchise and company-growth strategies (as many franchisors do).
- ► You can raise outside equity to facilitate faster growth (and raise your growth goals to offset the dilution you experience in the process).
- ► You can make adaptations to your business model to allow for greater returns.
- ► Or, of course, you can always reduce your goals.

It is best to remember that planning is a *process*. A plan is not a document you put on the shelf, but instead a progression of tactics you can use (and alter as circumstances dictate) to have the best chance of achieving a specific goal. Business plans change over time, as franchisors gain experience and continually evaluate the strengths, weaknesses, and opportunities of their business model.

THE BOTTOM LINE

"Me Too" Is Not a Plan; It Is a Recipe for Disaster

About 20 years ago, I received a call from a franchisor I will call Yummy Whip (some names and details changed for anonymity). With more than 200 locations, they wanted to fly in to meet with me and review the structure of their franchise program.

As soon as they walked into my office, they asked, "How many franchises do we have to sell before we get profitable?", and I knew we were in for trouble. I also knew they would not like my answer. I told them that with a well-structured franchise program, a franchisor can and should be profitable at virtually any size, but that the business terms in their franchise agreement were among some of the worst I had ever seen—and I went on to cite a number of examples for them.

The executives at Yummy Whip were none too pleased with my analysis and were not at all inclined to take my advice. "Obviously, you do not know what you are talking about," they said as they left. "We copied our legal documents word for word from Whippy Dip, and they are the leader in our industry with over 600 locations."

Two years later, Whippy Dip filed for bankruptcy protection, and the year next, my friends at Yummy Whip followed. Both companies have, since that time, successfully emerged from their bankruptcies, but both today have fewer than 100 locations remaining.

All too often, we find franchisors copying the legal documents (and the business decisions they contain) of their competitors and calling that a strategy. Unfortunately, it is not. It is a recipe for disaster.

As a new franchisor, you need to structure your franchise offering in a way that will make franchisees see you as different, and want to buy your franchise. And if the best argument you can make is "The other guy is already sold out," you are not doing a very good job.

In fact, many franchisors use their franchise business structure (the business terms in their legal documents) to differentiate themselves from the competition. But be cautious: One of the worst mistakes we see is franchisors offering a discount on fees and royalties.

Aside from the need to stand out, new franchisors need to understand that their existing situation is almost invariably different from their established competition. Almost everything, in fact, is different:

- ➤ Their goals for their business
- ➤ Their size
- ➤ Their experience with franchising
- ➤ Their investment
- ➤ Their costs
- ➤ Their staff and staff salaries
- ➤ The geographies they target
- ➤ Their site selection policies
- ➤ Their franchisees
- ➤ Their pricing
- ➤ Their marketing

☛ Their suppliers

☛ And a hundred other factors . . .

So your business economics will be different—and will demand a different franchise structure.

Even if your situation is nearly identical to that of your competitors, copying their structure has one more potentially fatal flaw: It assumes they were smart enough to do everything right in the first place.

The bottom line: Don't just dare to be different. Be different, and include unique and compelling aspects in your development strategy that allow you to create a strong value proposition.

CHAPTER 7

Getting
Legal

*"Knowing less and actually doing something is far better
than knowing everything and never doing anything at all."*

—FRED DELUCA, FOUNDER, SUBWAY

Once you have a good plan in place, the franchisor needs to find qualified legal counsel to develop the proper legal documentation.

This first sentence deserves to be read a couple of times, as it highlights two very important points (aside from the need to obtain proper legal documentation).

The first is that your business planning should be done before you get franchise counsel involved. While I have known some franchise attorneys who are very good at business, it is not a field in which most excel. As we have seen in previous chapters, the decision of whether your business can and should be franchised is largely a business decision. Many of your most important decisions as a franchisor (fees, royalties, territory, etc.) are almost entirely business decisions. These decisions are beyond the scope of an attorney's training and expertise.

The second important point buried in the first sentence is the importance of finding a *qualified* franchise attorney. There are more than 1.1 million lawyers in the U.S., and given the prevalence of franchising in today's economy, chances are that tens of thousands of lawyers have some franchise "experience." But while many of these lawyers, who like the rest of us are looking for business, will tell you they have franchise expertise, there are probably fewer than 1,000 who are really experts. And of these, perhaps less than half are in private practice. So choose your attorney carefully.

The Franchise Disclosure Document

As we briefly discussed in Chapter 1, if you choose to franchise your business, you will need to provide your prospective franchisees with an FDD 14 calendar days prior to taking any fees or signing any contracts with them (or upon their reasonable request). Since you do not count the day you provide the FDD or the day it is signed, you are actually able to sign on Day 16. There is no need to file this document with any federal agency: Simply present the document to your prospect, and the countdown begins.

The original purpose of the Franchise Rule dates back to the days when fast-talking franchise salesmen would often play fast and loose with the truth, resulting in a number of franchisees who would invest their life's savings into franchises that would ultimately fail. In order to protect these "consumers," the FTC promulgated the rule to more fully inform franchise buyers about the investment they were considering.

In essence, the FDD is just that. It is a document that is drafted in a prescribed format to provide your prospective franchisee with the information they need to make an informed decision. And while

>  **Franchise Agreement Changes Mean Delay**
>
> There is also a rule that states the franchisee must have a fully filled-out franchise agreement for seven days, which can run concurrently. So if you negotiate changes, those changes may require a longer waiting period. Again, this emphasizes the need for an experienced franchise attorney.

the quality and contents of these documents vary, each such document is required to contain the following sections in this order:

1. The Franchisor and Any Parents, Predecessors, and Affiliates
2. Business Experience
3. Litigation
4. Bankruptcy
5. Initial Fees
6. Other Fees
7. Estimated Initial Investment
8. Restrictions on Sources of Products and Services
9. Franchisee's Obligations
10. Financing
11. Franchisor's Assistance, Advertising, Computer Systems, and Training
12. Territory
13. Trademarks
14. Patents, Copyrights, and Proprietary Information
15. Obligation to Participate in the Actual Operation of the Franchise Business
16. Restrictions on What the Franchisee May Sell
17. Renewal, Termination, Transfer, and Dispute Resolution
18. Public Figures
19. Financial Performance Representations
20. Outlets and Franchisee Information
21. Financial Statements
22. Contracts
23. Receipts

The exact content and format of each of these required disclosure items is specified in detail within the text of the FTC Rule, but some of the more relevant aspects are listed below.

Initial Fees and Other Fees

As a franchisor, you must disclose in these two sections any fees you will be charging your franchisees. Hidden or undisclosed fees can be a source of disputes, so you will want to be careful here.

Estimated Initial Investment

You will need to provide your prospective franchisees with an estimate of their initial investment (often showing a low and high range), including an estimate that will cover their needed working capital. Be sure your range is realistic, as underestimating the high end of the range can also be a source of future disputes.

Restrictions on Sources of Products and Services

As a franchisor, you can sell goods and/or services to your franchisees, as long as you disclose that you (or an affiliated entity) are making money on the sales. You will also need to disclose the amount of revenue you are deriving from any required purchases (including rebates from unaffiliated vendors). Again, the rule here is to be sure you fully disclose all forms of revenue you generate through sales to franchisees.

Territory

You are not obligated to provide your franchisees with an exclusive or protected territory, but if you choose to do so, you will need to disclose it here. You will need to carefully consider a number of potential business conflicts and reservations of rights in this section should you choose to grant a territory.

Financial Performance Representations (FPR)

You are not obligated to provide your franchisees with any information on sales, earnings, or expenses (other than those outlined above). But if you choose to do so, you would need to provide it in this section of your FDD.

While you are welcome to discuss any information on these elements with your franchisees after they have signed the franchise agreement, prior to the sale of a franchise you will only be allowed to discuss what you have included in your financial performance representation (also referred to occasionally as an "earnings claim" by those who have been in franchising for a while), along with appropriate supporting data. These FPRs do not have to be in the form of income statements and do not need to be prepared in accordance with Generally Accepted Accounting Principles (GAAP), so there is a good deal of flexibility as

to what you can choose to disclose. But the bottom line is, if you plan to provide information that can help a prospective franchisee derive an income statement, it needs to be included in Item 19.

There are certainly advantages to providing an FPR as part of your disclosure document. It seems logical to assume that an FPR would make it easier to sell franchises, especially for the neophyte. That said, an iFranchise Group study of the disclosure documents of rapidly growing new franchisors several years ago showed no significant correlation between the use of an FPR and speed of growth.

There are also those who will argue that using an FPR will reduce a franchisor's legal exposure, as claims of misrepresentation would hold little weight in the face of a well-constructed earnings claim.

That said, there are often good reasons for not using an FPR. Your prototype may not be representative of the type of location, facility size, or other factors your franchisees will experience. Or you simply may not want your financial performance to be part of the public record. And the fact is that a number of franchisors choose not to do FPRs and still manage to sell franchises.

The bottom line is that whether to use an FPR is one of the more complex business decisions you will make as part of your business planning process, and you will need to take a number of factors into consideration when making your choice.

FPR Use Increases in Recent Years

The number of franchisors including FPRs in their disclosure documents has increased substantially over the years. As recently as a decade ago, it was estimated that only 20 to 30 percent of franchisors made any kind of disclosure. More recently, depending on the survey and the industry, various industry observers are reporting that FPRs are being used by about 60 percent of franchise systems. While the iFranchise Group generally advocates using FPRs, there are instances in which they are not appropriate. And we have not seen any correlation between their use and faster franchise sales.

Outlets and Franchisee Information

You must provide a table that will summarize, among other things, the number of franchises that were opened, the number of terminations, the number of franchises that were closed, and the number that were transferred over the past three years. You will also be required to provide contact information for all the franchisees in your system along with the contact information of franchisees that left the system (for any reason) in the past fiscal year.

While we will discuss this in more detail in Chapter 11, almost every book, article, and video discussing the purchase of a franchise encourages your prospects to call these franchisees—making franchise success the primary driver of franchise systems.

Financial Statements

You will need to provide three years of audited financial statements (balance sheets, statements of operations, owner's equity, and cash flows) as part of your FDD. Since most franchisors create a new business entity when they begin franchising, the FTC has developed a "phase-in" rule that allows a startup franchisor to provide an unaudited balance sheet in the first year of franchising and an audited one in the second year. *Note*: Some states have not adopted this rule. Moreover, if the franchisor is a subsidiary of an existing entity (or has obligations guaranteed by another entity), you may need to provide audited financial statements of the existing entity. Be sure to get legal advice on this issue before setting up your franchising business.

Contracts

You will also need to provide your prospects with any contracts they will need to sign. These will certainly include your franchise agreement and may also include financing agreements, product supply agreements, personal guarantees, software licensing agreements, and many other contracts that may be specific to your situation.

Receipts

The final section is a receipt page for your prospect to sign so you can document when he received the FDD.

In summary, your FDD will review the business decisions contained in your contractual relationship with your franchisees and provide them with additional information on you and the franchise that will aid them in making their decision. There are literally hundreds of issues that must be addressed, and the decisions behind those issues will ultimately dictate the franchisor's success. The FDD, and the underlying franchise contract, are complex legal documents that should only be prepared by an experienced franchise attorney.

State Franchise Laws

While there is no need to file your FDD with any federal agencies, the same cannot be said for all the individual states. Some states require franchisors to register and obtain state approval before they are allowed to sell franchises in that state. Some require you to submit franchise marketing material for approval. Other states mandate filing certain legal documents. Some of these filing states offer exemptions to franchisors who license the use of a trademark as part of the franchise offer. Some states regulate the franchisee-franchisor relationship in areas such as territory, termination, and other important rights.

Moreover, these laws are often inconsistent with each other, and may also be inconsistent with FTC Rule 436. The net result is a patchwork quilt of laws that requires specialized legal expertise to navigate. For example, in some states, the definition of a franchise combines the trademark and fee elements with "the right to engage in the business of offering, selling, or distributing goods or services, under a marketing plan or system prescribed or suggested in substantial part by a franchisor." So while the definitions are similar, these small differences can be important.

In addition, the instances in which you may need to register or file your franchise offer vary from state to state. Among the things that can trigger the requirement to register or file in a state are the following:

- ☞ If the franchisor is incorporated in the state
- ☞ If the franchisor is domiciled in the state
- ☞ If the franchisee who receives an offer is a resident of the state
- ☞ If the prospective franchisee's territory will be located in that state

Figure 7.1: **Franchise and Business Opportunity Legislation within the U.S.**

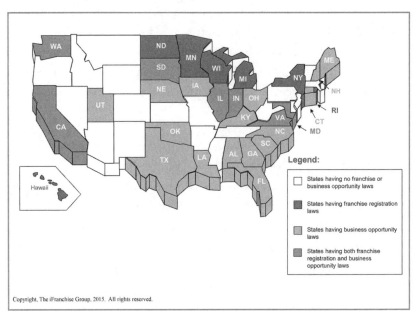

❦ If the offer for the sale of a franchise takes place in that state

The map in Figure 7.1 shows these state laws at the time of writing, but bear in mind they are changing all the time. And again, the purpose of this book is to provide you with a business perspective, not a legal treatise. So while these laws are relatively easy to follow, they do require an experienced franchise attorney to advise you during this process.

Obtaining Your Trademark

Whether you are planning on franchising now or at some point in the distant future, one of the first things you will want to do (if you have not done so already) is obtain a federal trademark on your brand. In a franchise, you are providing your franchisee with a license to use your name, so the last thing you want to do is license a name you do not actually own.

The trademark issue can occasionally pose a short-term stumbling block for new franchisors. If the name you have chosen is already trademarked or is not subject to trademark, you may have to go back to the drawing board.

Sometimes there are simple solutions—an intentional misspelling, a modified word added to your existing name, purchasing rights to the trademark from the owner—and sometimes there are not.

But even if there are not, take heart. Many of the world's most successful franchisors have weathered the name-change storm:

- ▼ Boston Market was originally Boston Chicken.
- ▼ Buffalo Wild Wings was Buffalo Wild Wings & Weck.
- ▼ Burger King was originally Insta-Burger King.
- ▼ Denny's was originally Danny's Donuts.
- ▼ Domino's Pizza was originally DomiNick's.
- ▼ Dunkin' Donuts was originally Open Kettle.
- ▼ KFC was originally Kentucky Fried Chicken.
- ▼ Subway was originally Pete's Super Submarines.

And as much as you may feel your name has been an integral part of your success, remember: Names don't make businesses—businesses make names.

If you find you cannot use your name and must change it, keep in mind names that are generic or descriptive are difficult or impossible to protect. And if the name is remotely descriptive, others may already be using it.

You can start investigating the availability of various names by searching the U.S. government's trademark database (TESS) (http://tmsearch.uspto.gov). With more than 3 million registered, filed, or dead trademarks, coming up with a name that is unique and protectable can be more frustrating than you might imagine. To complicate matters, you will ideally want to pick one that has a corresponding top-level domain name available online.

The good news is that trademarks are granted based on 45 different trademark classifications. So the trademark granted for medical supplies might be different from the trademark granted for hardware, which explains why Ace Bandage and Ace Hardware can coexist.

Once you have several names you like and feel you may be able to protect, it is important to engage the services of an experienced trademark attorney. The attorney may recommend a more thorough search (which will include other public uses of the proposed trademark, including derivatives) using specialized services like Thomson CompuMark. The relatively low cost of conducting a comprehensive trademark search is well worth it, as it may save you time and money in the long run. Once your search is done, the attorney can then complete the registration process, often for as little as $2,000 or so—assuming, of course, that the trademark is not contested.

The trademark process is relatively simple, but given the number of trademarks already established and the bureaucracy involved, it can take a year or more to complete. It involves several steps, including publishing the trademark in the *Trademark Official Gazette* of the U.S. Patent and Trademark Office. *Note*: You do *not* need to have completed the trademark process before you begin franchising.

Your rights to that trademark vest on the date you file your trademark application. When a company is committed to a franchise growth strategy, it will often initiate the franchise process (which can take four to six months or more) while it is still finalizing its name.

While the iFranchise Group does not undertake trademark work (or any legal work), we are happy to refer our clients to excellent attorneys in this field.

Protecting Your Intellectual Property

One key element of the franchise relationship involves sharing your intellectual property with your franchisees, which is often found in the trade secrets and business systems you will include in your operations manual.

As such, one key concern for any new franchisor involves protecting this intellectual property. Because a copyright does not protect the underlying idea but the way the idea is expressed, franchisors generally treat their operations manuals as trade secrets. The status containing confidential and trade secret information in these operations manuals must be addressed in the FDD and the franchise contract.

In addition, the franchisor will want to include the strongest noncompete and intellectual property language permissible (this will vary by state), both for in-term and post-term protection.

Legal Risk

We regularly hear concerns from companies that franchising is just too litigious. But, as we pointed out previously, litigation is not inevitable. In fact, about three-quarters of all franchisors did not report any litigation in their FDDs, according to FRANdata research. And there is a good deal of anecdotal evidence to suggest that of those that did report litigation, many were either larger companies (more relationships create more opportunities for conflict) or simply bad franchisors.

So why is there a perception that franchising is so litigious?

Decades ago, when franchise law was in its infancy, there were not many legal precedents that franchise attorneys could turn to when drafting franchise agreements. And, because franchising was so new, many agreements were drafted by attorneys with little or no experience.

As franchise-related cases were adjudicated, the best franchise attorneys constantly reviewed the outcomes of these cases and made adjustments to their franchise agreements to make them more favorable to their franchisor clients. As case law continues to evolve, these documents typically become even more bulletproof. Franchise agreements today afford franchisors much more protection than those written only a decade ago—as long as the right attorney is drafting the contract. Franchisors have also evolved and become more aware of best practices that help strengthen franchisee relationships and mitigate the risk of litigation.

Much of the litigation that was seen in early franchising is no longer an issue. Historically contested issues, such as use of advertising funds, territorial disputes, good faith and fair dealing, and a franchisor's duty of competence, have largely faded away as court rulings have set precedents and established case law. Franchise lawyers have learned how to write their contracts in a way that will largely avoid such litigation.

Today, a franchise agreement drafted by an experienced franchise attorney is almost always a very one-sided document in favor of the franchisor, and it is usually presented to the franchisee on a take-it-or-leave-it basis. They are substantially non-negotiable. In fact, most franchise agreements today are written in such a way that it is almost impossible for a decent franchisor to be sued for contract violations.

Mitigating Franchisee Litigation Exposure

When it comes to contract disputes, the two issues that remain ripe for litigation are violations of franchise law and fraud in the sales process. In fact, the vast majority of the claims we see between franchisee and franchisor are really centered on one of these two issues (or sometimes both).

But the good news is that these issues are relatively easily inoculated against.

Much litigation in the area of franchise law is triggered when businesses try to avoid being a franchisor (more on that later). Avoiding violations of franchise law and accusations of fraud are largely a matter of education, diligence, and hiring an experienced franchise attorney.

The following checklist will provide you with the basics:

- ⬇ Work with your franchise attorney to train all your salespeople on franchise law and make sure they go through refresher training once a year. As part of that training, have them take a test on the basic tenets of franchise law to ensure they have a good understanding of the issues. Keep these tests for your files.
- ⬇ Be sure your training includes all the following issues:
  - The importance of the franchisee screening and selection process (more on this in Chapter 11)
  - Where you are registered to sell franchises and what questions the salesperson needs to ask to determine if the proper registrations are in place
  - When they must make disclosure
  - The proper format for making disclosure (electronic, paper, etc.) and documenting that disclosure
  - What can and cannot be said in the sales process, especially when it comes to FPR issues
  - Remaining consistent with the FDD in the sales process
  - How to comply with the 14-day rule for FDDs and the seven-day rule for modified franchise agreements
  - How to document conversations and write bulletproof emails
  - When they should contact your attorney with questions

🙟 Provide similar less intense training to nonsales staff that will instruct them how to handle franchise sales leads without violating franchise laws and ensure they understand how to hand off these leads to people who are trained to properly answer questions.

🙟 Designate someone in your company as your compliance officer. The compliance officer should be the go-to person for questions about franchise law and should make sure all registrations are kept current.

🙟 Be sure everyone on your staff is scrupulously honest. Mystery shop your sales force once every year or two and keep a record of the results.

🙟 Ask every franchisee in their closing interview about any representations that were made during the sales process. Many franchisors use a written closing checklist, and some have gone as far as videorecording those interviews. If you find a problem, stop and call your attorney immediately.

🙟 Document all communications with franchisees and prospective franchisees. Simple contact management software costs less than $400, so an electronic system is best.

🙟 Finally, institute a no-tolerance policy if you find any infractions. Be sure your staff knows they will be mystery shopped. And be sure to include something in their employment agreement stating that violations of franchise law and/or misrepresentations made to prospective franchisees are grounds for immediate termination.

The Contractual Liability Trade-Off

Even with the best compliance and training programs and the strongest possible contract, every legal document you sign carries some potential to create legal exposure.

That said, any growth strategy contains some risk. For example, as a franchisor, you will take on incremental obligations with your franchise agreement. But compared to opening another corporate location, you will:

🙟 Avoid any incremental exposure for leases, leased equipment, or other purchases associated with opening an additional location.

▼ Largely avoid any liability associated with accidents in the workplace, slip-and-fall, etc.

▼ Largely avoid any employment liability for issues such as EEOC violations, sexual harassment, etc.

▼ Largely avoid any liability associated with worker accidents, workers' compensation, etc.

So in understanding your potential for liability, remember that the liability associated with franchising can be minimized and, more important, it is probably lower than the liability you might encounter when expanding using other growth strategies.

The Inadvertent Franchisor

As mentioned above, one of the simplest problems to avoid (yet one of the most common mistakes) in franchising involves the sale of inadvertent franchises. Often, company management created this relationship innocently. Some wanted to avoid a business strategy they perceived to be highly regulated. Others may not have liked the idea of calling their relationship a "franchise" and assumed if they called it something else, they were not violating franchise regulations. Some simply had no clue about franchise law.

What do these companies have in common? Often, unfortunately, it is bad legal advice.

Attorneys, like the rest of us, are fallible. And attorneys who are not experts in the complexities of franchise law will occasionally try to navigate these issues on their own. And when they do, the results can be disastrous.

▼ In *Mirza v. TV Temp*, the plaintiffs were awarded $1.45 million based on the defendant's failure to provide disclosure documents in a timely fashion.

▼ KIS Corporation paid $1.55 million in damages after agreeing its plan violated the FTC Rule.

▼ In *LASVN #2 v. Sperry Van Ness Real Estate*, a jury awarded more than $6 million in a case in which both parties had agreed in writing that the relationship was not a franchise.

☞ In *Charts Insurance Associates v. Nationwide Mutual Insurance*, a jury awarded $2.3 million for the sale of an insurance agency that triggered the Connecticut Franchise Act. In this case, only two elements were necessary to meet this test: "1) an oral or written agreement . . . in which a franchisee is granted the right to engage in the business of offering . . . services under a marketing plan or system prescribed in substantial part by a franchisor, and 2) the operation of the franchisee's business pursuant to this marketing plan or system . . . substantially associated with the franchisor's trademark . . ." In this case, the fee element was not even needed to create a franchise relationship under Connecticut law.

☞ And, in at least one case, a true nonfranchise relationship actually (and probably unwittingly) *evolved* into a franchise. As odd as it may seem, a business that started as a distributorship became a franchise without any change in the contract. In the case of *To-Am Equipment v. Mitsubishi Caterpillar Forklift America*, Mitsubishi granted a distributorship to To-Am assuming that since it was not charging To-Am a fee, it was not subject to franchise laws. But over the course of the eight-year relationship, To-Am purchased $1,600 worth of manuals from Mitsubishi, thus triggering Illinois state franchise laws and ultimately costing Mitsubishi $1.525 million.

Unfortunately, the problems associated with these inadvertent franchises may take years to arise, often catching the franchisor by complete surprise. And on occasion, these accidental franchises will even encourage competitors, who unknowingly replicate a flawed system and follow their lead into legally troubled waters.

Worst of all, these situations are entirely and easily avoidable. In virtually every case, these

> ☞ **Should Have Read More Carefully**
>
> Unlike FTC Rule 436, where the fee element of the franchise definition is triggered with a $500 fee paid in the first six months of operation, Illinois law omits this "first six months" language, which created a franchise relationship once this amount was exceeded.

companies (or their lawyers) simply did not realize they were franchising.

Quantifying the Risk

As you can see, acting as a franchisor without complying with franchise laws can create major problems.

At the federal level, the FTC has the right to seek both preliminary and permanent injunctions against rule violations—effectively banning you from franchising for years (or even forever!). It can freeze assets at the corporate and personal level. It can assess civil penalties of $11,000 *per violation* (the largest civil penalty in a Franchise Rule case to date is $870,000). And it can require monetary redress on behalf of those injured by Franchise Rule violations. (The largest consumer redress so far stands at $4.9 million.)

The good news is that under the FTC Rule, there is no private right of action. In layman's terms, that means franchisees cannot sue you under the act. That said, there are provisions for personal liability: "Franchisors and their key officers and executives are responsible for violations by persons acting in their behalf, including independent franchise brokers, subfranchisors, and the franchisor's own sales personnel."

State laws can be even more damaging. Under many state laws, franchisees have a private right of action. These laws can also provide for incremental fines of up to $100,000 per violation. And in some states, violations of franchise law are actually a Class IV felony.

Beyond the financial downside, if you are found to have violated federal or state rules or regulations, you may be required to disclose those violations in your FDD for ten years. Since your prospective franchisees will all see these violations, these disclosures could cost you lost franchise sales.

What's more, the franchisor may also find its contract is subject to rescission. So your former franchisee will have received all your training, intellectual property, and initial and ongoing assistance, and you will not be able to collect fees or enforce post-termination noncompetition clauses, allowing them to compete with you using your own intellectual property. To add insult to injury, you may be required to return the franchisee's entire initial investment—not just the franchise fee, but also any related expenses that were incurred in starting up the business.

Again, the important point is that compliance with franchise laws is relatively easy if you hire competent franchise counsel. The penalties for noncompliance are stiff. So the savvy franchisor will not try to shortcut the process by using their real estate attorney, their brother-in-law, or an inexperienced attorney just to save a couple thousand dollars.

Vicarious Liability Concerns

Aside from litigation that might result from your contractual relationship with your franchisee, there is also the issue of *vicarious liability*—the liability a franchisor may incur due to the actions of their franchisees or their franchisee's employees.

Almost everyone has heard of the McDonald's coffee case—where a customer named Stella Liebeck received third-degree burns on her legs when she spilled hot coffee on herself in a franchisee's drive-thru. McDonald's eventually settled for an undisclosed amount, but at trial Liebeck was awarded $640,000 (reduced by the judge from the $2.8 million originally awarded by the jury).

While this kind of case can appear frivolous, it serves to illustrate how a franchisor can be held liable for the actions of their franchisees in a vicarious liability suit. Remember, this happened at a franchisee's location and that franchisee was, in fact, an independent business owner.

So how can something like this happen?

The short answer is that vicarious liability may become an issue when a franchisor unintentionally creates an "agency relationship" with its franchisees (or their employees) by exercising control over their activities. And under the doctrine of *respondeat superior*, the party in control is responsible for the acts of its subordinates. In the McDonald's case, the franchisor required its franchisees to serve coffee at between 180° and 190° F—a temperature hot enough to cause third-degree burns—and the jury found that that the warnings on the cup were insufficient.

The good news when it comes to issues of vicarious liability is that the law is on the side of the franchisor. The franchisee is, in fact, an independent business owner and as such, they are in control of their actions and the actions of their employees.

So how is an agency relationship created?

Usually it stems from the franchisor's desire to be overly prescriptive about the way in which franchisees conduct their day-to-day business. In essence, the franchisor must be cognizant of the line between controls that impact brand standards and those that do not.

While a comprehensive discussion of vicarious liability is beyond the scope of this book, much of this type of liability is avoidable. Start by insisting that all franchisees clearly indicate (with signs, on letterhead, in advertising, etc.) that they are independent licensees. By requiring franchisees to hold themselves out as independent contractors, *and remembering to treat them as such*, the franchisor will take an important step toward insulating itself from the acts of its franchisees.

Aside from relying on the requirements of the franchise agreement, one of the best ways to avoid vicarious liability is to be sure that your franchise agreement, operations manual, and training programs are all properly and consistently written to specify the nature of the relationship. The operations manual should be written by someone with an understanding of how this liability can be inadvertently created.

A good operations manual will provide very specific direction in areas that impact brand standards but exercise less control over areas that do not. For example, a franchisor would want to specify the use of a certain piece of equipment if it had an impact on the consumer's brand experience. However, if there were ready substitutes for that equipment that would provide the same brand experience, the franchisor could allow it (including an approval process for substitutes), thereby reducing the amount of control being exercised and reducing its potential for liability.

As you can see, the process of writing to these standards is often part art and part science. But it is something a skilled professional will always keep in mind when drafting a manual.

And, of course, once the operations manual is written, have it reviewed by your attorney to ensure it properly addresses this issue. Well-written legal documents and manuals, along with appropriate internal processes, will allow you to minimize the potential for vicarious liability claims.

Beyond these tools, you will typically want to require your franchisees to carry comprehensive general liability insurance coverage that will name you as a coinsured on the policy. This will provide you with an extra level of protection. Be sure that your compliance officer routinely obtains and checks your franchisees' insurance certificates. Of course, you may also choose to carry your own insurance that will cover you in the event of a third-party action.

Any time you allow someone to use your brand, the possibility exists that you will be named in litigation. That said, for a vicarious liability action to harm you as a franchisor, someone would need to:

- ➤ Prove that excess control was exercised (so the franchisee/employee was not acting as an independent contractor)
- ➤ Prove that this control resulted in liability or that you were negligent
- ➤ Receive an award in excess of your franchisee's insurance and your own insurance coverage

So while it is a real concern, it is a manageable risk. And again, keep in mind that if you were to develop additional company locations as an alternative growth strategy, all this liability would fall to you in any event.

Finding the Right Attorney

When choosing your franchise attorney, you need to bear in mind that you are likely looking at a long-term relationship. In addition to developing your franchise's legal documents, you will need your attorney to update those documents (and perhaps file them or renew your filings with the appropriate state agencies) on an annual basis.

There are a number of factors you may want to consider when choosing your franchise attorney: industry expertise, location, firm size, franchisor focus, transactional focus, franchise experience, price, and fee structure. These issues are addressed in greater detail in Chapter 13. But the best way to begin your search is often with referrals from a trusted source.

At the iFranchise Group, we do not draft legal documents on behalf of our clients or provide them with legal advice. And, of course, we do not take referral fees from the attorneys we recommend.

If you are considering franchising and want a recommendation for a franchise attorney, we are happy to provide you with referrals—even if you do not choose to work with us—as we feel it is in the best interest of franchising to have franchisors represented by competent counsel.

Unauthorized Practice of Law

While the practice has been the subject of increasing scrutiny in recent years, some consulting firms and legal document preparation firms persist in selling the preparation of franchise legal documents to their franchisor clients. According to a recent case in the U.S. District Court, Northern District of Illinois:

> "Drafting franchise agreements, offering circulars, and licensing agreements and executing registration certificates is the practice of law . . . in-house counsel may not act as attorneys on behalf of their employer's clients . . . simply having a licensed attorney review and 'sign off' on those documents does not absolve the company from unauthorized practice [of law]."

Similar cases have more recently been heard in Ohio and Florida, and, in at least one of the cases, the courts have come to similar conclusions.

Still, these franchise packagers will tout their all-under-one-roof approach and continue to develop these legal documents on behalf of startup franchisors.

At the iFranchise Group, we believe strongly that consulting firms should never practice law. But it is a worthwhile exercise to ask why the unauthorized practice of law is prohibited and why independent and expert legal representation is so vital to implementing your franchise program.

By contracting with an experienced franchise attorney from the start, you can:

- ⌐ *Avoid conflicts of interest.* When you hire an attorney, the attorney represents you. When you use a packager's attorney, the attorney represents the packager. In the event of a conflict of interest, you will find that "your" attorney is actually working for the other side.
- ⌐ *Avoid having to pay for legal documents twice:* once for their creation and once for their review by outside legal counsel—something packaging firms often require to try to avoid claims of unauthorized practice. The fees quoted by packaging firms are only a fraction of what you will really pay to create these documents.

- ☞ *Use your law firm for legal proceedings*, such as franchise closings, transfers, negotiations, etc.
- ☞ *Receive expert legal advice on issues* such as real estate, capital formation, franchise finance, antitrust, and so on from professionals who understand the impact of these matters on franchising.
- ☞ *Have the peace of mind that the firm that developed your legal documents is properly insured in the highly unlikely event of a problem.* Packagers cannot carry legal malpractice insurance for obvious reasons.
- ☞ *Enjoy attorney-client privilege.* When you hire an attorney, you may have privileged conversations. With a packager's attorney, nothing you discuss is subject to privilege. Thus, your own attorney may be called to testify against you. Just imagine this scenario: one of your franchisees sues you over a particularly onerous clause in a franchise agreement, and your franchisee has the right to depose your attorney relative to all conversations you had on the subject.
- ☞ *Develop a relationship with professionals* who are well-established in the franchise community and well-known and respected by state examiners.

Perhaps most important, it has been our experience that turnover among lawyers in packaging firms is often very high. The best attorneys will leave the packaging firm after gaining experience to move on to more lucrative roles in private practice or as an in-house franchise counsel at a large franchise company. And since consulting firms cannot offer partnership opportunities in the same way a law firm might, these consulting firms may be forced to recruit from a pool of relatively inexperienced candidates.

(The iFranchise Group does not provide legal documents to our clients or participate in legal fees collected by the outside counsel, allowing us to maintain our objectivity in our recommendations of counsel.)

THE BOTTOM LINE

The Legal Stuff Sounds Scary But Really Isn't

The bottom line is that penalties built into these laws and regulations are severe—and can be a death trap for the unwitting. After reading about these penalties, it is a wonder anyone would want to be a franchisor. Multimillion-dollar fines and felony convictions are not what most entrepreneurs dream about when they go into business. But the fact remains that franchising remains one of the most robust sectors of the economy, with continued explosive growth and new, successful franchisors joining the market every day.

So how do franchisors sleep at night?

The fact is that being a franchisor is not all that difficult or scary, if you do it right and seek qualified legal counsel.

The short version:

- Hire an experienced franchise attorney.
- Always tell the truth to your prospective franchisees.
- Never say anything to a prospect that is not in your FDD.
- Follow some fairly simple disclosure rules.
- Be sure you have a well-written operations manual.
- Document what you have done.
- Be aware of what triggers state laws and when you need to be registered.
- Be sure your staff follows these rules.
- Require your franchisees to carry insurance.

Follow these steps, and you should be able to sleep soundly at night.

Growth comes at a cost, and part of that cost is becoming a bigger target. If you have 1,000 franchisees, the odds increase that one of them—or one of their customers—will not be happy with you. But there is much more liability associated with an equal number of company-owned operations than there is with franchising.

Ultimately, franchising is about relationships. The best franchisors are open and honest in their communications. They sincerely want their franchisees to succeed, and they are transparent and fair in their dealings with them. And while savvy franchisors will build their contracts as if they were brick houses, they will also recognize that the best contracts are the ones that get locked in a file cabinet, never to be looked at again.

CHAPTER 8

Controlling
Quality

*"You look at any giant corporation, and I mean the biggies,
and they all started with a guy with an idea,
doing it well."*

—IRV ROBBINS, CO-FOUNDER, BASKIN-ROBBINS ICE CREAM

Throughout this book, we talk frequently about the importance of franchisee success to your success as a franchisor. Successful franchisees are at the heart of almost every successful franchise system. And for most successful franchisors, quality control is at the heart of franchisee success.

In fact, if we start with the premise that a franchisor's core business model is successful, we have the following equation:

Franchisee Success = Quality Control

The Quality Control Myth

When it comes to franchising, one of the most pervasive myths is that corporate stores will outperform franchise locations when it comes to quality. This is born out of the notion that operational control is the same as quality control.

And while it is true a franchisor cannot control a franchisee the way it can control a hired manager (you cannot fire them at will, for example), there are a number of reasons franchisees typically outperform non-owner store managers:

- ☞ Franchisees are often recruited from a higher-caliber candidate pool than are store managers. To accumulate the capital necessary to purchase a franchise, most franchise candidates have already had some substantial (and successful) business experience.

- ☞ Franchisees typically invest in a franchise because they believe passionately in the concept and want to be associated with the brand. Managers often apply for a job because it was available and met their general compensation needs.

- ☞ Franchisees are motivated to follow the system because they believe it works and know that if they do not follow it, they could lose their entire investment. Managers follow systems because they might lose their jobs if they do not.

- ☞ Franchisees are typically highly motivated by the investment they have made. Managers invest no money and usually see a job only as a stepping stone in their long-term career plan. Even the best profit-sharing plans provide managers with much lower potential rewards and much less is at risk.

- ☞ Franchisees also have a pride of ownership. Most managers see their workplace from a very different perspective.

- ☞ Franchisees typically plan to stay involved with a franchise for a decade or more, where they will accumulate knowledge and experience that will allow them to better run their operations. Most managers look at the job with a much shorter time horizon.

- ☞ Under most franchise agreements, franchisees cannot jump ship and go to work for your competitors. The best managers are often recruited away by the competition.

- ☞ The ultimate goal for someone who buys a franchise is to sell it for a profit. Franchisees know this is not possible unless the business performs at a high level. They are thus motivated to maintain a high level of quality in the business. A hired manager has no such motivation.

So while your operational control will be reduced as a franchisor, the quality levels achieved by your franchisees will often exceed the quality in your corporate locations.

While a definitive study has never been conducted on the subject, there is plenty of anecdotal evidence supporting the theory that franchisees outperform locations run by corporate managers—both in terms of revenue and expense management. When corporations sell company-owned stores to franchisees, for example, they almost always see revenue increases (such as the Sterling Optical example in Chapter 2).

Bottom line: In our observations, franchisees historically outperform corporate managers by anywhere from 10 to 30 percent on the revenue side. And in a world where consumers are voting with their pocketbooks, improved sales are generally a strong indicator of increased quality.

Similarly, franchisees typically do a better job of managing expenses by:

- Managing labor better (sending employees home when the store is not busy, etc.)
- Keeping tighter controls on inventory (ordering more efficiently, reducing spoilage by rotating stock, decreasing shrinkage, etc.)
- Improving margins through opportunistic buying

Not only can franchisees outsell similarly situated corporate stores, but they can often out-manage them as well—occasionally allowing franchisees to succeed in markets the franchisor might find marginal for corporate locations.

The Pillars of Quality Control

Of course, the lack of direct operational control a franchisor can exercise has its drawbacks. Since the franchisor cannot fire a franchisee (or their employees) or employ similar levels of control over other aspects of the franchisee's operations, the franchisor must guard against franchisees who try to change its systems in an effort to "improve" it. But while the franchisor cannot exercise absolute control of its franchisees, it has the obligation to control the brand and the brand image. And the brand, along with what it stands for, will ultimately dictate the success of everyone in the system.

Remember: Franchisee Success = Quality Control

The factors that influence franchisee success are the same factors the best franchisors focus on to influence quality. We call them the four pillars of quality control:

1. Franchisee selection
2. Documented systems
3. Training and support
4. Legal documentation

While we will deal with franchisee selection in greater detail in Chapter 11, there are few things that will have a greater influence on the success or failure of a franchise than the quality of the candidate. If you award a franchise to someone who does not have the skill set, work ethic, or resources to succeed, you are setting up both the franchisee and, in the long term, your franchise system for failure.

Second, of course, you need to document your systems in detail so your franchisees will have a road map for success. Every successful business has systems, but they have not always documented those systems to a high degree. When it comes to franchising, this piece is vitally important.

Third, it is imperative that you provide your franchisee with the support they need. For virtually every franchise system, that will entail some level of training, although the amount and type of training can vary substantially. In addition, there may be many other things you will need to do to help ensure franchisee success. For some, it will involve assistance in areas such as site selection, lease negotiation, and construction. For others, it may involve the provision of back-office services and support. At a minimum, the vast majority of franchisors provide some level of field support to their franchisees.

Finally, while we discussed the importance of appropriate legal controls and contracts in the previous chapter, quality control in franchising means more than just having these documents in place. It also means you have to have the intestinal fortitude to enforce those controls.

In looking at these four pillars, you will note none of them fall outside the controls you have to place on your company-owned locations. You need to hire good people. You need to provide them with specific

tasks and have them done in a specific way. You need to train them and provide them with ongoing assistance to ensure they are following your systems. And if they are incapable or unwilling to follow those systems, you need to discipline or terminate your employees.

You will also note that each of these four pillars comes with an associated cost:

- The increased cost of marketing that results from being more selective in the sales process
- The cost of developing comprehensive best practices operations documentation—either in time or in fees or both
- The cost of the staff you hire to provide training and support to your franchisees
- The legal costs associated with developing and enforcing your franchise contracts

But the bottom line is that if you are willing to pay the price, controlling quality is simply a process like any other. High-performing franchisors ensure they budget properly in each of

Keep Your Manual Close

A franchisor may allow prospective franchisee to review its manual prior to purchase, but this poses a number of problems. It exposes the franchisor's intellectual property to the prospect. If the prospect is not granted adequate time with the material (and that adequacy would be something a court might choose to weigh in on), the franchisor could risk noncompliance. And if the franchisor provides the franchisee with as much time as he needs, the franchisee might be unimpressed or turn out to be a current or future competitor. Moreover, the franchisor would be exposing the operations manual to "the public" and thus might be compromising its trade secret status. And, of course, adding this step to the sales process adds to a franchisor's compliance burden, especially when dealing with remote franchise prospects. The net effect is that virtually all franchisors will choose to disclose the table of contents rather than risk the problems above.

these areas so corners are not cut, which would cause quality control to suffer.

The Franchise Operations Manual

The key to duplicating a franchisor's success lies in documenting the systems of operation that led to that success. And in franchising, this means developing an operations manual.

In recognition of how important the manual is to a franchise system, regulators actually included the requirement in FTC Rule 436 that the franchisor must disclose the table of contents of the operations manual to prospective franchisees, along with the number of pages devoted to each subject and the total number of pages in the manual.

In addition to meeting this legal guideline, a good franchise operations manual will serve several purposes:

- ☞ A well-written operations manual will be useful as a sales tool for prospective franchisees. A brief glance and riffle through the pages (not allowing an actual review, since you have provided the outline in the FDD) will demonstrate to prospects just how thoroughly you have documented your systems.

- ☞ Your operations manual will play a key role in training your franchisees, serving as the textbook for your training program. Franchisees can read the manual at home (after they have signed the franchise agreement, of course) and study for the training they are about to undertake.

- ☞ Your operations manual will serve as an ongoing reference tool for established franchisees, and you will want to train them to use it to answer any questions they may have before calling you.

- ☞ Of course, one of the main purposes of the operations manual will be to serve as a legally enforceable quality control document. Your franchise agreement will require your franchisees to meet the standards in your operations manual. Failure to meet the standards set out in the manual will be grounds for termination—thus it is the manual's role, when properly tied to the franchise agreement, to serve as the system's brand standards. By keeping your brand standards in the operations manual instead of in the franchise agreement, you can maintain them as trade secrets and change them as your operating systems change over time.

➤ A well-written operations manual can also save your franchisees money by improving and systemizing your operations (labor control, purchasing controls, etc.). Ultimately, this will result in happier and more profitable franchisees (and may have similar benefits for corporate operations).

➤ Similarly, a well-written operations manual will contain systems (local marketing and advertising requirements, sales scripts, etc.) that will help the franchisee improve sales. In addition to improving franchisee revenues, this will increase royalties for the franchisor.

➤ And, of course, the last two benefits will result in more profitable franchisees, lower franchisee turnover/failure rates, reduced support costs, improved marketability of the franchise, and perhaps reduced litigation.

➤ Finally, a good operations manual will help the franchisor avoid vicarious liability by clearly establishing the franchisee as an independent contractor and explaining important areas of compliance.

While some entrepreneurs choose to develop their operations manuals internally, this carries considerable risks. While many people are certainly capable of drafting a well-written manual, a franchise operations manual calls for more than good writing because of the legal issues involved.

Relative to contractual liability, the writing process is relatively simple. The rule of thumb is to never state in absolute terms that the franchisor will do something they are not prepared to do in every set of circumstances. So, for example, your operations manual should never say something such as "The franchisor will always provide you with 100 percent of your inventory"—even if that is your intent. The reason? If unforeseen circumstances were to prevent you from supplying inventory, the franchisee might claim you had breached your responsibilities as a franchisor. Thus, you always want to couch such terminology in less absolute terms: "the franchisor or its designated supplier . . ."

Of course, unlike your contract, your operations manual is subject to modification—so most of these issues are relatively easy to overcome as long as you regularly review your manual to be sure policy changes have not made certain sections obsolete.

The more serious concern when drafting an operations manual involves the issue of control. The more control you exercise over your franchisee, the greater the likelihood you may step over the line of creating an agency relationship, in which you become responsible for the acts of your franchisees or your franchisees' employees.

Thus part of the key to writing a good operations manual is understanding where to draw the line on the issue of control. In a franchise operations manual, you will want to exercise strong controls over any aspect of the franchisee's business that will impact the consumer's perception of the brand or brand standards. And you will want to exercise less control (often providing simply recommendations and best practices) over those issues that will not impact brand standards. (*Note:* This does *not* hold true for a corporate operations manual. In drafting your manual for company operations, you can exercise much more control without incurring incremental liability, since you already bear responsibility for your employees' actions.)

Thus, for the uninitiated, drafting an operations manual can be a minefield of potential liability. Worse, the offending section of the manual can go for years without incurring any problems at all until one day the time bomb goes off. Lawsuits in which an operations manual determined the outcome for a franchisor are not uncommon:

- ◆ In the case of *Decker v. Domino's Pizza, Inc.,* an employee at a Domino's in North Alton, Illinois, was robbed at gunpoint. When he could not open the drop safe, which operated on a time lock, Decker and other employees were assaulted. Prior to the incident, Domino's had mandated that all stores adopt a cash management system which included the use of this type of drop safe, as studies had indicated that this type of system tended to reduce store robberies. Nonetheless, Decker eventually won $300,000 in the lawsuit based on the premise that the franchisor's insistence on using this cash management system was the proximate cause of his assault and injuries.
- ◆ In the case of *Wu v. Dunkin' Donuts,* the courts reached the opposite conclusion. In doing so, they held that the franchisor did not have

any liability involving an employee who was brutally attacked, stating, "the weight of authority construes franchisor liability narrowly, finding that absent a showing of actual control over the security measures employed by the franchisee, franchisors have no legal duty in such cases."

➤ Jack in the Box nearly went bankrupt in the mid-1990s following a food poisoning incident involving E. coli bacteria. While the FDA requirement at that time called for meat to be cooked to an internal temperature of 140°F, the state of Washington required a temperature of at least 155°F—the temperature needed to kill the bacteria. A well-drafted operations manual that properly mandated the franchisee must comply with the stricter of federal, state, or local laws governing the preparation of food product might have saved lives as well as more than $160 million.

➤ More recently, in the case of *Ketterling v. Burger King Corporation,* a customer filed a vicarious liability against Burger King for the failure of its franchisee to clear snow and ice from their premises in a timely fashion. The court concluded that Burger King did not control the premises. While Burger King's operations manual did require the franchisee to clear snow and ice, the Idaho Supreme court stated, in part, that "a franchisor may be held vicariously liable for the tortious conduct of its franchisee only if the franchisor has control or a right of control over the daily operation of the specific aspect of the franchisee's business that is alleged to have caused the harm." In dismissing the claims against Burger King, the court focused on language in the operations manual that the franchisee was responsible for the day-to-day operation of the restaurant.

While there could be a number of additional examples, the key for the new franchisor is to understand the complexity of these issues when developing a manual. Failure could set the time bomb ticking.

With this as a starting point, the new franchisor will want to document every step in the development of a new franchise unit, starting with the most basic: finding a site, opening a bank account, obtaining a federal tax identification number and insurance, and even primers on general business practices. The operations manual should also include discussions on issues such as wage and labor laws, EEOC requirements, policies against sexual harassment, the Americans with Disabilities Act, and a variety of other laws affecting small business operations. The manual should not, however, attempt to dictate the franchisee's general employment policies such as wage or bonus structure, vacation policies, etc. And, of course,

---

▼ Tread Carefully

Where the line is drawn on employment issues is of huge importance given recent attempts by the National Labor Relations Board to try to classify franchisors as "co-employers." Any franchisor considered a co-employer would incur signif-icant potential liability—so you must take care in drafting your manual that you do not acciden-tally create this co-employment relationship. For these (and other) reasons, have your man-ual written professionally and reviewed by legal counsel.

---

the franchisor must include very specific instructions on business operations, franchise reporting requirements, and expected standards of performance. All these discussions should focus both on the franchisee's profitability and protecting the franchisor's brand.

One last word of caution: on occasion, companies obtain the operations manuals of other franchisors (or general industry manuals) and use them to create their own. And while it probably goes without saying, you should never copy a manual and use it as your own unless you have express written permission to do so. The use of this proprietary intellectual property can create significant liability under various copyright and intellectual property protection statutes. And that does not even account for the fact that the information contained in any manual could be poorly drafted from a franchise standpoint.

Keeping Your Operations Manual Current

When you develop your operations manual, bear in mind that it will be an ever-changing set of systems and standards—not a static document you develop once and never see again. As your business evolves to meet changes in the marketplace via new advertising, expanded product or service offerings, changes in pricing strategy, or any of a number of other factors that will evolve over time, your operations manual must evolve in parallel for it to reflect the most up-to-date systems.

Since the standards in your operations manual are legally enforceable, your legal documents will give you the flexibility to alter your system over time—and for those alterations to be enforceable (within reason) as a part of your contractual relationship with your franchisor.

With this in mind, you should plan on constantly updating and

▼ **Advantages of Online Manuals**
More and more, franchisors are migrating their operations manuals to a web-based format. Doing so allows greater flexibility in terms of updates, setting permissions on access to specific sections of the manual, and protecting the franchisor's intellectual property.

expanding your operating manual. Disseminating these updates electronically, in password-protected, encrypted files can make delivery efficient and virtually cost-free. And while the time and effort budgeted will be a function of change within the system, we recommend that you review your operations manual annually to be sure it incorporates the most recent information on operating the business, as well as changes in any relevant laws.

Keeping Your Operations Manual Confidential

Another important factor to consider once you have drafted your operations manual is how to keep its contents confidential. In fact, it is generally referred to as "Confidential Franchise Operations Manual" in your legal agreements and must be treated as such to be protectable as trade secrets. If you were to allow the manual to be freely circulated in the public domain, you would lose your rights to the trade secrets it contains (and would be unable to enforce confidentiality agreements involving the manual), as you would have failed, in the eyes of a court, to treat them as trade secrets.

Most franchisors therefore require their franchisees to keep their manuals under lock and key, disseminating copies of relevant parts to employees only as needed for training. They must understand that the manual represents the value of the system and the harm that can come if they were to lose control of your intellectual property.

Training Your Franchisees

With the operations manual completed, the franchisor must develop a strong training program to impart its contents to franchisees. But while the operations manual should be very detailed, training programs will often presuppose a certain level of knowledge or ability.

To develop a sound training program, the franchisor needs to start with an understanding of their franchisee. Is this new franchisee someone with industry-specific knowledge? Specific skills, such as sales or management abilities? Or will the franchisor need to treat their franchisee as if he were learning absolutely everything for the first time?

Ultimately, the training program must be good enough to ensure that the least-skilled new franchisee can represent the brand to the standard of quality associated with the concept.

Some franchisors feel they can cut corners and costs by limiting training to a brief initial session. In fact, the money *lost* by reducing a franchisor's commitment to training can be staggering—but, at the same time, it is exceedingly difficult to measure.

Training does come with a cost, in terms of time, salaries, and the expense associated with developing training programs and learning management systems. But the costs of undertrained franchisees start with the increased costs of supporting these franchisees. Add to that the costs of potential legal actions and other problems associated with failed franchisees. But perhaps the biggest loss will come from the royalties forgone when franchisees do not perform to their potential.

Meanwhile, the best franchisors are huge advocates of training and invest heavily in it. Even though the training conducted by newer franchise companies is often fairly informal, the best new franchisors make it a priority to develop more formal programs as soon as possible. These programs will prescribe in detail exactly what each franchisee and their personnel must master. By specifying exactly what must be taught and how the instruction will be conducted on an hour-by-hour basis, these training programs provide knowledge in a manner that will foster consistency. Finally, through the use of comprehensive tests, the franchisor can create accountability.

Once a new franchisor decides on subject matter, it must then decide how to conduct the training. Generally, this training takes several forms:

- ☞ Pre-training (either reading assignments or online learning) that is often completed prior to the start of classroom training
- ☞ Classroom training (generally at the franchisor's home office)
- ☞ On-site training (often including grand opening assistance)
- ☞ Ongoing training (which can be provided via video, online, at the franchisee's site, in regional meetings, or at annual conventions)

Once you reach a decision on how to provide training, you will need to decide on logistics.

- ☞ Where will the training be held?
- ☞ Will training be given on a regular schedule or on an as-needed basis?
- ☞ Who will conduct the actual training?
- ☞ Who must attend training?
- ☞ Who may attend training?
- ☞ How long will the training take overall?
- ☞ How much time will be devoted to each topic?
- ☞ What form or combinations of forms will the training take?
- ☞ How will trainees be tested on their knowledge?
- ☞ What will happen if a trainee fails? Does not attend? Demonstrates a poor attitude?

Because a healthy franchise system depends in large part on the ability and preparedness of its franchisees, the franchise agreement must define with great care and precision the franchisor's obligations and rights with regard to training and ongoing support. To ensure maintenance of brand quality, system-wide uniformity, and reliable quality, all franchisees should be required to attend and successfully complete an initial training course designed, refined, and staffed by the franchisor.

The duration of training should be determined by how long it takes the franchisor to adequately impart the contents of the operations manual in a way that will allow the franchisee to consistently meet the franchisor's standards of quality. And while holding the training process to this standard can be expensive and time-consuming, there may be no more important facet of quality control than this initial training.

Training at the Franchisor's Home Office

For most franchisors, the hands-on portion of training starts at their home office. This training can last for several days or weeks and, for newer franchisors, is often held in hotel conference rooms or temporary office facilities to keep costs under control.

Generally speaking, home office training starts with a tour of the prototype operation and corporate offices, and an introduction of staff and their roles. Once the formal training session begins, most franchisors focus on subjects best taught in a classroom setting. Among the dozens of topics usually included in this portion of training are corporate history and philosophy, site selection, lease negotiation, pre-opening procedures, daily operations, insurance requirements, vendor relationships, and reporting requirements. This segment of training often involves hands-on training within your franchise prototype (or perhaps a special training prototype constructed for that purpose).

Franchise training classes should be lively and interactive. A mixture of training formats such as video (for example, showing a key supplier's facility), lecture, discussion, and hands-on work (such as product preparation or how to provide the franchise services) creates an inviting training environment for franchisees. Moreover, various studies have shown that franchisees retain more information when the trainer uses a variety of training methodologies combining visual, auditory, and tactile learning. We often recommend that our clients involve their management staff in the home office training session as well. Exposing multiple staff members to franchisees energizes the process and helps build franchisee relationships throughout the organization.

The time, effort, and expense associated with developing appropriate training tools and materials will vary considerably. The more complex the business, and the more it relies on the franchisee's employees (as opposed to the individual franchisee) to deliver the product or service, the more the system will benefit from more sophisticated training tools like videos.

Home office training, like all training, should be accompanied by testing, evaluation, and other procedures to ensure that franchisees are indeed capable of top performance.

On-Site Training

The next step in the franchisee training process often involves spending several days to a few weeks (or more, depending on the complexity of your operation) assisting franchisees and their staff at the franchisee's location.

As with home office training, you should develop a detailed training agenda for this stage. Depending on a franchisee's prior business experience and sophistication, the on-site portion of the training can differ markedly from one franchisee to the next. The franchisor will thus need to be flexible in terms of approach and content.

Given that the on-site session will take place at the franchisee's location, training should focus on assisting the franchisee in becoming more familiar and comfortable with the day-to-day operation of the business. Franchisees new to the industry will have different questions and expectations than franchisees with prior experience in related businesses. One of the key objectives of the on-site trainer is to identify and prioritize the franchisee's needs during the first day or two so she can tailor the remaining training schedule to best meet those needs.

On-site training is an important extension of the franchisor's pre-opening training program. New franchisees can easily become overwhelmed and can sometimes momentarily forget everything that has been taught to them. Having the franchisor's representatives at the site—often in the form of an opening team—can ease this transition and ensure that customers get a good first impression of the brand and the franchisee's operations. An opening team helps franchisees break into day-to-day operations slowly, so they don't feel they're jumping into the deep end alone, without assistance from the franchisor.

My partner, Dave Hood, tells a story that illustrates this from his days at Auntie Anne's. Years ago, an opening team from Auntie Anne's traveled to a franchisee's grand opening. For those readers who are unfamiliar with Auntie Anne's, the locations (most of which are in malls) are typically 600 square feet with a very small back room that serves as an office. So when the grand opening got off to a raging start, the training team was celebrating what was sure to be a very successful location. The franchise owner, however, could not be located. After a brief search, he was found lying on the ground in the fetal position—afraid to even move. The staff got him to his feet, walked him back out front, and told him not to worry about anything—just watch. And the team finished the day for the franchisee, eventually working him into the day's activities. Over the course of the next several years, the franchisee became one of Auntie Anne's top operators. But if it were not for the support of the franchisor on that first day of operations, things might have gone a very different direction.

Within several days following the completion of on-site training, you should provide the franchisee with an overall written evaluation of his or her performance in the training program. The evaluation should reference both the franchisee's strengths and areas in which the franchisee needs additional work, and it should include a specific action plan with a clear list of objectives for the coming weeks and months. It is also a best practice to have the franchisee rate his training experience and suggest specific improvements you could make for future training classes. Surveying your franchisees again on their training experience after they've been operating for several months is also worthwhile, as franchisees will have an even better sense for how adequately they were trained once they've been in the business for a while.

Ongoing Training

For the best franchisors, training doesn't end once the startup period is over. It is a vital ongoing part of the franchise relationship. Unfortunately, while many franchisors provide extensive training to new franchisees, some fail to ensure that franchisees continue their learning process year after year.

For a franchisor to be competitive in the long run, its franchisees must remain current with industry trends and adapt to changes in the market, incorporating new products, services, marketing, and operating procedures into their businesses.

With this in mind, every franchise agreement should contain not only initial training requirements, but also specific requirements for ongoing training. To minimize the erosion of system standards over time due to a lack of training, you may want to consider requiring periodic recertification on core competency issues for franchisees and their key staff members. Such a program might include regularly scheduled refresher training for these top positions, as well as detailed training for all staff on any new products, services, or procedures that are introduced from time to time.

Web-Based Learning

Online training, often conducted over a dedicated learning management system (LMS), offers substantial advantages to franchisors when it comes to communications, training, reporting, and testing. And increasingly, franchisors are adopting these tools as an integral part of their franchise systems.

In addition to housing operations manuals, these sophisticated systems can also house training materials, videos, and links to outside information (e.g., government regulations, industry standards, etc.) that may change over time. Moreover, better LMSs will take their users through a prescribed curriculum, with prerequisites and demonstrated competence required to move to each subsequent lesson.

The advantages to these systems translate very rapidly to the bottom line, especially for larger franchise organizations:

- ☛ They allow the franchisor to pre-train their franchisees before the face-to-face training begins. This pre-training allows the franchisor to train franchisees who already have a standardized base of knowledge—saving the franchisor a great deal of time (and ultimately reducing the need for training staff).
- ☛ At the same time, this remote training allows the franchisees to save some of the out-of-pocket expenses associated with a longer period of on-site training.
- ☛ Just as upfront training costs can be reduced, an LMS allows the franchisor to reduce ongoing training costs and the costs associated with educating franchisees on changes in the system.
- ☛ The better LMS software allows the franchisor to test for competence and document the results. By documenting the fact that franchisees and/or their employees were trained and understood various

elements of the system, the franchisor may be in a better position to enforce quality control provisions of their contract or avoid vicarious liability issues.

☛ These software applications can also offer additional value in that the information housed on an LMS is both instantaneous and sortable. Have a problem installing a widget? With a few keystrokes and the right password, you can be watching a video on the subject on your computer, phone, or tablet without missing a beat.

☛ Moreover, because this training is password-protected and customized by user, it can readily be used to push training down to the lowest levels of the organization. The dishwasher's password will take him to a curriculum designed specifically for a dishwasher, without providing access to proprietary information that is not required for his position.

Most newer franchisors, however, do not invest in online learning right out of the gate. Developing the curriculum, tools, videos, and tests often requires a major investment of time and money. And since the greatest value for these systems comes from training low-paid, high-turnover positions (as opposed to training a franchisee), this investment is often delayed until the franchisor is large enough to justify it.

Testing for Competence

Training without testing assumes two things that may not be true. First, it assumes that you, as the franchisor, did a good job of training. Second, it assumes that your franchisee did a good job of learning.

With this in mind, franchisees should be given a number of written and practical tests (for example, on customer service procedures) throughout the home office training program. A final exam covering a broad range of topics should also be part of this testing process.

While most franchisees successfully complete their training program, some franchisees (or their managers) may struggle with the training or display undesirable traits during the training (e.g., rudeness, lack of sales ability, lack of focus, etc.). This should raise red flags as to their potential for success and their ability to meet your brand standards. In such cases, it is important you give your training staff the authority (and responsibility) to address deficiencies with trainees and, if necessary, fail them from the training program.

You may then give these trainees the opportunity to extend their training or retake their training, or you may simply decide they are not a fit for your organization. Your franchise contract should have specific provisions for how you will deal with franchisees who do not pass training; as difficult as it is, you are better off revoking the grant of a franchise than allow someone who is unqualified to fail or to damage your brand.

While the goal of the training program is to assist new franchisees in their transition to your system, not every franchisee or manager attending the training will demonstrate the ability to succeed. It's much easier to deal with these problems during initial training than after the franchisee returns to her location and opens for business.

How Much Training?

One question we are frequently asked is, "How much training is too much?" And we are always tempted to answer, "You can never do too much training." But the fact of the matter is that there are always trade-offs involved.

For franchisees, who are eager to open the business and are carrying the out-of-pocket costs for themselves and perhaps their managers, the longer the training, the more expensive it becomes for them. This is particularly true when a visit to the home office involves plane fare, car rentals, and room and board in the franchisor's city. Additionally, franchisees often attend training during the critical period in which they're preparing to open their business. Likewise, for the franchisor, time spent training is time not spent working on system development. As you grow, you'll need dedicated training staff—and the more training you provide, the more staff you'll require. So training involves an investment in both human and financial capital.

Thus it becomes incumbent on you to attempt to measure these costs—both for you and your franchisee. In doing so, you will need to account for the complexity of the system, the nature of your targeted franchisee, the potential for mistakes, and the damage that could result from those mistakes. So, for example, if you are in the food-service industry—where improper food preparation procedures can result in illness or worse—you will need to provide more training than you might in a simple retail franchise.

Ideally, you may want to pay a professional to develop a formal training program on your behalf. A well-crafted training program will provide your training team with a guide on how to train franchisees on everything from skilled technical tasks to operational and administrative activities.

Whether you develop the training program yourself or through the use of a consulting firm, you will ultimately want to have a teacher's guide or curriculum master that will ensure you are training new franchisees consistently and comprehensively. The curriculum master should include a detailed agenda for each day of franchisee training, with cross-references to the sections of the franchise operations manual that are being covered under each topic. It should also recommend the length of each learning module and the training procedures used (appropriate role-playing exercises, on-site activities, quizzes, etc.), and make provisions for all required testing.

Before determining how much training you should provide, it is often instructive to examine the FDDs of comparable franchise systems to determine the length and content of their training programs (both of which are required disclosure items). Just be sure you do not take their decisions as gospel. If you copy the training program of a franchisor that does not do a good job of quality control, you may find yourself in a similar situation. But a close examination of their training will at least provide you with a starting point.

Our last rule of thumb for making your final assessment is the "keys to the shop" test. When determining how much training a franchisee needs to succeed, imagine you are about to take a cruise down the Amazon for a month. No cell phone. No internet. Then ask yourself, "How much training would you want that person to have if you were going to let her run your company store for that month without you?" Add training on the pre-opening process (site selection, lease negotiation, etc.) to that equation, and you will have a good estimate of an adequate initial training requirement.

Finally, as you implement your franchise program, pay close attention to the time your training is taking and the results you are achieving. Can you cover the material in the time you have allotted? Are you running long or short on certain topics? Are your franchisees doing well on their tests? Or is additional training needed? The answers to these questions will help you refine your training program.

Train the Trainer Too!

The goal of the franchisor's pre-opening training program should be to enable the franchisee not only to operate the business successfully, but also to train new staff members at the franchisee's business location. With this in mind, the savvy franchisor will often develop a specific training program for each position in the franchisee's organization. These mini-training manuals become the tool used by the franchisee in training his staff. With many small businesses having annual employee turnover rates of 100 percent or more, the execution of your brand standards at each franchise location will only be possible if your franchisees have the tools and knowledge to train their front-line employees on an ongoing basis.

Since these train-the-trainer manuals will be distributed to staff who have less invested in your franchise and are often less-qualified than your franchisee, be sure the material is written at a level they will readily comprehend. The best of these documents make ample use of photographs but do not contain the franchisor's most proprietary, confidential information.

In developing these documents, it will also be important for the franchisor to teach the franchisee how to train their employees. Showing a franchisee how to conduct training is very different from training that franchisee on a particular topic.

Startup Assistance

Supporting franchisees properly—through site selection, training, startup activities, and ongoing operations, for example—is critical to the health of a franchise network. When franchisees feel underserved, unsuccessful, or singled out for criticism or penalties, they will invariably claim they are victims of the franchisor's inadequate training, support, assistance, or advice. So it is imperative that the franchisor provide the right balance of guidance and control without crossing the line into effectively operating the franchise units itself.

As part of this process, the franchisor will need to make a number of decisions about how it will support franchisees once they open their doors for business. And like most issues in business, there are often no right or wrong answers.

For those franchisors that have a business model that depends, at least in part, on real estate, there will be a number of pre-opening questions that will need to be addressed as a part of the strategic planning process:

- ☞ What role will the franchisor take in finding an appropriate site? Will it actually find the site? Provide guidelines for sites? Approve sites?
- ☞ Will the franchisor approve the franchisee's lease? Provide specific mandated lease terms? Require that its standard form letter of intent or lease be used? Will it provide input on appropriate lease rates?
- ☞ Will the franchisor own any or all of the real estate? Will it go on some or all of the franchisee's prime leases? Will it profit from these leases?
- ☞ Will the franchisor require the franchisee to use a specific architect for the design of the space? Will it mandate the use of a particular contractor? Will it play any role in the actual build-out? And if so, how will it charge for that (if at all)?
- ☞ Will it recommend that the franchisee works with specific third-party brokers or "store-in-a-box" build-out firms? And if so, who will bear the associated costs?
- ☞ Should the franchisor be involved in helping the franchisee order her initial equipment? Her initial inventory?

As a general rule of thumb, the more aggressive the franchisor's growth plan, the more formalized many of the above processes should be. Greater structure around the pre-opening processes helps minimize the number of moving parts involved in each opening, which in turn allows the franchisor to open locations more quickly and on a more predictable schedule. However, the issues underlying these questions are often more complicated than they may at first seem. Owning or subletting locations may seem like a nice profit center, but it carries with it substantial exposure should the franchisee fail. Moreover, it can create contingent liability on the franchisor's balance sheet, and thus, its access to capital.

The franchisor's role in finding locations for its franchisees carries with it obvious issues of staffing and capacity. As a franchisor, your primary expense is your people. And while your franchisee may

> **⟳ More NLRB Pitfalls**
>
> Again, given the recent efforts by the National Labor Relations Board to classify some franchisors as co-employers, the franchisor will not want to take responsibility for training the franchisee's staff—which further highlights the need for professionally designed training programs and legal review.

see this as a benefit (and may even allow your role to influence his decision making), you might also later risk claims that the location was not appropriate for the franchise business, making you (in theory) responsible for the franchisee's failure.

As the system continues to expand, the need for additional types of pre-opening support may become apparent, based not only on needs identified by franchisees, but also on the franchisor's perception of shortcomings in the pre-opening assistance program. Typical areas in which the franchisor may provide additional assistance include marketing, grand opening, public relations, programs to help the franchisee hire qualified managers, or franchisor-initiated marketing campaigns.

In deciding which, if any, of these services should be offered, the franchisor should attempt to measure the value received by the franchisee against the cost of providing them. As part of that process, the franchisor should also examine the extent to which these services should be provided by the franchisor as opposed to being provided by an outside vendor (e.g., public relations firm, etc.).

Ongoing Support

Ongoing support can come in many forms, including field support through on-site visits, new product development, advertising assistance, purchasing programs, public relations initiatives, technology development, national accounts sales programs, and backroom services (billing, collections, etc.), to name some of the most common. And while all have associated costs and may require staffing by the franchisor, the goal of all these ongoing services is to contribute to higher quality and more profitable franchisees.

Site Support Visits

Most franchisors consider periodic visits to the franchise location by qualified field representatives an integral part of system support. These visits have two primary objectives. First, they provide an opportunity for the franchisor to observe how the franchisee's business is being run and reinforce brand standards. But more important, they also allow the franchisor to coach the franchisee in the field on ways to improve business operations.

While many new franchisors think of their field consultants as the "brand police," the best field consulting programs incorporate a number of responsibilities into a single role:

- ◥ The field representative will be a *brand compliance and quality control officer*, going through a checklist of brand standards to be sure a franchisee is in full compliance and, if they are not, taking the appropriate corrective action.
- ◥ They need to act in the role of *field trainer*, providing the franchisee with ongoing training on new products, new initiatives, and improved methods—along with refresher training as needed.
- ◥ At the same time, they want to work collaboratively with the franchisee in the role of an *operations consultant* to help her run her business more efficiently based on observation, comparative analysis, and the use of key performance indicators.
- ◥ A closely related role is that of a *marketing expert* who will focus on ways in which they can grow their revenue base from the standpoint of advertising and sales.
- ◥ At a higher level, they need to be a *business planning expert*, who can use financial analysis to identify potential problem areas and, if merited, help franchisees plan to acquire additional units.

⟝ They need to act as a *cheerleader*, encouraging franchisees to continue their good efforts even when sales are down.

⟝ And finally, they need to function as a *brand ambassador*, fostering good relations between the franchisor and the franchisee.

As a new franchisor, you will need to institutionalize all these roles in a single person (and later in a team), so be sure you select someone who is highly qualified and who will be credible in the franchisees' eyes. And in developing your staffing plan, you will need to answer a number of questions:

⟝ Should your field representatives limit themselves to scheduled visits (which will ensure the franchisee is always present), or should they occasionally mix in surprise visits?

⟝ How frequently should your representatives visit, and should the frequency of visits decline over time as the franchisee gains proficiency?

⟝ Based on the frequency of visits, the length of visits, the complexity of the business, the nature of the franchisees (startup vs. area developer, for example), and the clustering of your franchisees, how many franchisees can a single field representative handle?

⟝ What other forms of communication should be incorporated into your field representatives' regular routine?

⟝ What steps should be taken in the event of various levels of non-compliance? And what follow-up should be planned for each?

⟝ Can this role initially be handled by the person charged with training? When will you need to hire additional staff? And what qualifications will they need?

⟝ How do you best institutionalize the role? Should you develop a field support manual for your field representatives? How do you train and test these field representatives?

Remember: It is imperative that your franchisees not only receive adequate support, but that they also feel you, as a franchisor, truly care about their success and their future. Perhaps one of the most common franchisee complaints in younger franchise systems is that they rarely see the franchisor and feel abandoned. While it is easy for a rapidly growing franchisor to overlook franchisees who appear to be doing things right, especially when the press of rapid growth puts so many priorities on your plate, remember that franchisee validation is at the heart of most successful franchise systems. Make sure your franchisees know how much you care. Without their respect, your ability to lead them toward a common objective will be greatly diminished.

Products or Services Purchasing Programs

Another key benefit of many franchise systems is the franchisees' access to purchase arrangements with key suppliers negotiated by the franchisor. Purchasing programs can provide very tangible benefits to franchisees and can have a substantial positive impact on both franchise sales and franchisee profitability.

Of course, franchisees with large purchasing needs can always negotiate with vendors directly. But it behooves the prudent franchisor to take the lead in this area, both to build value into the services it provides the franchise network and to retain quality control over the goods and services its franchisees buy. The franchisor's task, then, is to decide how much of its human and capital resources to devote to negotiating pricing on behalf of franchisees and how to be compensated for those efforts.

For many franchisors, the answer should come from a cost-benefit analysis. The larger the cumulative purchasing needs of the franchisees, the more benefit can be derived from staffing this function. The financial question then becomes whether and how the franchisor should recover the associated expenses for these services. Should you keep any rebates for yourself? Allocate some portion to the franchisees? Allocate rebates to some other system wide benefit such as a national advertising fund? Or simply negotiate the lowest possible prices on behalf of franchisees as a benefit to the system?

Some franchisors may take on a production role—providing either products or services to their franchisees directly. If you choose this path, it is imperative that you first understand the costs before completing your initial or ongoing fee analysis. Again, this decision is one in which tangible benefits must be measured against costs. The franchisor will want to consider the franchisees' increases in productivity (and the associated increased revenues and royalties), economies of scale when providing these services across a network, and the increased marketability of the franchise system, and measure those benefits against the costs of providing and administrating these services.

Approved and Designated Suppliers

As a franchisor, you will likely want to place strict controls on your franchisees' sources of supply. To the extent to which these decisions impact the quality of the product/service offered, you are within your rights to control the specific products carried and, often, the sources of those products. And, as the discussion of rebates above alludes, these provisions can be a profit center for you as a franchisor. Should you choose to profit from supplier programs, these relationships are subject to disclosure in Item 8 of the FDD. And more detailed disclosures must be made if the franchisor itself (or an affiliate) is acting as the supplier.

While the franchisor is certainly entitled to sell products to its franchisees, mandating certain purchases may subject the franchisor to antitrust issues, such as tying arrangements. To the extent a franchisor can show that *proprietary* recipes, methods, or products are being supplied, these supplier designations are readily justified. If, on the other hand, the franchisor intends to require franchisees to purchase products that are only differentiated in that they are imprinted with the franchisor's logo, it

Beware the Antitrust Act

Under the Sherman Antitrust Act of 1890, certain agreements that restrain trade are not allowed. Tying arrangements, for example, involve an agreement to sell a product (the tying product) only if the buyer also agrees to purchase another product (the tied product). In a franchise context, the question becomes whether the franchise and the products the franchisee must purchase are, in fact, separate products. Of course, there is much more to this (issues such as economic power come into play, for example), again illustrating the need for good franchise counsel.

may have to argue it is seeking to control brand standards or to provide franchisees with the buying power that results from group purchases. The startup franchisor should thus carefully consider whether it should use supplier designations as profit centers or forgo these additional revenues and instead get value by providing a real economic benefit to franchisees.

Advertising and Marketing Support

The best franchisors are constantly looking for ways to help their franchisees increase revenues, as this will impact both franchisee and franchisor profitability. Providing advertising assistance is perhaps one of the best ways to accomplish this. Franchisees are paying for the right to exploit the franchisor's market identity and reputation, and thus will typically rely on the franchisor to enhance the brand by developing national, regional, and local advertising programs, as well as assisting the franchisee with neighborhood or unit-based advertising and marketing programs.

As a franchisor, you will control every aspect of the advertising message and the media in which it is presented. Obviously, you will supervise all national advertising expenditures. But even local advertising undertaken by franchisees will need to use franchisor-created advertising materials or will need to be approved in advance by the franchisor.

Research and Development

A related responsibility of the franchisor is to keep the concept fresh in an ever-changing marketplace. More than 50 years ago when McDonald's was just getting its start, it had only 11 items on its menu (hamburgers, cheeseburgers, fries, Coca-Cola, root beer, orangeade, milk, coffee, and three flavors of milk shakes). Today, their menu looks very different, as do their ads, their buildings, and even their methods of service.

If you want to remain relevant as a franchisor, you will need to incorporate a plan for change into your business strategy. As part of that, you will eventually need to formalize a process for evolving your concept to stay ahead of the competition. And while you may be the head of research and development when you first get started, in the long run this function will play an invaluable role in franchisee success.

Other Forms of Support

Franchisors can also support their franchisees in any number of industry-specific ways. For example:

- ◄► Some advertising or publication franchises will provide editorial content, ad design, and printing services to their franchisees. This frees the franchisee from tasks for which they may not be well-suited while allowing them to focus their efforts exclusively on marketing and sales.

- ◄► With hospitality or travel franchises, a major part of the value proposition is often found in the reservation system.

- ◄► Some temporary placement franchisors will assist their franchisees with payroll financing, allowing them to better leverage their assets.

- ◄► In manufacturing and direct sales concepts, the franchisor may provide assistance in the areas of consumer financing with an eye toward helping their franchisees sell.

- ◄► While the practice has come under increasing scrutiny at the state level (where some are claiming it creates an employment relationship), franchisors in the janitorial services industry will sometimes sell accounts on behalf of their franchisees.

- ◄► And, in a number of industries, franchisors will provide backroom support services that can be better leveraged centrally. Such services can include call centers, national accounts programs, direct marketing, routing and scheduling appointments, centralized billing, and even collections.

THE BOTTOM LINE

Make Your Franchisees Successful

The bottom line when it comes to quality control and support is that the relationship you create and the responsibilities you undertake as a franchisor are a matter of contract—and, as such, you have a great deal of freedom when structuring them. The best franchisors are guided by two basic principles:

1. Do whatever needs to be done to vigorously maintain brand integrity, and

2. Provide any cost-justifiable service that will help the franchisees succeed.

CHAPTER 9

Franchise Marketing—
Your Unique Message

"Strategy is about making choices, trade-offs; it's about deliberately choosing to be different."

—MICHAEL PORTER, PROFESSOR, HARVARD BUSINESS SCHOOL

Your existing and successful operations may have already generated a list of strong franchise candidates. But to grow as a franchisor, you will ultimately need two things: a stream of qualified franchise prospects and professionally designed marketing materials that show those prospects your franchise is worthy of further consideration.

Ultimately, you will never sell a franchise on the strength of your marketing materials alone. But if you fail to develop these vital tools, you will certainly lose prospective buyers who might otherwise have considered a relationship. This brings us to the concept of the "Present Value of a Franchise."

The Present Value of a Franchise (PVF)

Some years ago, the iFranchise Group developed the concept of the Present Value of a Franchise (PVF) for use in a franchisor's decision-making process.

Since the PVF comes to our attention first in the context of marketing, I have addressed it here, although there are numerous applications of this concept, just a few of which are:

- ☞ When deciding how much to spend on advertising
- ☞ When deciding which people to hire
- ☞ When deciding whether to use a management recruiter
- ☞ When deciding which consultant to employ
- ☞ When deciding whether to retain brokers
- ☞ When deciding on the quality of advertising materials
- ☞ And many, many more

The underlying principle of the PVF is that the sale of a franchise is much like the purchase of an annuity. When you sell a franchise, you can anticipate that not only will you receive a franchise fee upon closing the transaction, but you will also receive revenues from that franchisee for years—perhaps decades. Those revenues, which come from royalties, advertising fund contributions, product sales, rebates, technology fund contributions, and conceivably many other fees, can easily add up to many hundreds of thousands of dollars over the course of your relationship with the franchisee.

Moreover, every franchisee contributes to the ultimate enterprise value of your franchise company. If they contribute an incremental $15,000 to your bottom line profitability, that might add $150,000 or more to your ultimate selling price.

The concept, of course, is a little oversimplified. To get a real Present Value, one would need to account for incremental expenses and discount the cash flow streams based on an appropriate cost of capital. But you get the idea.

Add it all together, and you have the PVF.

All too often, franchisors make their decisions based on a short-term view of their situation. They do not want to pay "excessive" brokerage fees of perhaps $20,000 because they "would lose money on that franchise sale." But as the PVF suggests, that is often the furthest thing from the truth.

Just as you would not make a decision about an annuity based only on the first year's returns, you should consider the franchisee's lifetime value when making decisions impacting the franchise organization. And while the franchisor must temper its decision making based on an understanding of anticipated cash flows, this longer-term viewpoint on the value received from each franchisee is perhaps the single most frequently shared trait of successful franchisors.

With that behind us, let's examine marketing from the messaging side.

The Motive Is the Message

In order to sell franchises, you must start by understanding the nature of your specific franchise buyer. Franchisors who target their prospects with a generic "be in business for yourself, but not by yourself" will often find their message falling on deaf ears. So before you begin your marketing efforts, be sure that you understand what it is you are selling, whom you are selling it to, and why they should be interested in buying.

The Many Sales of Franchising

The savvy franchisor realizes that when approaching a prospective franchisee, the franchise salesperson must make not just one sale, but rather FOUR separate sales if they are to succeed. The prospect will ultimately ask:

1. Should I go into business for myself?
2. Should I go into the "widget" business?
3. Should I go it alone or buy a widget franchise?
4. Should I buy *your* widget franchise?

To become a prospect in your franchise sales pipeline, you can be fairly sure your candidate has already answered the first question affirmatively. That said, not everyone is right for business ownership—even if they believe they are. You will need to be sure your prospect understands the positives and negatives of business ownership, or you will run the risk of awarding a franchise to a candidate who may be predisposed to failure. And, as we have discussed previously, nothing will doom a franchise as quickly as a track record of failed franchisees.

To answer the second question, the franchisor will need to develop a selling proposition for the widget industry, but chances are it will not be unique. Rather, all the franchisor's competitors in the widget market will be giving the same pitch. (*Note*: Only when a franchisor is in the enviable position of being the only player in a market segment can the answer to the second question yield a true USP. But being first to market is rarely enough. While early market entrants can gain a strong position by moving quickly, if the concept is a good one, there will be imitators sooner or later.)

The answer to the third question requires the franchisor to sell the concept of franchising, separately from the advantages of widgets. It is remarkable how many inquiries a franchisor will get from people who don't understand what a franchise relationship is all about. If the franchisee believes that he will have the freedom to do as he pleases, you are better off dispelling that notion early in the process.

This third question also presents the franchise marketer with a unique dilemma. On the one hand, the marketer wants to say they are offering a can't-miss opportunity in a great market. On the other hand, they need to tell the prospect that without the franchisor's assistance, the prospect will be doomed to failure (or, at best, significantly less successful).

And, of course, the fourth question is where the rubber meets the road—differentiating the offering from its *closest direct competitors*. This is where a new franchisor will need to focus its creative efforts—in terms of the concept itself, the structure of the franchise offering, and ultimately, in the way the USP is communicated to the prospective franchisee.

The Many "Buyers" You Need to Address

The marketing message is further complicated by the fact that it will ultimately be heard by numerous people other than the prospect who will influence the franchise sale. In most cases, the franchisor can anticipate that its buyer will be influenced by:

- 🪶 An attorney she will retain to review the franchise legal documents
- 🪶 The lender that will be providing her financing (and she may talk to several of these)

☞ Her personal accountant (especially for opportunities with more sizable investments)

☞ Her trusted advisors and friends (and her know-it-all Uncle Charley, who will tell her she is crazy, no matter how good the message)

☞ Her spouse and other close family members

☞ Google (and other search engines), which will determine who gets to read your message online

☞ State regulators in eight states, who will determine if you can use the material at all

For those entrepreneurs reading this book, you already know how unsupportive these additional "buyers" can be. So your website, videos, collateral materials, and other marketing pieces must address this audience as well as your prospective franchisee (who may often be the easiest of the group to sell to).

The Many Messages of Your Materials

In addition to the many sales and buyers you must address, you must also be aware that your franchise marketing materials will send more than one message.

The copy that is used in your marketing will need to send two messages:

1. A message that conveys the content of your offering
2. A message that imparts the emotional impact of your franchise

The franchise buying process is highly emotional. It is integrally related not only to a person's financial well-being, but also wholly intertwined with the way a person does (or wants to) perceive himself. So simply expressing the content of the offering and the value proposition, without accounting for the emotional impact of the franchise sales process, will considerably reduce your likelihood of closing a sale.

Beyond the copy, your photos will send messages. We often see websites and other collateral materials developed by consumer marketing agencies to promote a franchise opportunity that completely miss the mark.

One brochure I remember reading for a hair salon franchise featured three happy barbers standing in a pristine barbershop just waiting for a customer to show up. And to a potential customer, it looked great. But what the ad agency who designed the brochure failed to realize was that what looks great to a consumer (no waiting, pristine environment) is the franchisee's worst recurring nightmare (no customers while he pays those barbers to do nothing).

Aside from the content, the materials themselves will carry a message. Your first impression will often come from your website. Fail to make a good impression, and you are done before you start. Print a cheap brochure (or worse yet, a folder with inserts), and you will send the message that you are not serious about franchising. The quality of the paper stock you use can send a similar message. So do it right.

The Many Motives of Your Franchisee

It is also important to understand that your franchisee candidate will not be motivated by the same factors that motivate you. Many neophyte franchisors wrongly assume that franchise buyers are primarily motivated by financial returns. In fact, our experience has shown (and independent surveys back this up) that much more important are motives such as:

- Independence
- Being one's own boss
- Flexibility
- Control of their destiny

So you are well-advised to understand who your prospects are and what really motivates them before drafting the message you will use to attract them.

If you already have franchisees, talk to them about what motivated them—although you need to be careful to avoid a fallacy of composition. If, for example, all your prior messaging was focused on independence, you might expect to hear your franchisees echo that. To avoid that mistake, you may want to survey franchisees from similar systems to better understand the broader motives in your category.

Does Size Really Matter?

There are absolutely some prospective franchisees who will
not consider anything other
than a major brand. But there
are also franchise prospects who
are only interested in ground-
floor opportunities. For them, a
well-known brand is actually a
turnoff—so again, be careful with
your messaging.

> ### ➤ Brand Recognition
>
> Anecdotally, about 20 percent
> of buyers are looking for known
> brands. Of the remainder, about
> half say they prefer a known
> brand but would remain open to
> newer concepts, and the other
> half feel brand recognition is not
> vital to their purchasing decision.

If you are with a smaller
franchise chain, chances are the type of folks you have attracted are looking
for a venture that is more entrepreneurial—or perhaps are indifferent to
size. So don't try to be something you are not. If you have a ground-floor
opportunity, don't hide it (it won't work anyway). Flaunt it.

Structure and Motives

The business structure of your franchise offering will also impact the
marketing message you should use.

Franchisors expanding through conversion franchises find their prospects
are generally easily identified, reducing marketing costs substantially. But
a conversion sale is much different from the sale of a startup franchise.
The converting franchisee likely has his name (or his father's name)
over the door, so there is a pride of ownership that needs to be taken
into consideration. And a converting franchisee is likely to value his
independence more than a typical startup. Since a conversion franchisee
will ultimately have to pay royalties on his existing base of revenues (a hard
pill to swallow), the marketing message will have some weighty emotional
issues to overcome.

In conversions, franchisees generally sign out of fear. They have often
seen the handwriting on the wall (or it is your job to show them that
handwriting) and convert because they see change (the bad kind) on the
horizon. They feel they can no longer compete on their own. And if you

have done your job, they feel strongly that the incremental value provided by the franchisor outweighs the fees and loss of control.

Over the past decade, few trends have been as pronounced as the increase in area development or "multi-unit" franchisees. In fact, according to FRANdata, 2007 marked the year when multi-unit franchisees passed individual franchisees in terms of total U.S. units. In their 2007 Profile of Franchising, they reported that while only 18 percent of all franchisees were multi-unit operators, that group controlled more than 50 percent of all franchise units. An even more telling aspect of the report was the finding that the 3 percent of franchisees who own more than five franchises control a staggering 24 percent of all franchise units.

When it comes to established multi-unit operators, identifying these prospects can be much easier than selling to them. The first thing any franchisor targeting these operators should know is that the market is extremely competitive.

Much of this is simply a question of supply and demand. Again, according to FRANdata, between 11 and 15 percent of all multi-unit franchisees operate more than one unaffiliated franchise brand. Thus, if a franchisor wants to hunt for big game among the 37,000 existing multi-unit operators, it should realize it is probably not looking at that entire universe, but more realistically at about 6,000 multibrand, multi-unit operators. This number looks smaller still when we recognize that a significant percentage of the 3,000 or so active franchisors in the U.S. have these same operators in their sights.

Likewise, the message used to attract area developers will be considerably different from the message used to target startup operators. While startups will continue to be attracted to the "be in business for yourself but not by yourself" message, area development franchisees are much more likely to focus on the franchise as an investment. These operators will likely resent a pure emotional pitch, so the message needs to communicate the value proposition clearly and without puffery.

Additionally, area developer candidates, unlike single-unit prospects, expect the franchisor to hand over earnings data. A well-documented financial performance representation is virtually mandatory. Moreover, this more sophisticated operator will be intent on dissecting the franchisor's value proposition. A critical aspect of her buying decision will be her analysis of the franchisor's support structure in the areas of advertising, training, real estate, design, construction, and operations assistance. And, of course, she will scrutinize the franchisor's financial strength and management team.

Start with Your Story

To succeed in franchise marketing, you need to start with a powerful brand story that is compelling on both an emotional and logical level. It must inspire and motivate the prospect to action. And it must be uniquely your story.

The acid test is this: If you could substitute a competitor's name for yours in your messaging, you have failed to differentiate yourself. Remember, everyone will claim to have the best concept. Everyone will claim to have the best support. Everyone will claim to be the most responsive. If you cannot explain why you are better in a way that is unique to you, it is time to go back to the drawing board.

While it is certainly a behemoth now, the McDonald's juggernaut started with a single location. Before they captured the American consumer's mind share for fast food burgers, they had dozens of competitors.

Those of us over 50 may still remember companies like Burger Chef, Dee's Drive-In, Sandy's, Red Barn, and Druther's (which, to give you a feel for its originality, began its life as Burger Queen). Geri's Hamburgers, which was owned in part by a former vice president of McDonald's, had numerous similarities to McDonald's, including a cartoon icon that was very like McDonald's "Speedee" (their mascot before Ronald McDonald came along). Another concept, Wetson's, was designed to duplicate the McDonald's concept, but instead of "Look for the Golden Arches," Wetson's used "Look for the Orange Circles."

So why was Burger King successful while so many others failed? While there were numerous contributing factors, the answer can be summed up in a single sentence: "Have it your way." Burger King positioned itself to be *different* from McDonald's, not just a "me too" operation. More important, they positioned themselves in a way to which McDonald's could not respond competitively—because in order to do so, they would have had to revisit their entire kitchen operations.

More than a decade later, few believed any burger operation could crack the "Big Two," yet Wendy's did. Their secret: "We don't cut corners on quality." While McDonald's and Burger King were slugging it out trying to capture the hearts and stomachs of the nation's children with Happy Meals and cartoon characters, Wendy's hired an octogenarian spokesperson and touted their freshly ground "old-fashioned hamburgers." And when Clara Peller asked "Where's the beef?", Wendy's crafted an appeal to an entirely different customer. McDonald's and Burger King were powerless to respond—unless they wanted to abandon their core customers to do so.

More Than One Way to Skin a Cat

Of course, there are dozens of ways for a company to differentiate itself. The easiest is often found at the consumer level. Those fortunate enough to be the first into a new industry or niche can seek to attain the position of market leader. To achieve that status, the franchisor must generally grow rapidly enough to achieve brand recognition.

Aside from the concept itself, franchise companies can differentiate themselves based on the size of the initial investment, target market (either at the franchisee or consumer level), target geography, services provided to franchisees (quality or type), and even franchise structure. (Another cautionary note: For those with an undifferentiated concept, being the cheapest is often a road to perdition. If you choose to take this route, focus on minimizing the franchisee's investment, not on minimizing the royalty structure.)

Regardless of where this differentiation occurs, it is imperative that the franchisor stake out the areas where it wants to excel, develop a unique selling proposition (USP) around those areas, and acknowledge where it will allow its competitors to play unchallenged. Positioning is sacrifice.

Be Best at Something

When positioning yourself against your franchise competitors, there are numerous ways in which you can differentiate your offer. But whether it is based on the consumer or the franchise offer, if you want to capture a long-term market position, you need to be perceived as being the best at *something*.

To paraphrase from retail consultant McMillanDoolittle's groundbreaking study on successful strategy, you have to choose your "EST" and focus on that position. (See more at www.mcmillandoolittle.com.)

The model, in grossly oversimplified terms, states that a retailer has to be best in one of five essential areas in order to "win" in the retail game:

1. BiggEST—largest assortment
2. CheapEST—lowest prices
3. EasiEST—high-service orientation
4. QuickEST—fast-service orientation
5. HottEST—fashion orientation

Moreover, the theory states that while a retailer can choose to be two of these at once (biggest and cheapest, a la Walmart), it is a big mistake to try to be more than two. Companies that try to be all things to all people quickly find that they only succeed at being mediocre at everything—a guarantee of long-term failure. This leads a business to the black hole where bad companies go to die.

The essence of positioning is sacrifice. To be the low-cost retailer, you need to sacrifice the idea of selling high-fashion premium products, and vice versa. Likewise, to have the highest quality, you cannot have the fastest service. Speed (think fast food) requires you to sacrifice quality (think fine dining).

Figure 9.1 on page 186 from McMillanDoolittle illustrates what this looks like in terms of positioning. The best marketers pick their place and defend that territory—to the exclusion of others.

In franchising, especially when it comes to undifferentiated concepts, many of these same principles apply. Apart from the need for a strong value proposition, the best franchisors will actively seek to control their desired position in the marketplace. You may find other things to differentiate your concept—or perhaps new "ESTs" where you can command the high ground.

As mentioned above, the decision to invest in a franchise is often heavily influenced by the emotional response a candidate has to the franchise opportunity. This emotional response is often driven less by what

Figure 9.1: Sacrifice Positioning

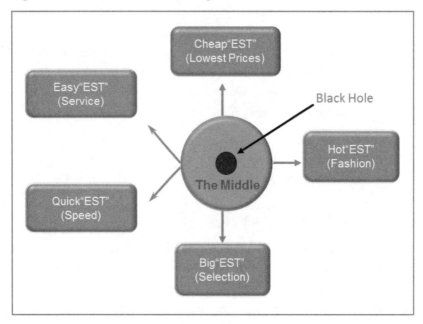

you do and more by why you do it. One of the most successful franchise brands today, Chick-fil-A, is a great example of this. Chick-fil-A sells a good product, but the quality of their food is not the primary reason for their incredible success. Truett Cathy, the founder of Chick-fil-A, built his company on a foundation of core beliefs and principles that guide everything they do as an organization. Chick-fil-A's strong adherence to their principles has created a culture that not only resonates with consumers but also helps generate more than 20,000 franchise leads each year.

One thing is certain: If you don't know how you want to be positioned in the marketplace, your prospects may end up being educated on your position by your competitors. And that is generally not a good strategy for sales success.

Buyers Don't Start as Buyers

Imagine for a minute you are looking to buy a franchise. Would you undertake a systematic analysis of all the nation's 3,000 franchisors and rank them until you got to the one at the top of your list? Of course not.

Chances are, if you are like most buyers, you will only seriously consider between six and 12 franchisors before making your final decision. So before you buy, you are looking to eliminate huge numbers of franchisors from consideration.

When it comes to franchise buyers, some will start their search by choosing a specific industry segment in which they are interested. Perhaps they have always wanted to own a restaurant. Or a dress shop. Or an MRI imaging clinic. Perhaps they want to buy a franchise that capitalizes on what they perceive to be their particular skills or experience. Often they will focus on industries they perceive to be fun or lucrative.

Likewise, they may use others to help them narrow their focus— whether through the use of brokers, trade shows, or franchise directories. Or perhaps they will use the internet to help them narrow their search using parameters such as investment size, number of operating units, years in franchising, or the presence of positive or negative public relations. Some will use social media or perhaps personal referrals to find a smaller handful of companies from which to start their search.

Some will be interested only in established franchisors. Others will be looking to get in on the ground floor with a franchise they believe is poised for explosive growth. Many will eliminate large pools of franchisors quickly based on the fact that the estimated investment exceeds their available capital.

In short, every buyer's process will be different.

From a messaging standpoint, it is important to remember this: Each buyer is looking for reasons to eliminate you from consideration. They are not looking for reasons to buy. They are looking for *reasons to cross you off their list.*

So when crafting your story, do so in a way that eliminates the nonbuyers while maintaining the interest of anyone who may actually be a prospective franchisee.

It may sound counterintuitive, but one of the basic principles of successful franchise marketing is to eliminate the time wasters. If you require a $1 million investment, you do not want to talk to folks who have $10,000 and a credit card to their name. They are time wasters—but they may also be your customers, so you will need to gently disqualify them without alienating them as consumers. You are far better off eliminating them with your message upfront so you do not need to do it over the phone. If you are looking only for dentists or real estate agents or experienced restaurateurs, don't wait until the phone call to let your unqualified prospect know. If you have qualifications a franchisee must meet, be sure you communicate that in your marketing message.

Beyond that, understand that the purpose of your marketing material is *not* to sell the franchise. It is to get qualified prospects to take the next step in your sales process.

If you are running print ads, for example, their purpose is to encourage your prospects either to contact you or to go to your website for further information. So the message of the ad may well be "This is a very interesting opportunity; learn more here . . ."

Looking at the website first (as many of your buyers will) and remembering that most new visitors are looking to eliminate your company from consideration, your goal should be to promise them more information (a brochure, a white paper, a video, a consultation, or whatever) in return for their contact information. That is the sale you are making. You are selling information, and your payment is their information.

So from a messaging standpoint, you want to avoid providing too much information—especially if it could be used to disqualify you in the eyes of your franchisee. The information you are holding back is your bargain with the website visitor. So, as Ludwig Mies van der Rohe once said, "Less is more." Or, as my mother once said, "You won't buy the cow if you get the milk for free."

Give visitors to your franchise opportunity site enough information to eliminate themselves if they are unqualified, but not enough that they can make a decision. Remember, a website never sold a franchise. Never. Your website should be designed to capture leads, not to sell your franchise. So be sure there is a value proposition associated with taking the next step.

Know Your Competition

To develop a truly unique position in the marketplace, most new franchisors need to understand the companies they are trying to position themselves against. The U in USP means Unique, so we need to ask, "Unique from whom?"

Let's face it: If you are like most franchisors, your business model is probably not unique and never before seen on earth. More likely, it is one of many of its kind. Think of the numbers of janitorial, doughnut, and hamburger concepts that have been successful virtually next door to each other.

Not every company can be Massage Envy—creating a franchise market where none existed before. But examples of startups succeeding in the face of established competition abound. Who would have thought that Popeyes could take on the Colonel? Or that Papa John's could enter a market dominated by the likes of Pizza Hut, Domino's, and Little Caesars? More recently, names like Krispy Kreme, Jimmy John's, LA Fitness, and Häagen-Dazs come to mind, having made inroads against giants like Dunkin' Donuts, Subway, Gold's Gym, and Baskin-Robbins.

In theory, each new franchisor competes with *every* established franchisor for franchisees. Obviously, this is not true in practice. But even the most innovative new concept will compete with companies in a similar market or of a similar investment size.

So where do you start? The first thing you need to do is identify the companies with which you are most likely to compete and learn everything you can about them. Pore over their web pages and other online information about them. Obtain their FDDs from online sources or brokers, and analyze the business and structural decisions behind them. Do detailed interviews with their franchisees. And always keep an eye out for new competitors by asking your prospects who else they are considering.

Once you have done this research, ask yourself, "How do I get my concept onto my potential investors' short list?"

Dealing with the Risk vs. Return Equation

One particularly effective way of differentiating a concept is by offering franchisees the prospect of better financial returns than your competitors. Remember, there is a risk-reward paradigm at work here: the greater the perceived risk, the more reward your prospective franchisee will require. So if you have managed superior earnings despite being relatively new to the market, make sure your prospects learn about this by using a financial performance representation. (Of course, speak to your attorney and/or consultant before finalizing this decision.)

Newer franchisors can reduce perceived risk by doing everything they can to build their credibility. Credibility can be enhanced in a number of ways aside from the size and age of a company. Recruit the best management you can find as soon as possible. Hire the best franchise attorney. Work with established franchise consultants. Join the International Franchise Association, and subscribe to its code of ethics. Build incredibly strong relationships with your existing franchisees. And retain a franchise public relations firm.

Going up against bigger competitors will require you to look better as well. Your corporate image, the look of a prototype unit, enthusiastic publicity, and strength of management are all taken into account by the franchise prospect. Websites, brochures, and other marketing materials should look *better* than those of your closest direct competitors. And don't forget the little things: Professionally designed logos, letterhead, correspondence, and other image pieces can have a huge impact on the opinion of a potential franchisee.

In the hands of a skilled marketer, even "me too" businesses can stand out from the crowd. Think back to some of the undifferentiated concepts we discussed earlier. What about janitorial services—why have they been so successful? Maid services. Lawn care. Carpet cleaning. Temporary and permanent placement firms. The list goes on and on.

The fact is that a significant number of franchise companies are in industries in which their products or services cannot be readily differentiated. But remember, the best franchisees are not afraid of competition. Maybe they looked at your competitors and found their territories were sold out. Or maybe they just have a high level of self-confidence—a trait common in most people who have the entrepreneurial spirit. These folks aren't seeking out some never-before-discovered secret to success. What they want is a franchisor that is committed to their success, a good business model, and a strong value proposition.

Developing a Value Proposition

You can differentiate a franchise company through a number of factors. While the first and most obvious place to look is at the actual product or service, we have also seen franchisors succeed by offering:

- A more affordable initial investment (by value engineering startup costs)
- Unique marketing strategies
- Different target markets (geographic or demographic)
- Larger territories (allowing for a higher return or a more sophisticated prospect)
- Smaller territories (allowing for simplicity of operations and a lower investment)
- Superior support services or technologies franchisees can use to help manage their business
- Different (not necessarily lower) fee structures
- And a hundred other factors

By this point, you have likely watched a number of your competitors come and go. Why did they fail, while you survived with a similar product or service? The answer, at least in part, is found in your system.

When someone buys a McDonald's franchise, they aren't doing it because they want the recipe for the special sauce on the Big Mac. In fact, they probably aren't doing it because they believe McDonald's serves the world's finest hamburgers. But few would argue over the quality of their systems, which are among the best in the world.

The system is the embodiment of all those things that make the difference between success and failure in business. Good site selection. Effective lease negotiation. Compelling advertising. Top-notch customer service. Professional branding. Positioning. Purchasing. Pricing. Merchandising. Hiring. Training. Managing. Quality control. Financial management. It can be found in everything from the products you buy to the way your people answer the phones.

The best companies not only have developed good systems, but they also use those systems to ensure consistency at the consumer level, whether the business provides a product or a service. And that is what your franchisees want to buy—a consistent consumer experience that has been proven in the marketplace.

Through some combination of services and support, you need to teach your franchisee how to achieve what you have achieved. That will likely mean developing some of the features of good franchise programs that we have already discussed: training programs, operations manuals, site selection criteria, advertising guidelines, and other elements of the system that will allow your franchisees to take advantage of the intellectual property you have created. Moreover, you will want to provide your franchisees with the benefits of your labor and the relationships—the brand, your purchasing power, etc.—you have developed over the years. Combined, these elements must constitute a valuable proposition if you hope to have prospective franchisees pay you for them. And while creating that value proposition is part art and part science, it is something the best consulting firms do with regularity—and can likely be done with your brand as well.

Delivering the Message

Once you have developed your value proposition and your message, your next step is to determine how you want to deliver that message. If you are like most new franchisors, it will be delivered in a number of ways: via your web page, ads, stories, brochures, videos, social media, and other tools of the trade. And depending on the nature of your franchise, your best delivery vehicles may be different from others in the market. So if you have a limited budget, it is important you use it effectively.

The Franchise Website

Today, your most important marketing tool will be your website. For virtually every franchisor (new or old), their website is the point of entry for new franchise prospects. Whether you run an ad, place a great story in the media, write a compelling blog entry, or send out an email campaign, chances are your franchise prospect will go to your website before contacting you directly.

Still, far too many franchisors rely on friends, relatives, or neighbors to develop their websites (or, worse, try to do it themselves) and end up with a site that looks like . . . well, like they did it themselves. Then they wonder why it does not generate leads.

So ask yourself as objectively as you can whether your website looks as professional as those of your competitors. Does it have a redundancy of capture mechanisms designed to give the reader a reason to provide you with their contact information—a value proposition in its own right? Does it effectively use calls to action?

In developing the franchise opportunity section of your website, remember, your site should be part franchise advertisement and part collateral material. Its purpose is to find your franchise prospects and present your message to those prospects in a way that will compel them to supply their information.

Putting too much information on a franchise website can be just as bad as putting nothing at all. Far too many franchisors treat the franchise portion of their websites as they do their consumer-oriented pages. They try to sell their franchise with an abundance of clever copy and copious information on every aspect of the franchise investment. But the goal of a franchise website should be simply to get the candidate's name and some basic qualifying information so the sales process can go from there.

Prospective franchisees faced with literally thousands of franchisors on the internet are looking to do only one thing: narrow down their options. In the early stages, they are looking for a reason to *eliminate* your franchise from consideration. So your website should be designed to get them excited about your franchise opportunity without giving them so much information that they can decide without you. *Never let the written word raise objections that a skilled salesperson would likely overcome.*

A good website is the cost of entry these days—franchisors without a professional-looking website will lack credibility. And, as was discussed above, do not provide too much detailed information on your website—unless, of course, you get your prospect's contact information first. Remember: the goal of your site is to find qualified prospects and harvest leads, not to answer every question they may have.

And, of course, a good website must be optimized (more on that in Chapter 10), not only from a consumer standpoint but also from a franchise marketing standpoint.

More Leads: Boon or Bane?

The good news in today's franchise marketplace is that the internet enables franchisors to present their message to a broader market than was ever before possible. And a good website allows franchisors to communicate with relatively new methods such as online forms and streaming videos—greatly reducing their costs.

But the bad news is that as the numbers of leads generated by a good website increase, the amount of chaff the franchisor needs to sort through is increasing exponentially.

More and more franchise buyers are examining a greater number of franchised concepts than ever before on the internet. Huge numbers of people respond to what they see, often producing similarly huge numbers of leads of varying quality that the franchisor must sort through and evaluate. So while the leads generated by the internet are soaring, the close rate on internet leads is falling.

Improving Capture Rates

One of the metrics we encourage franchisors to measure is the "capture rate," which is defined as the percentage of people visiting a particular page who provide you with their contact information.

Internet prospects like to get information by using clicks and keystrokes, not by making a phone call or sending an email. So every franchise website—or franchise section of a corporate website—should include a simple-to-fill-out lead form for a candidate's contact details and other relevant information such as available capital, timetable for making a decision, and the geographical area in which your prospect is interested.

The best franchisors are also careful to ensure that their lead capture mechanism is easy to find on the site. It should be no more than one click away from every other page on the franchise website—and the button or the link going to that page should be prominently displayed.

The best way to optimize your capture rate is to provide a tangible benefit to those who complete the form. We often recommend providing a free streaming video (usually one that is educational in nature and not purely promotional) to anyone who fills out your form. When properly used, this strategy can offer the added benefit of increasing clickthrough rates

<blockquote>

☞**Always Get Their Information**

It is never a good strategy to permit a visitor to your site to download materials such as an e-brochure without requiring them to first complete the lead capture form. While this sounds intuitive, many franchisors make this mistake.

</blockquote>

on pay-per-click (PPC) advertising while lowering marketing costs by using electronic distribution for these materials. This can improve response rates dramatically and improve capture rates by 40 to 60 percent or more—providing you more leads for your dollar.

As you improve capture rates, you will likely want to add some kind of autoresponder matrix to your site, which will integrate through your contact management software, so you can automatically send out customized messages to your prospects, depending on the nature of their answers.

For example, if someone is undercapitalized, you may want to send out one message. But if they are well-capitalized, you might want your contact management software to send out a very different message (and BCC your salesperson so they can reach out to that prospect immediately).

And while the details of how these interactions would be structured will vary substantially based on the nature of the franchise, these issues should all be thought through from a strategic perspective before you begin designing the franchise portion of your website.

The Franchise Brochure

If the franchise brochure took on a persona, it would likely be that of Mark Twain, who, on having his imminent death reported in a newspaper, quipped, "The report of my death was an exaggeration."

Yes, you need to develop a brochure even if you have a great website. And yes, you need to print it, even in the Digital Age, because the secondary buyers referenced previously (attorneys, lenders, accountants, spouses, and others) will not be impressed with the fact that you have a PDF brochure and a nice website.

In fact, the printed franchise brochure still remains the undisputed king of franchise marketing materials and is the one absolute essential in your marketing arsenal. At its heart, it is a credibility piece, so don't try to get away with photocopied materials slipped into an office supply pocket folder. Go four-color with quality copy and design, and use an experienced consultant or ad agency that really knows franchise marketing. (Remember, ad copy for this brochure needs to be reviewed by regulators in eight states.) Use excellent photography and paper stock. Depending on your message, consider a higher-end print process or even a varnished cover. Good brochures can cost $4–$5 apiece if you use an offset print process, but they are well worth the price. If you have to cut corners, consider a print shop with digital printing capabilities. While the price per piece will likely increase, digital will provide you with high quality even with a lower print run (offset would be too expensive for a short run), saving substantially on printing costs.

The Mini-Brochure

The Mini-Me of franchise marketing, a mini-brochure is a trifold rack piece that is given away much more freely. Printed in quantity, a four-color mini-brochure (and, again, yes, from a credibility standpoint, do a nice job with the printing) can be produced for as little as 30 cents per piece, making it much more economical and more practical to use in large quantities.

When making a decision on your need for a mini-brochure, remember it has an entirely different purpose than its big brother. While you want it to present a good image, it is not designed to be a credibility piece. Instead, it is designed for lead generation. So while a full-sized brochure can provide more information for serious prospects whose contact information you possess, a mini-brochure is a teaser to use as a trade-show handout, a direct mailer, or an in-store promotion to candidates you have not yet fully qualified.

Its goal is to get the prospect to take the next step—go to the website, fill out the application, and tell you a little about themselves. So while the design elements of the mini-brochure should be consistent with the full brochure, its messaging should focus on why your franchise is worth further investigation.

Video

No discussion of franchise marketing is complete these days if it does not include video. While many people do not consciously realize it, video results are showing up in 70 percent of all Google searches (perhaps the fact that Google now owns YouTube has something to do with this), and YouTube itself is one of the world's top search engines. So while videos promoting franchising were once seen as an expensive adjunct to the franchise brochure, today video has evolved from luxury to virtual necessity—at least for franchisors looking for more rapid growth.

Videos come in a variety of flavors. The longest video format—the franchise opportunity overview—is typically a professionally produced piece, about eight to ten minutes long, that is hard to beat for effectiveness. With sound, music, narration, and vivid videography, a quality video draws the prospect into the franchise experience like no other medium. It is also great for Discovery Day events and group presentations, drawing people into your trade show booth, and sending to distant prospects who have not seen the excitement of your concept in person.

Once you have developed this full-length video, you can chunk it down into smaller bites that are more appropriate for your website or for YouTube searches. And since these videos can all be delivered electronically, the post-production costs are virtually nothing. But again, bear in mind your rationale for each video. If it is going to be used as a credibility piece, you may want to deliver it to your prospect in a nicely designed package (called a Digipak)—even if you know your prospect can simply view it online. If it is going to be used on your website, be sure you do not give away too much information, which would allow your prospect to leave your site satisfied that they need no more from you. If it is for YouTube, be sure it has a strong call to action and all the content needed to get your prospect to come back to you—otherwise you may have educated him in vain.

Done right, videos markedly improve the effectiveness of your franchise website. Our studies have shown that the use of free videos (best positioned as educational, not promotional) in PPC ad campaigns can increase clickthrough rates by 60 percent or more. Assuming a similar level of prospect qualification, that fact alone can increase your advertising effectiveness. So, for example, if you were spending $50,000 a year on PPC advertising, you could get the equivalent of $70,000 worth of leads from that campaign. And that should translate to about three incremental franchisees in today's market.

The other thing these educational videos can do is increase your website's capture rates (the percentage of site visitors who provide their contact information to the franchisor). By making your prospect fill out a contact form to access the video, you can increase your capture rate by as much as 40 percent—both for PPC leads and for those who responded based on your SEO efforts. And since these videos can be delivered instantly at virtually no cost, a professionally developed video can increase credibility and communicate a more complex message in a format that is much more likely to receive the full attention of the next generation of franchise buyers.

Autoresponders, Correspondence, and Drip Campaigns

The internet can create a massive number of unqualified leads you will ultimately need to sift through in the sales process. To solve this problem, we often recommend a system of customized autoresponder messages that encourage interested prospects and filter out unqualified inquiries without wasting valuable staff time. While the appropriateness of this strategy varies from franchisor to franchisor, the messaging remains important. These autoresponders are often the first communication prospects receive from your franchise organization, and, as such, they must deliver your message in a professional way.

And regardless of whether your correspondence is automated, there is no excuse for spelling mistakes, poor grammar, or any communications that run afoul of franchise regulations. At the end of the day, you will be judged on your professionalism, so you must train your staff on maintaining an appropriate image in all your communications.

Legal Review

Finally, be sure to have your franchise attorney review anything you will use in the franchise sales process before you finalize your promotional efforts. As discussed earlier, eight states will require you to submit your franchise marketing materials for approval. Even if you are not selling in those states, your franchise marketing must be consistent with your FDD. So you will want to seek your attorney's advice on promotional materials, referral programs, and any formal communication you have with prospects.

THE BOTTOM LINE

Sell Them on What Makes You You

If you have gotten this far in the book, you have (or plan to have) a strong value proposition that will make your business attractive to certain buyers. In crafting your message to attract those buyers, bear in mind that the vast majority of prospects will *not* buy your franchise. So don't try to be everything to everybody. And don't try to be your competitor.

Find what makes you unique (or craft that uniqueness). Develop a strong value proposition. And focus on making your franchisees wildly successful. If you turn your franchisees into your biggest fans, they, far better than you, will carry the message of your value proposition to future buyers.

PART THREE

Building Your Franchise Empire

CHAPTER 10

Franchise Lead
Generation

"You don't get what you expect unless you inspect."

—TOM MONAGHAN, FOUNDER, DOMINO'S PIZZA

While having a strong message is important, it is meaningless unless you have an audience to whom you can deliver the message.

Let's start with a basic premise. Franchise sales rarely happen by accident. And while an occasional serious prospect may just wander in your door, most franchises are sold because a franchisor executes against a marketing plan designed to attract that prospect.

Our affiliate, Franchise Dynamics, sells literally hundreds of franchises a year, year after year, for concepts that have included restaurants (Newk's Eatery), weight loss (Medifast), shelving retrofits (ShelfGenie), home renovation (101 Mobility), and even indoor trampoline parks (Sky Zone). In each case, the success of their sales efforts was directly related to their marketing plans. In selling some 1,500 franchises over the past few years, Franchise Dynamics had to process more than 100,000 franchise leads—and those leads did not just happen by accident.

Budget: Let Speed of Growth Be Your Guide

The first step in creating your franchise marketing plan involves setting a budget. And defining an appropriate budget is almost always a balancing act between goals and available resources.

When I ask my clients about goals, however, I find that many business owners simply haven't given the subject much thought. They often respond with vague platitudes about "aggressive growth without sacrificing quality" or suggest they would like to open a stated number of units without having considered all the factors that go into making that decision.

As discussed earlier in this book, the best way to develop your growth strategy is to set a long-term goal (exit, business value, cash flow, etc.) and time frame (five years), translate that goal into a hypothetical business that can achieve it (100 franchises paying $30,000 a year in royalties, for example), and work backward to a more specific short-term objective (selling 12 franchises in the first year).

After creating growth goals using these kinds of measures, the franchise marketing budget can be developed based on industry averages. The annual franchise marketing budget can be arrived at simply by multiplying the desired number of franchises to be sold by the assumed marketing cost per franchise.

So, using the figure of 12 franchises to be sold in the first year, you would multiply the average cost of marketing a single franchise by the number of sales to be made ($8,000 x 12) to determine that you will need a $96,000 franchise marketing budget for the year.

> ### ◤ Those Numbers Can Change
>
> The 2014 Annual Franchise Development Report published by Franchise Update Media indicates that the median marketing cost per franchise sale in 2013 was $8,000 and the average cost per franchise sale was $7,503. More detailed analysis of their data (and of data compiled by iFranchise Group and Franchise Dynamics) indicates that certain factors (such as lower total investment costs, good PR, and strong validation) can reduce those numbers to below $3,000 per sale, while higher investments and/or poor validation can increase those numbers.

Since the franchise sales cycle lasts about 12 to 14 weeks (and it takes some time to fill the salesperson's pipeline with leads), the new franchisor can expect to begin recapturing that budget in 12 to 26 weeks through franchise fees. (For higher-investment franchise opportunities, the sales cycle can be substantially longer.) Still, the new franchisor trying to sell 12 franchises in the first year would be well-advised to budget at least half that amount ($48,000) in working capital for franchise lead generation, spent at a rate of about $8,000 per month.

If, after completing this analysis, the franchisor determines the plan is too aggressive or the required capital is not available, there are several choices:

- Reduce the short-term goals (e.g., try to sell six franchises in the first year and more in later years)
- Lengthen the time frame for achieving the goals
- Bring in outside capital (and increase goals to offset the effect of equity dilution)
- Alter the strategic approach to incorporate more aggressive tactics (e.g., plan simultaneous development of company-owned units, include an area development or area representative option)

Your other option is to decide how much you can afford to spend on marketing and let your budget dictate your growth. So, for example, if you can only afford to spend $2,000 a month on franchise marketing, you would plan on selling about three franchises in your first year ($24,000 divided by $8,000).

But regardless of how you get to the budget number, you need to know how much you will spend before starting the planning process, since knowing your budget will help you prioritize your ad spend. For example, if you have a very limited budget, you might want to focus on PPC advertising to the exclusion of other media, as it is easily controlled and a reliable lead generator. And while other lead generation expenditures (such as public relations) have higher close rates, they are less predictable.

Geographic Markets for Expansion

One mistake we see again and again involves new franchisors starting their process with a national franchise rollout. Often, their initial expansion is serendipitous: they get a hot lead from Timbuktu and decide they should pursue it. Frankly, it is easy to spot a franchisor that has not benefited from professional advice just by looking at their location strategy. If they have locations all over the map, chances are they are being opportunistic and unfocused in their marketing efforts.

Many of these franchisors suffer from the misconception that there are a limited number of franchisees in any given market, and if they do not take advantage of every opportunity, it will never happen again. Unfortunately, that strategy is very likely to come back to haunt them.

The truth is that franchisee prospects are not in short supply. When you are ready to go into a new market, they will be there—as long as you know how to find them. If a franchisor adopts a reactive approach to isolated candidate leads in remote markets, it's also unlikely that they're pursuing the best candidates in that market. Focused lead generation within targeted markets will generate more leads that the franchisor can qualify to determine the candidates who will best represent its brand.

For most startup franchisors, a regionalized approach to their initial franchise development efforts has several distinct advantages while avoiding some major pitfalls:

- Initial training costs associated with franchisees are reduced when on-site training can be done locally, and corporate staff can be leveraged more effectively.
- The franchisor can minimize support costs by clustering units. Clustered units improve the efficiency of your support team by minimizing travel times between locations, thus reducing your staffing needs. And, of course, travel costs are reduced, as the franchisor does not need to pay for a plane ticket and hotel room every month (or every time a problem arises).
- Clustering locations will also provide for closer monitoring and increased support of the franchisee, increasing the likelihood of success. And the franchisor can respond more quickly (and perhaps with more people) if an issue arises requiring franchisor support.
- A local or regional strategy will provide your franchisees with consumer marketing economies of scale—again improving their business economics. And, in larger media markets, the regional group of

franchisees can afford media purchases that might otherwise be out of reach.

➤ In many businesses, having multiple locations in a single market will improve brand presence. The increased number of signs on the street (and the amplified word of mouth) will improve franchisee performance. In service-based businesses, multiple locations may also decrease service times and improve availability.

➤ At the same time, franchise marketing can be more effectively focused, reducing overall costs per sale.

The truth of the matter is that the failure to focus geographically puts most new franchisors in an untenable position. If they have a franchisee who needs additional support in a distant market, they can get on a plane, stay in a hotel, and work with that franchisee to make him successful—but they will conceivably lose money (and certainly a great deal of time) in the process. Or they can refuse the necessary support and run the risk of poor validation, decreased franchise close rates as a result, and even the risk of litigation.

With that in mind, our standard recommendation is that an early-stage franchisor should restrict its initial franchise sales to a three-hour drive radius. That way, if a franchisee needs assistance, the franchisor can get up in the morning, drive to the franchisee, provide support, and drive home in time to sleep in her own bed.

There are occasional exceptions to the rule. If a franchisor plans to expand using subfranchise, area representative, or area development strategies, the larger territories and more sophisticated nature of the targeted franchisee may argue against the more localized approach. If the franchisor is looking to do a very aggressive national rollout *and has the resources necessary to sell and support locations in multiple markets,* there is an argument to be made as well (although increased risk would still factor into that discussion). If the concept being franchised only works in a limited number of sites (such as a mall-based franchisor that requires "Class A" malls), the franchisor may need to adopt a strategy of locating sites first and later finding franchisees to fill them. Similarly, if the franchisor plans to offer only a limited number of franchises in any particular market (as might be the case for a staffing company, for example), a national approach may be more appropriate.

But with these few exceptions, the new franchisor is well-advised to take care of business in nearby markets before venturing too far from home.

Mix and Distribution of Corporate Locations

Another factor you will need to take into account will be your mix of franchise to corporate locations. For many new franchisors, the best course of action is to put the further development of corporate locations on hold as they get established as a franchisor. This approach allows you to learn the business of franchising and concentrate all your resources and efforts on this new business. Of course, if your short-term plans involve both franchise and corporate expansion, you should account for that in your marketing planning—especially when it comes to your location strategy.

There are several location strategies you can employ if you go this route:

- ▼ *The Home-Sweet-Home Strategy.* One would be to reserve markets that are "close to home" for corporate locations while franchising in more distant markets. This allows the franchisor to manage corporate locations more economically while minimizing market conflict with franchisees. On the downside, as the home market becomes fully saturated, you will be forced to open new operations in local secondary and tertiary locations, affording you a lower per-unit ROI and potentially cannibalizing sales from your existing corporate stores. This strategy also has the disadvantages of more distant franchising discussed in the previous section, so a close examination of costs is imperative.

- ▼ *The Spiking Strategy.* A spiking strategy involves opening locations in distant markets that will serve as a showcase for future franchise efforts and a hub for support. For example, a New York franchisor might open a location in Philadelphia where no franchise locations existed. That unit itself might attract franchisees and help them get local publicity. It could be used for hosting Discovery Days or other franchise lead generation efforts. And once the franchises are sold, the Philadelphia store could be used for training and support. This strategy might be accompanied by the sale of the "spiked" store as a franchise once the Philadelphia market is saturated. That sale would then provide the franchisor with enough capital to open a new spike in Baltimore. While good from the standpoint of lead generation and support, this strategy is both slow and expensive. If you're only opening a single corporate location at a distance from your home base, it is also risky because one location is unlikely to support the infrastructure needed to oversee a remote operation. Clustering remote locations is often most efficient, as it enables you to locate stronger field management in the market.

☞ *The "Cherry-Picking" Strategy.* If you were to opt for a cherry-picking strategy, you would reserve either the prime markets or the prime locations within those markets for yourself. The advantages of this strategy are self-evident—you will be reserving the best returns for yourself and providing your franchisees with access to secondary and tertiary locations. This is often driven by a short-term exit strategy or the availability of assets for corporate expansion. Franchisors with limited capital may want to reserve fewer markets for corporate growth. Moreover, a franchisor with a short-term exit plan will often choose not to reinvest in additional hard assets, making it likely that it will choose cherry-picking to obtain the most return on its locations. The disadvantages to this strategy, of course, are that franchisees may be less successful, resent the franchisor, and validate poorly.

☞ *The "Reverse Cherry-Picking" Strategy.* While we have not seen this often, the reverse cherry-picking strategy is employed when a franchisor is asked to take subprime locations as part of a package that includes prime locations. This is occasionally practiced by mall developers—or it would be the natural result if you were to acquire a group of corporate stores with the plan to sell them as franchises. While she may not have invented the strategy, I need to give credit to Anne Beiler, the founder of Auntie Anne's, for this one. When she was forced to take subprime locations, she would often take the lesser locations for corporate stores and franchise the prime locations. While the strategy seemed illogical to many, it paid off in spades when her franchisees became super-promoters of the brand, provided great validation, and bought additional locations.

To the extent that you will be developing corporate locations simultaneously with your franchise efforts, these factors will need to be taken into account in developing your franchise marketing plan.

Narrowing Your Market

One of the most effective ways to improve your franchise marketing is to narrow your prospect profile. If your target franchise audience comprises the entire universe of franchise buyers, you will be forced to use a very general message to attract them. More important, you will likely need to advertise in general business or franchise publications, where you will be competing with many additional franchise opportunities.

Competing with other franchisors head to head is part of the business, of course. But unless you have a very compelling, very short message that will attract prospects' attention quickly, a startup franchise will find lead generation more difficult in this environment. Far better to narrow the scope of your franchise prospects, narrow the focus of your message, and advertise in media that are less saturated with franchise competitors.

Armed with this knowledge, the franchisor should actively work to narrow the buyer profile as much as possible. While intuition alone can provide you with a starting point, the best marketers supplement their intuition with primary research.

In franchising, this research can be surprisingly simple. In addition to working with consultants who have access to this research, you can do your own by speaking to franchisees of similar brands or by going to industry trade associations and speaking to other franchisors. Franchisees are often happy to tell you about themselves and their buying decisions if you know how to ask the questions, as they are accustomed to fielding phone calls from potential franchisees on the same subjects.

The Marketing Funnel

While it is almost a cliché, it is worth restating here. Sales, and in this case franchise sales, is a numbers game. The more money you spend on franchise marketing, the more franchises you will sell. Franchise marketing dollars generate leads. A percentage of those leads fill out applications. A percentage of those will come in for meetings. And a percentage of those meetings will turn into franchise sales.

Of course, it is a little more complex than that. There are numerous sources of potential leads, and each of those sources has different associated costs and close rates.

To understand the process better, the iFranchise Group has developed a paradigm called the Franchise Sales Funnel. The Franchise Sales Funnel can help the franchisor analyze the effectiveness of current marketing efforts as well as identify areas for potential improvement. Figure 10.1 provides a visual representation.

The numbers in this diagram, which come from a combination of our own internal analysis and the previously cited annual survey conducted by Franchise Update Media, illustrate how the franchise sales and marketing process works at a general level.

From left to right (highest cost-per-lead to lowest), you will generate franchise sales leads from public relations, print media, trade shows, direct mail, the internet, brokers (who provide leads for "free" but take referral fees when the franchise sells), and referrals.

Figure 10.1: **The Franchise Sales Funnel**

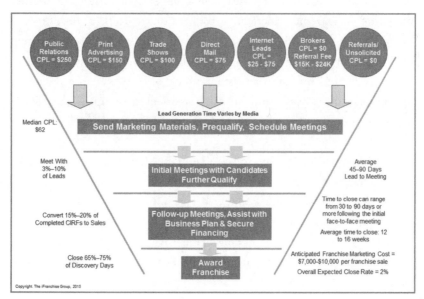

Not only do each of these lead sources have different associated costs for a lead, but each will have their own associated close rates.

- ☞ Leads from brokers, which are pre-qualified, will close at the highest rates.
- ☞ Public relations and referral leads will close at the next highest rates.
- ☞ Print media and trade show leads will close at about an average rate.
- ☞ Leads from the internet will generally have the lowest close rates.

But this only tells part of the story.

Each of the lead sources has its own anticipated cost-per-lead, and each has a varying level of effectiveness. Public relations, for example, while providing extremely valuable leads, supplies them at a lower level of consistency than will the internet—which can deliver numerous lower-quality leads with great regularity.

So as much as you would like to get all your leads from public relations, referrals, and brokers, you will likely need a mix of most of the above if you hope to sell franchises with any degree of predictability.

Moreover, this is made much more complicated by the fact that the media mix that is best for some franchisors will be the absolute worst choice for others. If, for example, you are trying to sell a restaurant franchise to an experienced area development franchisee, the internet would be an extremely ineffective tool, as these prospects do not shop for franchises online. Even the best franchise-oriented trade shows will not be effective, as only about 6 percent (at last count) of their attendees had more than $1 million to invest (and most of these were not restaurant operators). At the same time, restaurant-oriented or multi-unit, food-service–oriented trade shows might be some of the best vehicles for your lead-generation efforts.

And if you were looking to sell a lawn care franchise, you might take a very different strategy.

So the Franchise Sales Funnel, in isolation, is an excellent tool for analysis, but absent either your own historical data or (ideally) the data compiled for your industry by consultants such as the iFranchise Group, it will not be instructive in and of itself. That said, in general, you can anticipate:

➤ Lead costs of between $50 and $150

➤ About 13.5 percent of those filling out your confidential information request form (CIRF) to convert to a sale

➤ Overall close rates of about 2 percent of all inquiries

➤ A time-to-close of about 12 to 14 weeks (longer when you first get
started to account for the need to fill your sales pipeline)

The good news is, the more money you pour down the top of the
funnel, the more franchises will come out the bottom. The bad news, of
course, is that it is somewhat expensive (estimated at about $8,000 in 2014)
to generate enough leads to sell a single franchise.

While we will continue to refer back to the Franchise Sales Funnel
throughout the next several chapters, the important takeaways at this point
are just two:

1. Franchise sales are relatively predictable, assuming a strong value
proposition exists.
2. You need to track everything if you want to optimize your franchise
marketing and sales efforts.

Timing

In developing your franchise marketing plan, you should be aware that
timing will play a major role.

For franchisors that do not have major issues with seasonality, the
franchise marketing budget can be optimized by spending advertising
dollars more aggressively at certain times of the year.

Generally speaking, franchise buyers go into hibernation in November
and December. At that time of year, most of us are preoccupied with
the holidays and are less concerned with making life-altering decisions.
Likewise, there is a period of doldrums in the heart of summer, when
prospective franchisees are more focused on family time and vacations than
they are with buying a business.

By contrast, January through March is prime lead-generation season
for most franchisors. When January comes, it is time for New Year's
resolutions and reflecting on where our lives have taken us. Moreover, the

franchise buying process always starts with something—a bonus, the lack of a bonus, the lack of a raise, a bad review, a layoff—and the beginning of the year is often filled with those special "somethings."

The spring and fall tend to bring relatively average franchise buying activity. But bear in mind that it takes about 12 weeks to close the average franchise sale, so factor that in when determining the timing of your ad spend.

That said, there are certain instances in which seasonality is irrelevant. If, for example, you are targeting multi-unit operators and area developers, chances are that they will be far less impacted by the time of year. Larger operators will have staffs dedicated to development—and it is their job to keep the business growing regardless of season.

The more complicated situation, of course, occurs when you are selling a franchise that is itself highly seasonal. Some businesses (lawn care, tax preparation, mall-based retail, Christmas lighting, driveway refinishing, mosquito abatement, to name just a few) have their own busy seasons. The seasonal franchisor is thus well-advised to account for this timing when developing its franchise marketing plan.

If the seasonality of a business is profound, the savvy franchisor will probably not want to have its franchisees opening their doors in the beginning or the middle of the season (when they might be overwhelmed) or at the end of the season (when they might struggle until the following season). Instead, that franchisor would be well-advised to have its franchisees open at a strategic interval prior to the opening of the season.

To accomplish this, the seasonal franchisor should start with the ideal opening time and work backwards into its franchise advertising "high season." In a retail environment, that might mean working backwards from the grand opening through build-out through site selection through training through the sales process. So if a mall-based retailer wanted to open in September or October to allow their franchisee some time to work out the bugs before the holiday rush, it might schedule its franchise marketing as shown in Figure 10.2 on page 215.

So in a situation such as this, the franchisor should start its franchise marketing efforts in January (which is coincidentally a good time) but

Figure 10.2: Franchise Development Timetable

Activity	Time Required	Earliest Date	Latest Date
Grand Opening	One Week	September 1	October 30
Build-Out and Hiring	One Month	August 1	September 30
Vet Contractors	Two Weeks	July 15	September 15
Negotiate Lease	One Week	July 7	September 7
Find Site and Site Approval	One Month	June 7	August 7
Train Franchisee	Five Weeks	May 1	July 1
Franchise Sales Process	Twelve Weeks	March 1	May 1
Fill Sales Pipeline	Two Months	January 1	March 1

complete most of its marketing activities by March 1. While there might be some minimal advertising allotted for the remainder of the year, if a fall opening is important to franchisee success, the franchise marketing budget may be highly concentrated in just those two months.

The implications for seasonal businesses are significant. Working capital requirements at the beginning of the process will be increased, as the franchisor cannot offset them with franchise fees until after it has spent most of the year's franchise marketing budget. Moreover, from a fulfillment standpoint, the organization will need to be built in a multifunctional way (or outsource certain functions) to accommodate different organizational needs throughout the year.

Of course, none of these are hard-and-fast rules. Franchisees for most systems can be recruited throughout the year, and openings for almost any business can be accommodated out of season—as long as the franchisee is adequately prepared (financially or operationally) for the implications of this counter-seasonal opening.

But from a marketing perspective, seasonal franchises have to account for increased working capital needs (or otherwise modify their growth plans) to accommodate this need for seasonal openings.

Media Mix and the Allocation of Scarce Resources

Marketing planning is, more than anything, the art of allocating scarce resources effectively across unlimited uses for those resources. And as you begin your efforts at franchise lead generation, chances are you will be confronted with a lot of conflicting information.

Public relations professionals will tout public relations. Print salespeople will tout their publications. Internet professionals will talk about the sheer volume of leads they can drive. Brokers will rightly tell you about how well qualified their leads will be. As the saying goes, "When your only tool is a hammer, every problem looks like a nail."

What's more, all of these folks will be right. And, to the extent that they peddle the exclusive use of their particular lead-generation vehicle, all of them will be wrong.

The best marketing plans take into account several factors when allocating media dollars, including:

- Historical performance of similar franchise concepts
- Historical performance of franchises of a similar investment size
- Historical performance of your franchise marketing efforts
- The profile of the franchisee
- The message
- The size of the investment
- The value proposition of the franchise
- The complexity of the franchise (e.g., the need for more of a story)
- The franchisor's desired speed of growth
- The franchisor's budget
- Seasonality
- Franchisor growth goals

With this in mind, a comprehensive approach to how every franchisor should allocate their franchise marketing would clearly be beyond the scope of this book—and would likely be outdated by the time it is published in any event. The information that follows is intended to provide some general guidelines, but it will need to be adapted to your situation to be really effective.

Public Relations: The Power of Media

Effective public relations can be one of the most powerful tools in the franchisor's lead-generation arsenal. Because public relations does not come with a call to action and is not subject to predictable placements, the number of leads produced will likely be smaller than more traditional sources such as the internet or print media. Despite the relatively high cost per lead, however, few methods of lead generation provide the high quality of leads generated by publicity, as these leads carry the weight of a third-party endorsement.

And, depending on the nature of the placement, the results can be overwhelming. In the 1990s, a client of mine made the cover of *Entrepreneur* magazine. That story generated thousands of leads, and, over the course of the next year, the company sold 70 franchises without spending a penny on franchise advertising.

A few years later, another client, Krispy Kreme, was transformed from a regional chain to the hottest franchise in the country overnight largely as a result of massive publicity.

About that same time, my current partner at iFranchise Group was winning just about every award in franchising for his efforts at Auntie Anne's. Although Auntie Anne's has historically spent very little on franchise lead generation, the company boasts about 1,500 franchises today.

More recently, a number of our clients have jump-started their franchise sales efforts with similar fame:

- ⬥ *The Original SoupMan* received national publicity long before *Seinfeld*'s characterized its founder as the "Soup Nazi"—and continues to gain worldwide attention. Just by announcing its new franchise program, the company received more than 2,000 franchise sales leads.

- *GarageTek* was featured prominently in *Inc.*, *The Wall Street Journal*, and numerous other publications and then sold 52 franchises in their first year with virtually no advertising.
- *Tasti D-Lite* was featured on episodes of *Sex and the City* and *The Apprentice* and today has dozens of locations in countries around the world.
- *How Do You Roll?* was featured on *Shark Tank* and was immediately inundated by franchise leads; it ultimately sold a major development deal as a result of the exposure.
- *College Hunks Hauling Junk* did them one better by being featured on both *Shark Tank* and *Millionaire Matchmaker*. They have more than 150 locations to show for their efforts.
- Probably half a dozen clients have been featured on *Undercover Boss*, including *Checkers, 1-800-Flowers, Subway, Popeyes,* and *Sky Zone*—and all have had remarkable success.

While the list could go on and on, the results are always the same. Publicity generates a large number of high-quality leads that often convert to franchises.

Of course, most public relations is not found on the national stage. It is local. It is in the trenches. And most of all, it is on the internet.

The internet is increasingly where people go to get their news—and because stories that run on the internet typically have backlinks, this type of PR also contributes to your search engine optimization (SEO) efforts. Our staff at TopFire Media emphasize the importance of these backlinks, pointing out that virtually every media outlet today has an internet presence—and almost every story is duplicated on their internet site either as a podcast, video link, or text story. And each of these stories contributes to your SEO through the backlinks it provides.

The first rule in generating media coverage is that you *must* have a story. The second is that you should incorporate an angle or a slant in that story that makes it unique and interesting to the reader (and editor).

So what should you do first? Unless you have people on staff with the necessary skills and background, most new franchisors will want to hire a good PR firm that specializes in franchising as soon as they can afford to do so. While most people read the day's news oblivious to how it got there, the surprising truth is that 60 percent of "much of the news" was placed there by a PR firm.

A good PR firm—ideally specializing in franchising—will have numerous advantages over internal staff:

- ⬗ They understand how to create a story that "sells."
- ⬗ They have contacts within the industry who will take their calls.
- ⬗ They have third-party credibility when pitching your story.
- ⬗ They have knowledge of editorial calendars, as well as what has run in different publications over the past year.
- ⬗ They have the ability to provide a full-time and dedicated public relations effort and can turn up the jets when a big story arises.

Moreover, a PR firm can provide public relations both for you and your franchisees with equal effectiveness, providing your franchisees with increased value when they open their doors and on an ongoing basis.

Trade Shows and Expos

As the use of the internet began to rise by the late 1990s, trade shows and expos declined in popularity. In more recent years, they have bounced back. And while they no longer generate the foot traffic they once did, many franchisors have found that the ability to get up close and personal with their prospects in a specific location can be a very strong combination indeed.

But before signing up for a variety of shows, it's important to decide which, if any, trade shows are right for you.

In determining whether a particular trade show is a good fit for your franchise, you need to start by understanding the profile of the investor you are looking to reach. Virtually all trade shows track this kind of information, so it becomes a matter of evaluating your target against these statistics. For example, if you are looking for a multi-unit food-service operator who can invest more than $1 million, you probably do not want to exhibit at a general franchise show—especially if less than 10 percent of the attendees have more than $1 million to invest.

In addition to looking at the statistics from past shows, talk to past exhibitors or consultants to determine just how effective the shows are.

Some shows are just better than others, and given the time and money involved, it is important to focus only on the shows that will generate positive returns for you. Most shows will pre-publish exhibitor lists, making a quick survey of exhibitors relatively easy, even if references are not provided.

But before you sign up for any shows, we should draw a distinction between *franchise* shows and *industry* shows.

FRANCHISE SHOWS

Franchise shows cater to people who are actively shopping for a franchise opportunity or looking to learn more about franchising. These events can be fertile hunting grounds for new and growing franchisors. At the better shows, you will typically find that 75 percent or more of the attendees describe themselves as potential franchisees, and more than 45 percent of these potential franchisees have more than $100,000 to invest.

Most franchise shows attract a relatively local audience, although the larger shows in the U.S. will also attract some international attendees and exhibitors. So generally speaking, if you are not targeting franchise sales in the area where the show is located, a franchise show in that market may generate few, if any, leads that will be of value to you. (*Note*: Exhibiting at franchise shows in registration states may also require you to be registered in that state or file an exemption. Be sure to check with your attorney if there is any doubt in your mind.)

Another thing to keep in mind is that at franchise shows most of the action takes place over the weekend, when people take time off from their jobs to think about investing in their future. Since most of these prospects are local, some franchisors elect to stay an extra day after the show is over to meet one-on-one or even to hold seminars with their most qualified prospects.

And since franchise shows will expose franchise prospects to the competition, the savvy franchisor knows not to invite its pre-existing prospects to the show, although post-show seminars can be made more effective by including them in the mix.

Trade or Industry Shows

Industry shows, by contrast, do not focus on franchise buyers but instead target a particular market in which franchises may be offered. They often draw a national or even international audience. The National Restaurant Association (NRA) Show, which is held in Chicago each May, gathers tens of thousands of restaurant industry professionals for four days, while regional shows attract a similarly focused audience on a smaller scale.

While the vast majority of attendees at industry shows are not thinking about franchising, there are often enough prospects to make them very worthwhile for franchisors with a highly targeted franchisee in mind. In fact, over the years, some industry shows like the NRA Show have received enough interest that they have designated a separate Franchise Pavilion to allow franchisors to promote their opportunities.

Since large industry shows are often held during the week, attendees are eager to go home once the show is over. So seminars, receptions, or other activities scheduled for the day after the show may meet with a lukewarm response. Such events are often better hosted during the show itself.

Costs Associated with Shows

The most important thing to remember about shows—trade, industry, or franchise—is that they are all about lead generation, not sales. You will want to do everything you can to generate as many leads as possible. It is very important that the people representing you at the show have the personality and drive to actively engage with as many people walking by your booth as they can. If your team sits back in the booth and waits for attendees to engage with you, your investment in attending the show will be wasted. It is also important to limit your time with each prospect to the time necessary to build rapport and qualify them. Since a good show will provide you with a constant stream of traffic, that traffic may pass you by if you are too busy with another prospect to engage them.

One solution: bring more people to help you work the booth. This leads us to the matter of show costs.

While booth space will start at several thousand dollars, there are numerous hidden costs that need to be included in your trade show budget—and which should be accounted for when tracking costs per lead and costs per sale. Aside from booth space, you may want to develop or rent a professional trade show display. You will probably want to get extra padding under the carpet and a place to sit down with prospects. Everything comes a la carte, so be prepared.

Perhaps the biggest cost is that of travel, food, and lodging for those working the booth. While the shows will often have special deals with local hotels, there may be less expensive options. And booking flights in advance can save you quite a bit of money.

Another cost is for the printed or electronic material you provide to attendees. On the one hand, you will be meeting with prospects who just met your competitors, so you will want to put your best foot forward. On the other, with hundreds of prospects stopping by over a four-day period, you could go through a small fortune handing out brochures that cost $3 or more apiece. One solution: Pass out your mini-brochure or small handout to all the "bag stuffers" who pass your booth, but keep a supply of your full-sized brochures under the table to pass out to your more serious prospects.

All told, you can probably expect to spend $10,000 or more on a typical trade show if multiple people will be attending.

Print Advertising

When it comes to franchise sales, print advertising is not dead. Almost . . . but not quite.

Print advertising can be effective in certain instances, but given the associated costs, the savvy franchisor needs to be very careful about where that money is spent.

There are, for example, some franchise directories that compile lists of franchisors that can be effective. And there are certain franchise-specific or industry-specific publications that can also be effective, depending on the profile of your targeted franchisee. So print should not be entirely overlooked.

That said, print tends to have higher costs per lead than most other forms of advertising. And from a close rate standpoint, it is about the middle of the pack. So for most franchisors, print would not be at the top of the priority list—and if you have a limited budget, it is not likely to make the cut.

Unfortunately, when it comes to print, one of the big problems is measurement. These days, when someone sees a print ad and wants to know more, they usually turn to the internet. So while the print ad may have generated the interest, the lead source may appear to be an organic search or direct traffic (the people who type your URL directly into the browser).

The advantages to print, of course, are that you can convey a longer message in a medium that itself will have some shelf life. Print is often easy to localize if you are not looking at a national rollout by focusing on local publications and/or regional editions of national publications. And the circulation of a print publication may be increased by the "pass around" value of the magazine (either at trade shows or just among friends and colleagues) and further enhanced by the ability to tear out and file something for later reference.

So in making a decision about the value of print, the savvy marketer will need to do more analysis than simply measuring the cost per thousand (CPM), cost per lead, and cost per sale.

Direct Contact, Direct Mail, and Cold Calling

Some franchise marketers have shunned direct contact strategies as time consuming and inefficient, due to their low close rates. In years past, the rule of thumb was that a direct-mail piece might be expected to achieve a 1 percent response rate. So once you figure in the cost of buying or renting a mailing list (at a cost of 5 cents to 50 cents per name), materials, and labor, a list yielding 1 percent might generate a cost per lead of $100 to $150— which is not bad for a franchise lead.

But depending on the nature of your targeted franchisee and your proficiency at direct mail, it may, in fact, be much more effective. For example, a 2012 study by the Direct Marketing Association indicated that direct mail achieved an average 4.4 percent response rate for business-to-business and business-to-consumer mailings. And obviously, that level of response would cut your cost per lead to a quarter of the estimate above—a very attractive CPL indeed.

Response rates, of course, will be influenced by a number of factors, including:

- List quality
- The targeted nature of your franchisee
- Personalization
- The quality of the message
- The quality of the materials and inserts
- The size of the envelope
- Timing

The next question you may want to address is whether to use direct mail or email. Email campaigns are typically much less expensive as you forgo all the mailing costs and most of the labor, but they generally have much lower response rates.

And, last but not least, there is the question of cold calling. Linda Brakel, the former vice president of franchise operations at Bath Fitter, once told me she sold 40-plus franchises using cold calling alone because at the time, Bath Fitter was "such a new concept that it needed to be explained."

Often, a combination of these techniques can have a synergistic effect. Robert Stidham, president of Franchise Dynamics, has found that a combination of direct mail and cold calling can substantially increase lead yields if done right.

Of course, it is important to understand that direct contact strategies in markets like the U.S. and Canada are regulated. And given the vast chasm between a direct-contact strategy that is well done and one that is not, direct contact is often best done through a specialist who will improve close rates.

The Internet

Perhaps more than any single other factor, the internet has helped level the playing field for the new franchisor. Never before could someone get the message of a new franchise to such a broad market so quickly. And seriously, if you were considering the purchase of a franchise, where would you go to do your research?

Today, a startup franchisor can create a website over a weekend (not a very good one, of course), run pay-per-click (PPC) ads on the first page of Google results for targeted keyword searches, and be talking to prospects by Monday. And while the ability to maintain a top position on PPC ads will be limited by your budget and desired keywords, your website can be just as impressive as the one used by McDonald's. Especially in markets where there is not yet a well-established brand, new franchisors can dominate a niche very quickly.

By virtually all accounts, the internet represents the single biggest lead source for most franchisors. Some report they receive more than two-thirds of their leads from the internet. *Indeed, some franchisors spend virtually their entire franchise marketing budget on the internet.*

But when it comes to franchise marketing, calling the internet a marketing vehicle is almost as meaningless as saying, "You need to advertise." The fact is, there are a number of very different strategies for marketing your franchise on the internet.

Today's franchise marketing professional needs to take many different forms of internet advertising into account when allocating a budget:

- ➤ Search engine optimization (SEO)
- ➤ PPC advertising and remarketing
- ➤ Web portals and other site-based advertising
- ➤ Social media

Moreover, the internet has created a new way to calibrate time. Internet years are the inverse of what people used to call dog years—with everything changing seven times (or more!) faster than time in the rest of the universe. In fact, things change so quickly on the internet that almost anything specific that is written here may be outdated by the time it is read. So I will stick to generalities.

SEARCH ENGINE OPTIMIZATION

SEO is one of the single most critical steps a franchisor can take to increase lead flow. Generally speaking, SEO is the art of helping position a website so it comes in at the top of organic (nonpaid) search results. These efforts (and most related statistics) generally focus on Google, as it is currently responsible for 64 percent of all search activity in the U.S.

Why is SEO so important?

According to estimates from an advanced web ranking study by Google Webmaster Tools in 2014 (https://moz.com/blog/google-organic-click-through-rates-in-2014), more than 71 percent of Google searches generated clicks on the first page of results. Pages two and three combined get less than 6 percent of all search clicks. Moreover, according to the same study, the first five search results get an astonishing 67.6 percent of all clicks. A slightly older 2010 study by Optify indicated that the top five organic positions received 72.4 percent of organic clicks. Various other studies over the years have shown similar results. Moreover, these studies have shown that the top spot alone receives between 36 percent and 46 percent of all clicks!

The bottom line: If you are not at the top of search results, the odds are two to one against your being found. And your odds are only about 50/50 if you are not one of the top two organic positions.

It is also important to know that SEO is a moving target. Google, for example, is said to make 400 to 500 changes to its search algorithm each year—some minor and some very important. In the fall of 2013, for example, Google rolled out the biggest change to its search algorithm in more than a dozen years. This change (dubbed Hummingbird, for those of you who want to Google it yourselves) has greatly changed the focus of SEO strategies, so if your site has not been overhauled since then, it is almost certainly out of date.

Today, according to a 2014 Ranking Factors Study from Searchmetrics, the five biggest factors affecting search results are:

1. *User Signals*. Clickthrough rates, average time spent on the site, bounce rate, etc.
2. *Coding*. URL length, position of keywords in the title, keywords in the description, existence of H1 and H2 title tags, and the overall speed of the site. Less relevant since the Hummingbird introduction are keyword domains and keyword density.
3. *Content*. Internal links, number of words, number of keywords in the copy, the presence of keywords in external links, the presence of keywords in internal links, and the number of images and videos. Negative correlations include—somewhat surprisingly—the

use of keywords in H1 and advertising (even Google AdSense PPC ads).

4. *Backlinks.* The absolute number of backlinks, the SEO strength of backlink URL, the length of the anchor text, and the percentage of backlinks containing keywords. There is a huge disparity between top-ranking sites looking at this factor in isolation. Using major keywords, Searchmetrics found that the number-one page rank contained more than 6,000 backlinks, whereas the 30th page rank—the last result on page three—had only about 167. So if you do not have a backlink strategy, you should get one fast. While you might need 6,000 backlinks if you want to optimize around the word "franchise," you will not need that many to rise to the top of page one if your search terms are narrower.

5. *Social Media.* Even if you believe social media is not a huge source of franchise leads in its own right—and I would argue most are just doing it wrong—there is no disputing its strong positive SEO correlation. Again according to Searchmetrics, seven of the top 11 SEO correlates involved social media signals, including Google +; Facebook shares, post totals, comments, and likes; Pinterest; and tweets (not to mention local SEO techniques such as Google Places).

If these criteria read like Greek to you, you will need to hire a professional who understands both SEO and the web if you are to attract qualified franchise candidates in significant numbers online.

Moreover, SEO efforts have to be ongoing. Optimization is largely about an active social media presence and fresh content. And, since your competitors are constantly trying to improve their sites, you may need an active optimization effort just to stay even.

So why not just avoid the hassle and stick to PPC advertising?

While PPC can get you to the top of the first search page, it cannot make people click. In fact, another recent study published by Econsultancy used a sample of 1.4 billion clicks to compare organic to paid search. What it found was, frankly, astounding. In the study, 94 percent of the clicks went to organic search and only 6 percent went to PPC. So clearly, PPC alone will not absolve you of the need for a strong SEO effort.

FRANCHISE WEB PORTALS

Another way to reach the franchise buying public is through web portals—sites that are specifically designed to advertise franchise opportunities. These sites, some of which use a pay-per-lead model and others of which simply sell flat-fee advertising, can provide the franchisor with significant lead flow.

In fact, according to Franchise Update Media, online portals were ranked as the top sales producer on the internet—accounting for 35 percent of internet sales in 2014. In that same study, franchisors reported that online ad portals were their single biggest source of internet leads.

And in many respects, these portals are perfect for franchisors. Prospective franchisees can sort through a wide variety of franchise opportunities to find those that suit them best. Franchisors often pay only for the leads they receive. You can customize who sees your ad based on geography. And franchisees will often self-select their investment range—providing you with a further level of qualification.

Unfortunately, all is not a bed of roses when it comes to portals. Our anecdotal experience and the statistical information we have developed at iFranchise Group, Franchise Dynamics, and TopFire Media indicate that portal leads have some of the lowest overall close rates in franchising. Moreover, portals that use a pay-per-lead model thrive by getting prospective franchisees to request information from multiple franchisors (thereby getting paid multiple times for the same visitor), so you are virtually assured that any lead you get from a portal is also looking at numerous competitors.

Then you will have to deal with choosing the best portals for your franchise. There are more than 100 web portals that advertise franchise opportunities, and most of them have different rate plans (depending on the area you want to target and the prominence of your ads, among other factors). Most of them will negotiate on price. Some are pay-per-lead and some are flat-fee. Some provide statistics on unique visitors and others provide information on page views. Some have content and some do not. Some actively drive traffic to their sites through SEO and PPC while others do not. And almost all of them are continually looking to improve their performance vis-à-vis their competitors—so today's best performers may not be the same as tomorrow's.

In short, all portals are not created equal. And since advertising on 100-plus portals would be tremendously expensive and hugely inefficient, franchisors that do not have access to databases of franchisor performance on these portals must make these decisions by trial and error.

PAY-PER-CLICK ADVERTISING

PPC advertising with search engines such as Google and Bing constitutes the majority of some franchisors' internet ad budget. While PPC ads will typically underperform SEO results, they do have the advantage of getting you seen on the first page of search results. And if your choice is an ad on page one or an organic link on page two, the ad will almost always generate more traffic.

A PPC advertising campaign can be launched in less than an hour with no more than a credit card. Simply set up an account with the search engine, choose a budget, set some keywords, bid on them in an auction-like setting, write a short ad, and choose a landing page, and voilà!—instant leads.

But like most advertising, it's never that easy. The position of your PPC ad (just like your organic position) will influence your clickthrough rate. Your PPC position will be influenced not just by your keyword bids, but by competitor's bids, ad content, clickthrough rates, and other factors. And your choice of a landing page will influence capture rates for these ads.

The emergence of remarketing campaigns (where a cookie is attached to your website, causing display ads to follow visitors around the internet) has been another new development that has improved PPC performance.

And while performance-based advertising sounds great in theory, the evolution of click fraud has meant disaster for some franchisors. Click fraud can occur when ads run on affiliate sites that receive a portion of the revenue when visitors click on those ads. Some unscrupulous operators have set up sites and then paid people to simply click on ads all day long—providing them with revenue and some franchisors (and others) with big bills that resulted in no legitimate leads.

Moreover, unless you have an unlimited budget, it is almost impossible to maintain a top ranking if a competitor is intent on being listed first on a particular keyword. That is because bid rates and budgets are set independently. Thus, a franchisor with a $100-per-day budget can bid $25 per click and—until their budget runs out—their ad will be served above the franchisor with a $200-per-day budget who pays only $10 per click.

This PPC conundrum can be exacerbated by chasing your competitors up the ladder on bid rates. If the top bidder for a keyword is offering $20, you would have to pay more than that for the number-one position, but if the next bidder on that keyword is at $2, you could come in between them to snag the number-two slot for a mere $2.05—so deciding which strategy is best for a particular keyword becomes much more complex.

And since search engines do not publish competing bids, optimizing your PPC advertising involves extensive trial and error: keywords must be identified, inserted, and tested; ads developed, coded, and tested; landing pages developed and tested; bid rates adjusted and readjusted; ad positions analyzed and reanalyzed—and this may need to be done for hundreds of keywords. Beyond that, inefficient keywords need to be discarded and negative keywords need to be added based on an ongoing analysis of your leads (you would not want your ad to show, for example, if someone is searching "Chicago Bears franchise," but you might want to be shown for "Chicago franchise").

The bottom line: "Set it and forget it" is not a winning strategy when it comes to PPC advertising.

Social Media

Social media is a relative newcomer to the field of internet lead generation.

At recent IFA conventions, virtually all the sessions and roundtables dealing with social media were spilling out into the halls. By some estimates, Facebook alone has nearly 1.5 billion active users and LinkedIn (often the better choice from a franchise marketing perspective) has more than 97 million. So with such huge audiences, it is easy to understand what all the fuss is about—assuming you can crack the code of franchise marketing on these sites.

The problem is that far too many franchisors view social media as an easy opportunity for free publicity that can drive leads. But marketing on social media is neither free nor easy—and the sheer number of people using it does not dictate the size of the opportunity. And nobody wants to see posts that are simply self-promotional.

Social media is all about engagement. But engagement happens one-on-one (or perhaps in focused groups), where you can encourage conversation. So your marketing needs to focus on providing information that is of interest to a particular audience and building credibility with that audience. Ideally, you will get others who share your viewpoint to pass your message along, lending you third-party credibility.

Consider the difficulty of optimizing social media marketing efforts. Wikipedia lists more than 600 social networking sites—and that list does not even include sharing sites like YouTube or SlideShare. It does not include blogs, RSS feeds, social search sites, or social bookmarking sites. Moreover, many of these sites have dozens of different apps (Twitter alone has more than 500) designed to make your social networking life "easier."

Clearly, if you want to have a meaningful presence on social media, you would need several full-time people. For the vast majority of franchisors, that kind of commitment is simply out of the question—especially if the effort is focused solely on franchise lead generation.

So for those of us in the real world, the key to success is to have and execute a highly focused plan. That starts by understanding that having a random listing on LinkedIn and a Facebook page is not a plan—it's a prayer.

When you first start out, take care to make the right choices and employ the right techniques:

- ☞ Inbound links from social bookmarking sites can increase your site's traffic—and simultaneously boost its organic SEO efforts—but they have to be from the right sites.
- ☞ Publicity on blogs can enhance a franchisor's reputation—but, of course, they have to be the right blogs and it has to be good publicity.
- ☞ Fan pages and recommendations can build credibility and traffic—but only if you are clever enough to generate a substantial number of followers.
- ☞ Videos posted to sites like YouTube, Yahoo! Screen, and other video sites that have business channels can increase traffic while

building credibility—but they may only be seen if they are first optimized.

🐦 Just to complicate matters further, a franchisor looking to build traffic or gain more attention can use PPC advertising on social media sites to gain followers or otherwise encourage specific action.

🐦 And, of course, a franchisor's effective use of consumer-facing social media will demonstrate to potential franchisees that it understands cutting-edge marketing techniques.

Often, the first strategy a new franchisor should employ is to create a blog to disseminate news and commentary relevant to the franchise. Blogs can be used as the hub of a social media strategy, with content created on the blog pushed out to the social media channels you choose to optimize.

The next part of your social media strategy needs to focus on obtaining followers—and, in particular, the right followers. One of the great things about social media channels like LinkedIn is that you can target very specific people for your connections. So if you are targeting people from a certain geographical area with specific experience in your industry, you can easily identify and connect with them on social media.

But of all the forms of internet lead generation, social media is often the least understood. First, many people look at social media in a vacuum—believing that if it does not generate franchise sales, it does not deserve consideration as a part of your lead-generation budget. But at the risk of being redundant, remember: *Seven of the top 11 SEO ranking factors involve social media signals!* So to evaluate social media without taking its SEO impact into account is somewhat misleading.

The simple truth is that most franchisors do not execute proper social media strategies. This lack of engagement is again brought into sharp relief by the previously cited study from Franchise Update Media. That study found that 73 percent of respondents did not have a franchise page on Facebook and only 13 percent responded to negative reviews. It also showed that 69 percent of franchisors had no LinkedIn group and 67 percent posted on social media less than once per week.

Despite this lack of effort on the part of most franchisors, about 17 percent of the franchisors who participated in the survey reported that they could attribute sales directly to social media, with each franchisor averaging about 4.5 franchise sales through this channel. (Blogging and LinkedIn accounted for more than two-thirds of these sales.)

For franchisors who know the ropes, social media can clearly be an effective lead-generation tool above and beyond its relevance to SEO.

Referrals

In franchise sales, not all leads are created equal.

While the internet is the most prolific producer of franchise sales leads, if you really want to see a salesperson's eyes light up, start talking about referrals. By that, we mean recommendations by existing franchisees, suppliers, or other people "in the know" about the value of your program. Also include people who have seen your operation and are so impressed that they inquire about your franchise program—even though they were not technically referred by anyone.

Leads from genuine referrals have some of the highest close rates in the industry. Prospects who come to you through a referral almost always have a greater level of interest than other prospects and are far less likely to aggressively "shop" your competitors. Moreover, referral leads view the franchisor with greater credibility and are thus easier to close. In fact, in the previously cited Franchise Update Report, referrals were mentioned as having the highest close rate—almost three times as frequently as the next highest lead source.

But as valuable as these leads are, they are often not developed to their full potential. So what does a franchisor do to turn up the volume of these top-quality prospects?

The best generator of quality referral leads will ultimately be successful franchisees who have already invested in the system. The number and quality of referrals generated by the franchisee community will be in direct relation to the success franchisees enjoy and the franchisees' respect for the franchisor's support organization. Moreover, successful franchisees who trust their franchisor will also want to open more locations themselves and be less inclined to look for new business investments outside their current franchise system.

Any good franchisor should also inform its staff and relevant business associates about the advantages of the franchise, the skills it is looking for in its franchisees, and the costs of the program. They should ask employees and other associates to provide the names and relevant contact information of prospective franchisees. Our clients have struck gold by targeting their employees, customers, dealers, salesmen, bankers, and even attorneys! Each of these groups is likely to have a good knowledge of the business and the management team behind it, providing solid credibility in the sales process.

Note that you do not need to have a long-standing relationship with someone to turn them into a referral source. Some of the best referrals may come from people you have only recently met. One great source, when you find it, is the franchisee of a noncompeting system who is looking to join your network. Not only is this person likely to be financially and operationally qualified, but chances are they know dozens of similarly situated prospects who would be eager to hear about a great business opportunity.

In short, every new contact can be a source of referral leads. So it boils down to two simple steps: Network at every opportunity, and ask. Blasting away with the internet will certainly generate plenty of leads and somewhere in the mountains of ore, you will eventually find a nugget or two. But to grow as fast as you can, stake your claim around several strong veins and mine them for all they are worth.

If you already have a number of franchisees in place, recruit them as a source of referrals. Typically, they are proud of how smart they were to have joined your network and of what they have accomplished, so they are usually thrilled to talk to prospects, especially if the prospect is in a different region. Such franchisees are some of the best salespeople you will ever find. They love to talk about their businesses, and they have instant credibility with prospects who will know their enthusiasm is based on real experiences.

If you are targeting a market near a qualified franchisee, call him and discuss your plans to add a new neighbor. Some novice franchisors may fear this call, thinking the franchisee may complain he is being encroached upon. But this call provides you with an opportunity to emphasize what everyone will gain from network expansion. Educating your franchisees about the advantages of system wide growth—increased buying power, advertising power, brand awareness, and support services, and an improved ability to resell their business—will often soften the blow while depriving them of the chance to complain that they "never knew." Since you will need to make the call eventually, it is always best to make it early.

Moreover, when you make that call (ideally before you have identified prospects for that market), you may find the idea of selling an adjacent territory is enough to spur the franchisee to multi-unit ownership. In fact, the best franchisors often start talking with franchisees about their plans to add units from day one, even if they are not operating on an area development contract. They train their field support team to discuss this option on a regular basis and, assuming the franchisees are deemed capable of growth, coach the franchisees on the management, performance, and financial requirements they will need to be eligible for growth.

At the same time, this call provides an opportunity to ask the franchisee if he knows anyone who would be a good prospect for that territory. Assuming your franchisee does not want to invest himself, he may provide you with referrals to friends or relatives who might. Your franchisee certainly has as good an understanding as anyone of what it takes to succeed in your business, and by having input into his new neighbor, he is far more apt to develop a collaborative relationship with them.

One way to further motivate people to provide these referrals is to pay referral fees for franchisees that end up signing with you. While there is nothing illegal about these fees, and many franchisors use referral programs, they may trigger some disclosure obligations—so be careful to speak with your franchise attorney before implementing them. Moreover, if you are thinking about paying referral fees to your franchisees, you will need to exercise extra caution. Franchisees are generally not bound by the same disclosure rules as you are, so they can speak openly to franchise prospects about sales and earnings. But if you compensate your franchisees for referrals, there is an argument to be made that they now have a conflict of interest and should not be having this discussion. So again, speak to your franchise attorney about how such a situation might work if you want to offer referral fees.

Finally, aside from networking to generate referrals, be sure you are leveraging all your other assets as well. If you do consumer marketing, make sure you mention "franchises available" somewhere on each ad.

Whether you have a menu, a placemat, or a physical store, always look for opportunities to spread the word.

Brokers

Many people confuse franchise sales outsourcing companies (such as Franchise Dynamics) with broker networks (such as The Entrepreneur Authority). In fact, they are two entirely different types of organizations.

Franchise brokers, also known as Lead Referral Networks (LRNs), have one basic role: to provide prequalified leads to associated franchisors, generally in return for a success fee that is paid once the sale closes. A typical broker will represent numerous franchisors—often hundreds of them—and will act as a matchmaker by finding and funneling prospective franchisees to franchise companies that are a good fit. And while a broker can add some third-party credibility, once the selling starts, the broker will exit the picture and leave the heavy lifting (i.e., making the actual sale) to the franchisor. Thus, the broker is not part of the franchise sales process, but is instead an extension of the franchisor's advertising budget.

Programs targeting rapid franchise expansion may benefit from the use of LRNs in the sales

> ◥ **Creative Broker Compensation**
>
> In recent years, broker networks have become increasingly creative in their compensation structures. Some require entrance fees to join their networks. Some mandate monthly fees or participation in their annual conventions. Some encourage sales spiffs (think cruises!) or even contests provided to individual brokers who achieve certain performance objectives. And some ask for a piece of the royalty as ongoing compensation. While the iFranchise Group works with many reputable brokers, we *strongly* advise our clients to avoid any brokerage company that asks for a piece of the royalty or any other ongoing compensation. Such compensation is entirely unjustified and will place a significant long-term burden on the company.

process. This outsourced form of franchise lead generation provides the benefit of a variable cost structure, but with average success fees ranging $15,000 or more, these brokers can be far more expensive than internal lead generation.

Still, from a franchisor's perspective, brokers offer some notable advantages. While some brokers will take fees to accept a franchisor into their network, most are paid only once a franchise is sold, providing some comfort in the pay-for-performance nature of the relationship. Moreover, franchisors do not have to pay these fees until after they have received the franchise fee, which provides some cash flow advantages.

Additionally, each broker lead will come to the franchisor prequalified. These prospects take much less time and effort in the franchise sales process and close at a much higher rate than virtually any other type of lead. Franchisors who work closely with brokers can also use them to obtain feedback from the prospect and guide them more effectively through the sales process.

That said, brokers are not without their disadvantages.

Foremost on the list of disadvantages is the fact that although brokers are not directly controlled by the franchisor, they can make representations that may subsequently expose the franchisor to liability, claims of fraud, or franchisee dissatisfaction. With this in mind, prudent franchisors will make it their responsibility to monitor how the brokerage network is representing them, provide the brokers with ongoing training and feedback, and ensure that potential franchisees are fully informed about the franchise from the franchisor's perspective.

Brokerage networks are not a magic pill for lead generation. They take work. Franchisors who rely heavily on brokers will often spend money to attend or sponsor conventions for each brokerage network and develop formal communications plans to keep their concepts "top of mind" within their broker networks.

And, of course, brokers do not substitute for an internal sales force. Once the lead is generated, the franchisor remains responsible for the franchise sales process. In most cases, that will mean paying a sales commission to the franchise salesperson over and above the brokerage fees generated by that sale.

And, as was mentioned above, a broker lead is already more expensive than the cost of advertising for a lead internally.

Finally, being represented by a broker (or several, as they generally do not require exclusivity) is not a guarantee of franchise sales success—or even of increased lead flow. Sometimes, as the new franchisor on the block, you may find yourself with little brokerage action despite major expenses. Individual brokers within each network want to send leads to franchisors that will close deals (or that pay higher commission rates), so getting on an individual broker's short list may be more difficult—especially for newer franchisors.

In deciding whether to use brokers, factors to be considered include the aggressiveness of your franchise sales goals, the size of your marketing budget, the desired geographic coverage, and your willingness to monitor the brokerage network closely. Select your brokerage network (or networks) with the same care you would use in selecting an in-house franchise sales force.

The bottom line: While brokers can be a tremendous boon, driving high levels of franchise sales for some franchisors, they are not right for everyone. They should be viewed as a means of supplementing franchise sales leads, not as the exclusive mechanism for generating those leads.

The Importance of an Integrated Approach

Before leaving the subject of media selection, we should touch on the need for an integrated approach to franchise marketing efforts. All too often, we see franchisors taking disjointed approaches to their franchise marketing— to their ultimate detriment.

This is often most evident when it comes to messaging. The public relations firm hired by the franchisor tells one story. The website developed by their internal webmaster tells a second story. The brochure created by their ad agency tells a third. And so on.

The problem is that in today's interconnected world, all the different stories ultimately end up on the web, and these disjointed efforts fail to communicate the brand position the franchise hopes to occupy. Moreover, the lack of a coordinated approach can also impact lead generation efforts based on media choices.

If you have a limited franchise marketing budget (and who doesn't?), remember that every marketing professional you speak with will have their own ax to grind. And while there will likely be some truth in each of their sales pitches, you will need to be the ultimate arbiter of how you allocate your marketing dollars.

The best franchisors feed what is working and starve what is not—knowing that what works today may not work half as well tomorrow.

Measuring Results

As with all marketing, you need to be able to measure results to ensure your dollars are working to produce quality leads affordably.

As a franchisor, the most meaningful measure of success is cost per franchise sale—which in today's marketplace range between $7,000 and $10,000. But unfortunately, cost per sale is one of the least effective means of measuring success, especially for new franchisors. This is a result of the "law of small numbers."

To illustrate this law, imagine you have two sacks, each containing 100 marbles. In Sack A, there is one black marble and 99 white ones. In Sack B, there are ten black marbles and 90 white ones. If you drew a black marble from Sack A on your third pick while failing to draw a black marble in three tries from Sack B, you would be

> ### ➤ Why Cost Per Sale Can Differ
>
> There are a number of things that will influence your cost per sale—investment size, experience, quality of marketing materials, messaging, and sales process, to name a few—so your numbers may be different.

inclined to believe that Sack A was a treasure trove of black marbles and Sack B was a waste of time. The problem, of course, is that a single anomalous event has skewed your beliefs because your sample size—three marbles—was not large enough. And in determining an adequate sample size when dealing with small numbers, proper statistical methods dictate you must base the sample size on the number of occurrences of the desired outcome (black marbles), not on the size of the universe (all marbles in the bag).

For this reason, other measures with greater accuracy must be used in determining results. So while you should certainly track cost per sale, when it comes to media buying decisions, we recommend you also track variables like cost per lead (by media and media type), cost per application, close rate (by development officer), and speed to close. Then, on a quarterly basis, weed out the bottom 10 to 20 percent of your marketing performers and substitute in alternative media.

▼ A Shameless Plug

At the iFranchise Group, we have access to the data collected from our clients and affiliates (Franchise Dynamics and TopFire Media) representing hundreds of thousands of leads generated from virtually every franchise-oriented media in North America—and we can parse this data based on a number of relevant factors to provide our clients with marketing solutions that work.

If you are new to franchise marketing, your best bet is to work with professionals who have a database of this information. Absent that database, you will need to develop an estimate of that information from a variety of public and private sources.

For example, in trying to measure the effectiveness of websites prior to advertising on them, you could obtain information from the media representatives themselves. Or, if you find they are not providing you the information you need in a measurable format, you could go to TrafficEstimate.com and type in the websites you are comparing. Then simply divide the monthly advertising cost by their estimated traffic divided by 1,000, and you can generate a measurement tool to calculate cost per thousand (CPM) visitors. Similarly, you can measure site quality by going to Alexa (www.alexa.com), which provides its users with an estimate of page views per user—and of course, the more page views, the better your chances of being seen.

Critics (and salespeople) may argue these are only estimates, not precise numbers. But in the absence of better information, it is a start. In a recent study, CPM numbers ranged from $7.40 to $263 for two similarly priced sites—and the lower-priced site actually showed page-view estimates that were twice as high as the higher-priced site! It doesn't take a genius to figure out which of these sites is likely to generate better results, yet the latter site continues to attract advertisers.

Another method involves measuring capture rates on custom landing pages. Even without that effort, you can approximate the number of leads generated by applying your overall capture rates to inbound hits generated by a site, allowing you to derive a rough cost-per-lead measure. Your PPC capture rates, which are derived on Google by placing a cookie on the appropriate pages, can serve as a rough proxy in this calculation. The use of the free Google Analytics program can also help you measure key indicators across PPC campaigns (including total clickthroughs, conversions, costs per click, costs per conversion, and clickthrough and conversion rates).

The performance of specific inbound links can be measured through "link coding," in which the link string can identify the specific source even when the click came from a generic source such as Google PPC. A franchisor's capture rate can then be measured with a relatively simple formula: divide the total number of leads generated from your website by the number of visitors to the franchise section of the site.

Once you have established a baseline performance, you can alter variables to optimize performance. For example, you may choose to change the text or landing page (i.e., the first page visitors see on your site), or even create a series of landing pages for different inbound links. You may alter the text in your PPC ads on a keyword-specific basis. But whatever you do, remember to measure the results and make changes designed to produce improvements. And remember the law of small numbers: Each test must be large enough (i.e., long enough) to provide you with a meaningful measure of impact.

THE BOTTOM LINE

Marketing Done Right Yields Predictable Results

Franchise marketing is nothing if not frustrating. You need to generate large numbers of leads that have very low close rates to be successful in franchise sales—and if you do not know what you are doing, you can spend a lot of money on trial and error.

But if you develop a plan based on a carefully crafted message and a good understanding of your franchise candidate, you will certainly generate leads. And if you have a good concept and continually measure and refine your results, your marketing efforts will generate prospects who will be ready—even eager—to buy your franchise.

The only thing that will be left for you to do is . . . sell them.

CHAPTER 11

Selling
Franchises

"Take a chance! All life is a chance. The man who goes farthest is generally the one who is willing to do and dare."

—DALE CARNEGIE, FOUNDER, DALE CARNEGIE INSTITUTE

Franchise sales are easy.

Whoa! What? For a lot of new franchisors, saying that franchise sales are easy is counter to every instinct they have.

But I think it is important to start with that premise, because I all too often run into new franchisors that get a prospect who is ready to sign—and because they are new and because they have just spent a lot of money launching their franchise, they go for the close. And they should not have.

When new franchisors jump at their first opportunity to sell without giving a second thought to qualifications, geography, or organizational fit, they will regret their decision for the next decade—or more.

So while the franchise sales process is certainly not easy in a traditional sense, it is easy in that if you do the right things—if you have a proven process—franchise sales have a predictable outcome. Yes, you will have a low

close rate. And yes, you will need to be prepared for rejection on a scale unknown to most salespeople.

But if you can steel yourself for rejection and follow best practices, you don't need to jump at that first check. Another franchise prospect will be in line right behind the first.

The ability to sell franchises is fundamental to the success of a franchise system. Without the franchise sale, your legal documents, business plan, and marketing materials are just an expensive pile of paper.

> ### "Sale" vs. "Award"
>
> Some people in franchising steadfastly refuse to talk about franchise "sales" but will only refer to the "award" of a franchise. While we philosophically agree with the importance of an award process, we feel it is disingenuous to ignore that a sale is taking place and thus do not shy away from that terminology.

But as all franchise development personnel know, sales is a numbers game. The more and better leads a company receives, the more sales will result. But this can't be left to chance. Leads must be worked effectively and persistently. So let's get started.

A Sale Like No Other

Despite the abundance of prospects who are chasing after the dream of business ownership, the franchise sale is a sale like no other.

As a franchise salesperson, you need to get up every morning knowing your sales message will start with telling prospects, "I would like you to . . ."

- Quit your job
- Give up the security of your current salary
- Give up your benefits and insurance
- Give up your paid vacations
- Trust me with your life's savings
- Invest that money in a business you may know nothing about

And by the way, I cannot tell you how much money you will make.

Selling franchises is easier if the salesperson has experience in franchising. But at a minimum, she must truly understand the life change her candidates may need to make. Salespeople with a strong background in B2B or B2C sales can translate their prior success to the world of franchising, but they must understand that selling a life change is far different from selling advertising, electrical components, or insurance.

Who Is Your Buyer?

When starting the franchise sales process, remember that your buyers may not be who you think they are.

Most people think of a logical sales process in which a buyer starts with the universe of franchise opportunities and systematically narrows his focus until he is ready to sign (hopefully) with you. They assume the prospective franchisee is looking at quantifiable values such as buying economies, advertising economies, and shared support, and that the ultimate decision will be made after a thorough financial analysis.

 **"Read That FDD!"**

You should make sure you encourage candidates to read your FDD and urge them to have outside legal counsel review it as well.

But very few prospects take such a logical approach to franchise ownership. For most, franchise selection is a highly personal and emotionally driven process. Few candidates will have done systematic or comprehensive research on your industry. Many will not even read your FDD.

Based on our experience, most franchise buyers do not choose a franchise because they want to earn more money. Most make the move because they want to be their own boss, do something they love, control their own destiny, build something of value, or enjoy the independence associated with business ownership. So when designing your sales process, keep these motives in mind.

The Franchise Sales Process

Let me start this section by acknowledging that there is no single correct process for selling franchises.

☞ What works to sell individual franchises may be much less effective when selling area development franchises.

☞ The sale of a low-investment service franchise that requires little to no discussion of real estate and franchising will be very different from selling a more capital-intensive investment.

☞ What works for well-established brands may not work as well for you when you first start franchising.

☞ What works for a professional franchise salesperson may not be the best sales process for someone with less developed sales skills or a sales background outside the world of franchising.

So please bear in mind that there are many different versions of the sales process—none of which is right or wrong. Figure 11.1 will, however, illustrate the general flow of the process, with additional steps depending on the nature of the franchise, the source of the lead, the need for financing, and the nature of targeted franchisees.

In addition to the factors listed above, there are a number of issues you will need to address from a strategic perspective. For example, do you want to try to close franchisees at some point after Discovery Day or on Discovery Day (sometimes renamed "Decision Day" by franchisors adopting this approach)?

Figure 11.1: **Flow of the Sales Process**

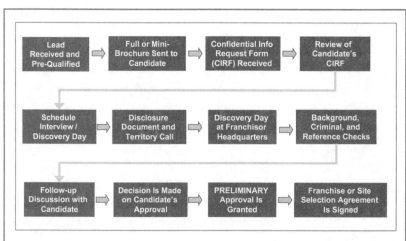

Below are some of the best practices in franchise sales.

Just Say No—The Hardest Job in Franchising

Prospective franchisors regularly ask me about the most difficult aspect of franchising. Is it franchise sales? Ensuring franchisee success? Quality control?

And my answer always surprises them: "No, it is turning down a check for $40,000." This is because the single biggest mistake made by novice franchisors is to sell franchises to candidates who are not truly qualified.

The temptation is understandable. When a new franchisor begins to market franchises, it will likely experience lower closing rates and longer sales cycles than it has ever encountered before. It feels like that first franchise sale will never take place. Doubt creeps in. *"Will I ever sell a franchise?"* And then a prospect the franchisor secretly knows is marginal indicates she wants to sign the franchise agreement and pay the initial fee.

So what do you do?

Before you take that check, remember *you are in this for the long haul.* And nothing is more important to your success than the success of your franchisees.

Don't forget, marginal franchisees require much more support than their stronger counterparts. This means you will need to devote more resources to, and incur more costs for, supporting these franchisees, and they will generate lower-than-average revenues and pay less in royalties—if they pay them at all. Failed franchisees, of course, pay nothing. Furthermore, they are much more likely to bring litigation against their franchisor.

▼ Don't Close on a Decision Day!

At iFranchise Group we advise our clients not to close sales on a Decision Day for a variety of reasons—not the least of which is the need to be sure the sale is the right choice for everyone involved. So we are rather strongly opposed to this practice, which we view as a hard sell. That said, there are those who swear by this approach. Thus we will refrain from advocating a single right approach here—despite our philosophical inclinations on this issue.

And that is just the start. For franchisors that use a financial performance representation in their disclosure documents, a bad franchisee's performance will drag down reported averages—making the disclosure less impressive. And as every franchise salesperson will tell you, a system characterized by poor franchisee validation and failed locations will be harder, if not impossible, to sell.

You should also remember that every one of your failed franchisees (and your franchise-related lawsuits, should you have any) must be included in your disclosure document. A savvy franchise candidate will always speak with these franchisees as part of his due diligence.

Now, if a marginal candidate is your 25th franchisee, you can probably weather the storm, though I am not advocating that you relax your standards as your franchise grows. But if this franchisee is among your first ten, you have a problem. And if he is your *first*, you may be so distracted by his demands that you never get

Ask Your Attorney

You will want your attorneys to provide you with specific advice on what is allowable (and what is not), including how to avoid charges of steering prospects to specific franchisees.

your franchise program in line again. Moreover, your first franchisee will often set the tone for your entire franchise program.

Suppose you accept a franchisee who is unqualified, undercapitalized, and lazy. Do you really think he will tell a prospective new franchisee, "The franchisor was a great teacher, and the system is flawless. The only reason I failed is because I am stupid, undercapitalized, and lazy."

Not likely! Instead, your prospect is more apt to hear, "This was the worst decision I ever made. The business is failing. The franchisor was absolutely no help. This business is much harder than I ever thought it would be—and much more expensive. It looks like I am going to lose everything. My wife has left me and taken the kids. I'm about to lose my home, and by this time next week, I will be living in a cardboard box underneath the highway."

If your prospect talks to this franchisee, I can pretty much guarantee you will never hear from her again, regardless of the quality of your marketing materials or how well your development staff prepares them for "the one or two franchisees who may not be doing so well."

Consider, on the other hand, if they hear a chorus of: "This was the best decision I ever made. I didn't have any experience and was worried at first, but the franchisor was great. They helped me every step of the way and were always there for me. My earnings are far better than what you are looking for, and frankly, after only five years, I am planning on buying a fifth franchise out of the profits." Any worries your franchise salesperson may have had about overcoming objections have just disappeared. Start preparing the paperwork!

Qualifying Prospects: The Award

One of the most important concepts for a new franchisor to master is that franchises are *awarded*. That is, they are granted to deserving prospects and not given to those who are unlikely to succeed. This must be taken very seriously by everyone in your organization.

Franchise sales is *not* a hunt for the next check. It is a true screening process through which you will identify the best candidates to join your franchise family. The success of your system depends on the success of your franchisees, and the biggest factor in franchisee success is not the system—it is the people. A great system with many unqualified franchisees will almost certainly fail. But even a mediocre system populated with great franchisees will likely succeed. In our experience, a well-executed sales process in which franchisee candidates are heavily qualified will result in selecting the right franchisees most—but not all—of the time. If a franchisor starts cutting corners and placing too little emphasis on franchisee qualification, it will be lucky to select the right franchisee half the time. Choose the wrong franchisee too many times, and the franchisor's focus on growth will be quickly diverted to quality control problems and managing disputes with franchisees.

Setting Standards

Before the franchisor spends its first dime on franchise marketing, the company must determine the nature of its ideal franchise candidate. Ask yourself if you would be better off with experienced prospects or if you should look for those without prior experience so you can train them from scratch with your philosophy and methods. Franchisors should ask themselves the following types of questions:

- 🐦 What resources do you have to train and support new franchisees?
- 🐦 Do you have an adequate value proposition to sell people who already have experience in your industry?
- 🐦 How important is prior experience in terms of the franchisee's ability to become profitable in his first year?

Going into the franchise sales process without this knowledge invariably leads to accepting marginal candidates. The savvy franchisor will start by establishing objective standards that can later be subjectively modified based on further examination of its specific situation.

Beyond capital requirements, franchisors should look at the hard skills needed for success in their system. These skills will be determined based more on the role the franchisee will play in the operation than on the ultimate product or service deliverable. A franchisor selling handyman services, for example, would look for one set of skills if the franchisee will deliver the service personally (trade skills, mechanically adept, etc.) and an entirely different set of skills if the franchisee's role will be to sell services and supervise a work force. This will influence the lead generation strategy, the sales process, and ultimately the types of support franchisees will require to succeed in their business.

As you build a larger pool of franchisees, you should be able to identify commonalities among your top performers. Look for those traits in new prospects, and learn from your mistakes as well as identify potential red flags.

Ultimately, your role in assessing and turning down candidates who are ill-suited to your business is perhaps your most important job. And it may seem counterintuitive, but in the long run, a franchisor who is willing to walk away from the wrong sale will sell the most franchises and build the strongest network.

The Big Three

So how should you go about qualifying your prospects? What criteria should you use? We generally recommend that you start with the big three and then add any preferred skill sets (e.g., sales ability, restaurant background, etc.).

The big three are:

1. Capitalization and credit
2. Work ethic
3. Personality and fit with your organization

Let's look at these one by one.

CAPITALIZATION AND CREDIT

Your new franchisee must have—or have access to—the necessary funds to start up the business and carry it until it is profitable. A franchisee's capital requirements will vary depending on a variety of factors, including the speed at which the business typically achieves positive cash flow, but most franchisors can readily identify a number at which their franchisees will have sufficient capital to open a unit and get it to profitability. In fact, this number is required as part of your disclosure of initial and recurring expenses in Items 7 and 8 of your FDD.

Undercapitalization is perhaps the number-one reason for franchisee failure. Adequate capital gives the franchisee time to learn on the job and recover from missteps, so every franchisor should take a conservative approach to franchisee approval in this area. Generally, the criterion is based on net worth, liquidity of assets, and the candidate's credit score.

Your franchisees may be able to finance a portion, if not all, of their initial investment. The *amount* financed will be, at least to a certain extent, a function of *what* is being financed (e.g., equipment is easier to finance than working capital because equipment becomes its own collateral) and the creditworthiness of the franchisee. You will want to establish standards to ensure franchisees are not taking on more debt than they can handle during the critical startup period. Take a conservative approach to determining these standards and walk away from franchisees who are going to be too highly leveraged.

As part of your qualification process, you will want to ask each prospect to complete a personal net worth statement that shows where their investment dollars will be coming from and secondary sources of

income that may help them support any initial losses during startup. Be sure to verify that those funds truly exist by requesting confirmation from the prospect's bank.

If the prospect doesn't have much in the way of liquid assets, home equity can provide a source of some of the needed funds. But be careful. You do not want to allow your franchisees to become overleveraged. And bear in mind that illiquid assets (cars, boats, art, etc.), especially if they are the bulk of a prospect's assets, will not be available to produce cash to pay advertisers and salaries as needed in the startup days.

In some instances, franchisees even use retirement savings to fund the purchase of a franchise. Known as ROBS (or Rollovers as Business Startups), accessing retirement accounts involves creating a new C corporation. The corporation creates its own 401(k) plan, and the franchisee rolls her existing retirement capital into that plan. The retirement plan then acquires stock in the new company, which can then use the capital for its growth.

> ## Do Your Background Checks
>
> If your franchisees will be inside customers' homes or have exposure to children, it is vital that you undertake full and detailed background checks for any criminal history.

Before going the ROBS route, be aware the IRS has been looking into these transactions very closely—and that certain uses of capital (paying yourself a salary, for example) are prohibited. So the transaction needs to be structured very carefully by a professional to ensure compliance.

And of course, be sure to check your prospect's credit and other references. TransUnion, Experian, and Equifax are the three primary players in the credit reporting industry. Their websites have options for creating a subscriber account, and all three offer credit and related reports online. Credit checks can be run nationally or by state. Additional checking can be done through SentryLink, an excellent resource for conducting background checks including criminal history, property ownership, and driving records. Intelius focuses on criminal checks, bankruptcies, small claims activity, tax liens, address history, and court judgments.

WORK ETHIC

The more difficult part of the screening process involves looking at the prospect's work ethic. Unfortunately, as with other screening processes, the prospect knows how to play the game, too.

Remember: candidates often come to you because they want to buy your franchise and they will give you the answers you want to hear. Obvious questions (e.g., "Are you a hard worker?") will get you obvious answers and will likely teach you nothing.

So it is imperative to ask your prospects questions that elicit meaningful information. Today's increasingly sophisticated franchisees know what most franchisors want and may tailor their answers to suit the situation— even when the ultimate result is not in their best interest. Simply asking, "Do you mind long hours?" will garner the expected response. And calling references will likely yield the same nonresult if the prospect has chosen his references well.

The iFranchise Group has, over the years, developed a number of approaches to draw out meaningful answers. For example, in addressing the question of work ethic, one might envision the following conversation:

Q. *So what do you do in your spare time?*

A. I like to work around the house and golf.

Q. *Really? I'm a golfer too. What's your handicap?*

A. I'm a six. How about you?

You now know that this prospect may be spending too much time on the links to be an effective business owner. I have nothing against golf, but it is not often that you meet a low handicapper who is eager to put in the kind of hours most new businesses require.

The point is to examine how the prospect lives her life, her outlook, and her expectations. Ask about an average day, about hobbies and achievements. If your prospect is a "nine-to-fiver" who reports that after a "brutal" eight hours, she feels a need to go home and unwind before a leisurely evening of television, she is unlikely to have the energy level or drive needed for your business.

Let your prospects know what they are in for, and don't hold anything back. Franchisees expecting to sit back and watch the money roll in may wash out early, so it is in the best interest of both parties that such prospects fully understand the required depth of the franchise commitment.

ORGANIZATIONAL FIT

As important as financial readiness and work ethic are in choosing your franchisees, the subjective value of how well the candidate fits into your organization's values and culture may be even more important. My partner, Dave Hood, once turned down a prominent actress for a franchise, despite the name recognition it would have brought to Auntie Anne's, because her image was inconsistent with the wholesome image associated with the brand.

Use Expert Profiling Tools

We typically caution against using standard assessment platforms. Instead, there are several profiling tools (e.g., the Nathan Profiler from Australia) that have been developed by franchising experts.

When it comes to fit, some franchisors swear by personality assessments. They will go about identifying top-performing franchisees (if they have them) or company-store managers and have them complete an assessment, hoping to isolate the characteristics that distinguish the strong from the weak. Results in hand, they will ask franchise prospects to take that same assessment and compare them. Franchisors with fewer operators may simply rely on the experience of the assessment designers.

But even the best-designed and properly administered personality assessments will only go so far. Their greatest value is often to provide guideposts for the franchisor as they probe deeper into various aspects of the candidate's background during the qualification process.

Ultimately, some part of the screening process must involve your own judgment. How well do you and your prospect get along? Do you share the same philosophies? Or is your relationship contentious from the start? Many of our clients have told us they accepted a candidate who looked good on paper, but who they "had a bad feeling about"—and they lived to regret it. Sometimes we have to trust our instincts, despite what profiling assessments may tell us.

With this in mind, it is incumbent on you to get to know each candidate one-on-one, the way you would get to know a life partner. For larger franchisors, it is vital that they work to institutionalize a practice of screening for cultural compatibility.

As you continue the evaluation process, you will also want to assess other criteria such as intelligence. While franchisors often work to simplify business operations, even the simplest business model requires some intelligence to run. And as the saying goes, "You can't coach 'smart.'"

Be sure to look at those personal skill sets that will help the franchisee succeed. Are natural sales abilities important? Do they need to know how to manage people? Is financial analysis key? What about marketing skills? Does your franchisee need a background in a particular industry or professional certifications or licenses? Will franchisees with a certain type of personality be more likely to prosper?

Since almost all applicants will tell you they are smarter than average, you need to independently determine if they are good judges of their own talent. Short of intelligence tests, a candidate's work history, academic achievements, vocabulary, and general presence will provide the clues you're looking for.

The problem is often largely one of the franchisor's own creation. By promoting their "highly selective, mutual qualification process" in which the franchisee must qualify for the award of a franchise, franchisors unwittingly encourage prospects to be on their best behavior. Franchisors may end up selecting the person who interviews best rather than the one who may best fit the role of business owner. A series of standard interview questions will help add a degree of objectivity when measuring and comparing candidates over time.

When making these assessments, it always helps to involve multiple people in the vetting process. Many franchisors require serious prospects to travel to their home office to meet their management team. Afterward, the department heads are often asked to evaluate the candidate before the final decision. In some cases, franchisors give members of the management team veto power over franchisee acceptance.

We also recommend to our clients that they educate their candidates on the advantages and disadvantages of joining a franchise system. Candidates should be aware of the responsibilities they will have as franchisees and the expectations the franchisor will have of them. For example, you should stress the importance of franchisee engagement in the system, emphasizing that the ultimate success of the system relies on franchisees being willing to invest their time, money, and effort in areas such as mentoring other franchisees, sharing best practices, completing ongoing training, and attending franchisor-sponsored seminars and conventions.

As you go through the evaluation process, think about traits like honesty, integrity, and compatibility, because you may be living with this franchisee for the next 20 years or more. If a candidate is confrontational in the interview process, constantly questions your established systems, or otherwise provides you with indications that he may not be a long-term fit, listen to your inner voice and walk away.

> ### ◄ Franchisee Reluctance Diminishes Benefits for All
>
> We recently conducted a survey on behalf of one of our clients to measure franchisee satisfaction and solicit input from franchisees on how the franchisor can become a better resource for them. One of the system's larger franchisees, with three units open and more committed to under their development schedule, declined to be interviewed because it was their policy not to take surveys. The franchisee's reluctance diminished the quality of feedback the franchisor received and lessened the benefits to the entire franchisee community through the survey process.

Passive Investors vs. Owner-Operators

Another important question is whether the franchisor will allow for passive investors, as opposed to owner-operators who will work day-to-day in the business. The trade-offs are easy to understand.

Owner-operators, if properly selected, will typically have better unit-level performance from both a financial and a quality perspective. Because they will own the franchise where they work, they will be more attentive to details and more concerned with quality and customer satisfaction than most hired managers.

On the other hand, opening the franchise opportunity to passive investors can mean faster growth and a larger pool of prospective franchisees from which to draw. Moreover, these larger investors will often have more capital and may be more sophisticated and better positioned to survive any downturns in their business. In fact, some of them may already have management in place.

Like many decisions in business, there is no right or wrong answer. Companies have succeeded with both approaches.

> ⬧ **Designate an Operating Partner**
>
> You can always require investor groups to designate an operating partner who holds some equity in the franchisee's company and brings the skills you're seeking to the daily operation of the franchise.

You should ask yourself what is needed to succeed at the unit level—and what you ultimately want the franchise network to look like.

The Entrepreneurial Prospect

When it comes to franchise sales, one of the most hotly debated questions involves whether franchisors should sell franchises to "entrepreneurs." Many franchisors—including some that are well-established—believe this is precisely the kind of franchise prospect they are seeking, while franchise consultants, lawyers, and others who don't sell franchises for a living often argue that managing entrepreneurs can be similar to herding cats.

From the perspective of the franchise salesperson, an entrepreneurial candidate may look otherwise qualified, but might be a little too creative. Is the salesperson expected to walk away from a sale over that? Isn't entrepreneurship the backbone of small business? And isn't the entrepreneurial work ethic legendary?

The entrepreneur-averse among us, however, will dig in their heels. New franchisors, who ironically tend to be extremely entrepreneurial, will be advised that if they "ever see someone who reminds them of themselves, they should turn tail and run! Lock the door behind you and throw away the key! Never sell a franchise to an entrepreneur!"

Why this aversion to entrepreneurs? In a word: *rules*. Franchise dogma holds that real entrepreneurs don't like rules, and franchisors do.

It is, of course, axiomatic that quality control is the key to successful franchising. And, of the factors affecting quality control, franchisee selection is far and away the most important. So if a franchisee will not follow the rules, the franchisor cannot control quality. But does this mean the franchisor can only sell to those who are entrepreneurially impaired?

The key lies in the definition of an entrepreneur. Of course, anybody with the nerve to invest what might be their life's savings in a franchise certainly has an entrepreneurial spirit. So when this question is raised, the underlying issue is really not whether they are an "entrepreneur," but instead whether they are a candidate that is so independent as to eschew the brand standards that a franchisor might impose in favor of their own ideas.

The folks you should avoid are the ones we refer to as "flaming entrepreneurs." These are the rule breakers—in fact, my short definition of a flaming entrepreneur is "someone who never saw a rule he did not want to break."

In general, we suggest it is best to avoid a prospect who is too strongly entrepreneurial. Flaming entrepreneurs can't help themselves: They will want to change any system no matter how good it already is. They always know better and want to do things their way. And an entrepreneurial franchisee can set the tone for every subsequent franchisee who joins the system, who will take the cue that the franchisor's rules are really only suggestions.

But entrepreneurial spirit—a willingness to take risks, supreme self-confidence, dedication, and tenacity—is to be coveted. The best franchisors will often avoid the former while cultivating the latter.

So how do you draw the distinction? Look for the typical characteristics of the flaming entrepreneur. They are likely to have changed jobs frequently; started numerous new businesses (whether successfully or not), often at an early age; displayed a spotty driving record; and built a less-than-stellar record of academic achievement.

The flaming entrepreneur is likely to drive a fast car with a glove box full of traffic tickets. They are more likely to be divorced. They are more likely to have been C students in school, if they finished at all—not because they were incapable of getting good grades, but because they simply weren't motivated to follow someone else's program.

Franchisees as Inventors

Iconic items like the Filet-O-Fish (Lou Groen), Big Mac (Jim Delligatti), Baked Apple Pie (Litton Cochran), and the Egg McMuffin (Herb Peterson), to name just a few, were all invented by McDonald's franchisees.

Of course, none of these symptoms, taken by itself, guarantees a rebellious franchisee. But if you see these signs in your prospect, dig a little deeper. Some revealing screening questions to test for flaming entrepreneurship might include: "Tell me about your first business," or "How would you feel if you thought of a great new idea, but we decided not to allow you to introduce it?"

More important, watch for signs the candidate wants to change your business model. If she starts questioning the way you do business before she has even signed on, her further involvement with you will probably not convince her she is wrong, but will instead embolden her thinking.

The best franchisees are often great at following rules. Many are A or B students, perhaps coming off a long career at a corporate job or a stint in the Armed Services (where rule following is even more fervently treated as dogma). They tend to drive the family car through the right lane of life!

But don't avoid prospects just because they have entrepreneurial characteristics. Ray Kroc, the man behind McDonald's, once said, "None of us is as good as all of us." And at McDonald's, many of their most successful products were invented by franchisees. The best franchisees, like entrepreneurs, constantly look for ways to improve their business—but they must do it within the context of the rules.

The First Call: Knowing Your A-B-Cs

After that lengthy prelude, let's talk about the actual sales process. The first rule of thumb when it comes to franchise sales is that each step in the process is designed to fulfill a specific goal. The first step in the process—and the first goal—is to either advance the sale or kill it.

The goal for the first call is to try to qualify the prospect as quickly as possible, without scaring them away or giving them any ill feelings about your brand if they are not qualified. In most franchise sales situations, the franchisor can anticipate closing rates in the range of 2 percent—and as few as 10 percent of inquiries may be qualified. So perhaps the greatest skill required of franchise salespeople is the ability to quickly qualify prospects so they can allocate their time to strong candidates.

Your goal as a salesperson for the first call is to qualify the prospect, explain the process, and establish a timeline for the next steps. Ideally, you want to be well into the qualification process within the first five minutes (and be able to end the process as soon as it is warranted).

Robert Stidham, the president of Franchise Dynamics, breaks these candidates into three types of prospects:

1. *"A" prospects, who represent about 3 to 5 percent of the calls for most franchise systems.* An "A" prospect is one who will fully engage in the evaluation process. As you take them through the first call, they are responsive, and will make a commitment to complete assigned tasks to stay involved. Typically, an "A" prospect will complete her CIRF and return it promptly after receiving it. And while it is occasionally more difficult for a neophyte salesperson to achieve this level of response, Franchise Dynamics expects about 80 percent of their "A" prospects to complete the required paperwork within 48 hours of receiving it.

2. *"B" prospects, who typically represent about 12 to 15 percent of inquiries.* "B" prospects are willing to partially engage in the process. They are not communicative, may lack trust, and lack energy. The "B" prospect can evolve into an "A" prospect but will need to be guided through the process. History shows this type of lead will take longer to close. The "B" prospect may have money issues and/or a less-than-supportive spouse or partner, be evaluating many different opportunities, or may just be unsure if he wants to be in business for himself. You will need to ask probing questions to determine if

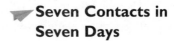

the "B" prospect can be moved to "A" status or should be removed from your pipeline.

3. *"C" prospects, who represent about 80 to 85 percent of inquiries.* The "C" prospect either cannot or will not engage in the process or is financially unqualified. Many internet leads who fail to return your calls will fall into this category as well. The "C" prospect should be put in a six-month contact file. Generally, you should not aggressively pursue "C" prospects, as there are simply too many variables in the mix to understand, manage, or resolve.

The goal of that first call is to determine where your prospect falls. You should not be trying to sell "C" prospects on your franchise. File them as inactive and move on. Remember: Every minute spent on a "C" prospect takes away from moving an "A" to a close and moving a "B" to an "A."

> ### Seven Contacts in Seven Days
>
> We typically attempt to contact a new internet lead seven times in seven business days (three calls and four emails) before closing their file.

The best franchise salespeople spend the vast majority of time listening and asking questions during that first call—not talking. They will never "sunburn" their prospects by spewing a long list of sales messages. They understand that people want to talk about their favorite topic—themselves. They also understand that no one ever sold a franchise on the first call, and that many pushy salespeople have lost prospects by giving too much information too quickly.

The franchise sales process is a courtship—not a one-night stand. So leave a little mystery to it.

The typical agenda for the initial call will look something like this:

- Get the candidate's contact information, including the source of the lead, if you have not done so already.
- Qualify the candidate financially.
- Qualify the candidate based on other criteria (experience, desired territory, etc.).
- Determine how quickly he is looking to move forward (urgency).

- ◢ Determine why he is thinking about franchising (motives).
- ◢ Determine why he is thinking about your franchise in particular (hot buttons).
- ◢ Understand his buying process and find out which other franchises he is actively considering (positioning).
- ◢ Provide a brief overview of the opportunity emphasizing any appropriate hot buttons.
- ◢ Tell him you will be sending materials and discuss the process and timetable.
- ◢ Ask him if he has any questions.
- ◢ Ask for an advance—usually for him to complete and send you the CIRF—and schedule your next call.

Note that the qualification process is at the beginning of the call. If the prospect is unqualified, the salesperson will want to let him down easy and get him off the phone quickly. If there is a way to remedy his shortcomings as a franchise prospect, give him some guidance as to how he might remedy the situation.

Stalking vs. Calling: Frequency of Follow-Up

You should end your first call with an "A" or "B" prospect by setting timetables and expectations. There is a fine line between stalking and persistence, so the best strategy is to discuss timetables with the candidate upfront. Whenever possible, schedule these calls. This level of commitment will keep your prospect on a timetable and will get them to commit to taking a certain action at a specific time. Moreover, it will limit

---

◢ Rejecting a Prospect Gently

If a prospective franchisee is financially unqualified, the salesperson might say: "Our top priority here is franchisee success, and we have determined you need a net worth of at least $100,000 to have a reasonable chance at achieving that success. Since you only have $50,000, you might want to consider looking for an investor, or, if that is not something you are comfortable with, waiting until you have a little more in savings before pursuing our franchise."

the downtime that would otherwise be spent playing telephone tag with prospects.

Often, the franchisor will establish a timetable with its good prospects during the first call, saying something along the lines of, "Our process typically takes about 12 weeks. If we can answer all your questions about our franchise and allow you to complete your diligence in that time, will you be ready to make a decision one way or the other?" Establishing this timetable (and candidate readiness) is often the key to keeping the sales process on pace and one of the primary tools in candidate qualification.

As a general rule, you should respond to an initial inquiry within one business day. Materials should be sent out that same day. Your initial follow-up call should be within the next seven days. And subsequent calls, with intervening tasks assigned to the prospect, are typically scheduled about a week apart.

Eating the Elephant: Goals and Advances

As the saying goes, "When eating the elephant, take one bite at a time." These are particularly apt words when it comes to franchising. Prospects do not make a decision to franchise based on a single phone call or after reading a single brochure. And if you, as the salesperson, try to rush the process, you will be viewed as pushy and untrustworthy.

The essence of franchise sales is the knowledge that selling a franchise is not just about making a sale. It is about making a series of small sales—with each one inching the candidate closer to the final decision about investing in your franchise. Each of these small sales is called an advance.

So when you have sales calls with your candidates, you should have specific goals for each call. Each call should be targeted toward an advance, which is defined here to mean an action taken by the prospect that moves the sale closer to resolution.

Some examples of advances would include a commitment from the prospect to:

> ☛ Review your printed materials, your website, your Franchise Disclosure Document, or other information on your company

- Submit the CIRF
- Schedule a call to review your FDD in detail
- Get his spouse or partner to participate in a scheduled conference call
- Research the local market on numbers of competitors, pricing, or consumer marketing
- Measure market demographics or evaluate the market for potential sites (talking to brokers, landlords, etc.)
- Schedule a face-to-face or Discovery Day meeting at your home office
- Complete validation calls with your franchisees
- Talk to his banker or investor about financing/capital
- Talk to his lawyer and/or accountant about your offering
- Schedule a closing meeting

In each of these instances (and there are more), the candidate is moving the process forward and becoming more emotionally invested in purchasing the franchise. So your goal is to get the prospect to make some kind of progress every time you interact with him.

"Selling" Discovery Day

Whichever franchisor came up with the concept of Discovery Day is an unsung hero in the history of franchise sales. Prospects who might otherwise be scared off by the thought of flying out to meet a high-powered franchise salesperson were put at ease by this event that would help them learn more about the franchisor while the franchisor learned more about them. Many were attracted to the name, which had a wonderfully nonthreatening ring to it.

And soon, franchisors worldwide sold it in just that way. "Bring your spouse but leave your checkbook at home" was the mantra. But make no mistake; getting someone to Discovery Day is still a sale—and perhaps the most difficult one short of the close. You are asking your candidate to take a day or more out of her busy schedule, spend time and money to travel to your location, and ideally persuade her spouse to come along.

The purpose of Discovery Day is fourfold. First, the candidate can learn more about you and your franchise. Second, you can further qualify the franchise prospect, both in terms of commitment (by coming to see you) and in terms of getting to know her better. Third, you can get feedback from your management team on the candidate. And finally, you can put your best foot forward and make a good impression on the prospect.

Remember, from a sales perspective, the candidate is (or should be) looking at more than just the franchise concept. Part of what she is buying is you and your team.

The key is building value around the Discovery Day event itself. If the candidate believes Discovery Day is simply a tool to evaluate her, she will delay deciding whether to attend until she is ready to say yes. If, on the other hand, she believes Discovery Day will help her make an informed decision, she is much more likely to attend earlier in the sales process—allowing you to put your best foot forward sooner rather than later.

This leads us to a problem I call the "founder's trap." Often, a franchise's founders (or even some salespeople) want to be helpful and answer every question a prospective franchisee has as fully as possible. But the trap in this approach is that it eliminates the need to come in for Discovery Day.

The better alternative is to answer some of the candidate's questions by pointing out the value she will get out of Discovery Day, rather than providing a comprehensive answer. You want to sell the strengths of your team and the value of the meeting, so while you might give them a partial answer, be sure she knows she will get a much more detailed understanding when she comes in to meet your team and see the concept firsthand.

This sometimes means checking your ego at the door. After all, you are the genius founder of the franchise—of course you can answer every question candidates might have over the phone. But even if you *can* answer a question, that doesn't necessarily mean you *should*. Sometimes it's better to wait and address it in person at the Discovery Day, when you can really sell them on the concept.

It is important to have a well-choreographed process in place for your Discovery Days. While there is no definitive agenda for these meetings, these events will often involve:

- 🠖 A casual dinner the night before where you can get to know the prospect on an informal basis
- 🠖 A tour of one or more operating units (if you have physical locations)

☞ A tour of your home office with introductions to various members of your team

☞ Interviews with team members, during which each side will have the opportunity to ask and answer questions

☞ A PowerPoint presentation outlining the concept, market, support provided, and other aspects of the franchise

A Discovery Day should not simply be a rehash of information you have already shared with the candidate via email, over the phone, or through webinars. If she's making the investment to travel to your office, she should receive additional value that will help her in her decision-making process and overall understanding of the franchise opportunity. This again emphasizes the importance of carefully placing Discovery Day within the overall context of your entire franchise sales process.

At the end of the Discovery Day, you should let the candidate know how the management team felt about the meetings and, of course, ask for an advance. At this point, you should be looking to close, so assuming you are still impressed with the candidate, your parting conversation might sound like this:

"I have not had a chance to speak to everyone on the team yet, but I think they were all impressed with you. If the team decides to award you a franchise, are you ready to move forward?"

If, on the other hand, you do not want to move forward with the candidate, you will want to let her down gently. Make sure she knows you are not accepting her into the franchise system for her own good—not simply because you dislike her. But do not go into specific reasons for the rejection. Simply tell her something like:

"As much as we like you as a person, our number-one concern here is always that our franchisees succeed. And while you certainly could bring some tremendous skills to the table, the team was not sure that your skill set was a good match for our business model."

While a rejection is always painful for all involved, remember that it is generally in everyone's best interest.

The Salesperson's Best Friend: Objections

Once you begin the sales process with your prospective franchisees, it is vital to know what they are thinking—and, in particular, to understand what might keep them from moving forward. But all too often, neophyte salespeople shy away from uncovering objections to the franchise sale because they would rather not address the negative.

That can be a deadly mistake.

Uncovering objections is perhaps the most important role you will have when selling franchises. Knowing the nature of an objection gives you the ability to overcome that objection. Not knowing objections will invariably lead to lost sales.

Remember: Objections are a salesperson's best friend. It means your candidate is interested enough to move forward—if you can answer the objection. If a prospect does not raise any objections, he has either already decided to buy (unlikely) or he will never buy from you.

So how do you identify a prospect's objections? You ask.

- ➤ "What's preventing you from . . . ?"
- ➤ "What other information do you need to . . . ?"
- ➤ "It seems as if you are concerned about . . ."
- ➤ "Based on our initial conversations, I understood you were looking to . . ., but it seems that is no longer the case. Has something come up that is bothering you?"

Once you have uncovered the objection, you can try to overcome it and move the sales process forward. So you will want to think through potential objections in advance so that the first time you try to overcome those objections is not under live fire.

Selling Your First Franchise

For example, what if your prospect's primary objection is that he does not want to be a system's guinea pig as its first franchisee?

One new franchisor I recently spoke with found out the hard way that it takes more than boasting of being a ground-floor opportunity to get people excited when one of its prospects remarked, "If the program is that good, it will still be a great opportunity in a year." A valid point! And while the availability of prime territories may be a mildly motivating factor, we counsel our aspiring franchisors to address their newness head-on.

What is important to some prospective franchise owners is not important to others. So while some prospects will be looking for well-established franchises with a long-standing track record, others will like the idea of buying into a new business, hoping to get in on the ground floor of the next big thing.

 **Higher Tolerance for Risk**

As a new franchisor, the prospects who approach you will tend to have a greater risk tolerance, as they certainly knew you were just starting out when they first inquired.

For prospects with a greater tolerance for risk, a franchisor's youth can have advantages that large franchisors cannot offer. Most notably, the first franchisee in any system is likely to get much more attention and care than, say, the 50th franchisee.

In most franchise systems, the first franchisee can expect to receive the personal involvement and support of the founder and senior management. And, because of the priority given to a new franchisee's success, the amount of training and hands-on support is often far greater with early franchisees. Simply put, a new franchisor cannot afford to have its first franchise fail, so many early-stage franchisors use that in the selling process. Tell your prospect how vital he is to you and why—and, most important, what you are going to do about it. Emphasize that he will receive nothing short of your full attention.

In the same vein, your first franchisee can expect a higher degree of input in the development of the franchise system. He will often have a greater voice than any other, and while the ultimate decision on direction will always come from the franchisor, the franchisee's feedback will be critically important when it comes to shaping the system. This appeals to the ego of many prospective investors.

That said, the first-time franchisor should make it crystal clear there are risks as well as rewards associated with joining an emerging concept. While there may be benefits to having that level of input, if there are shortcomings in the areas of brand, service, or support due to the newness of the system, you must discuss them. It is vitally important to build a solid relationship with your early franchisees, so the franchisor is well-advised to properly manage their expectations.

The newness of your concept is, of course, just one example of the type of objections you are likely to encounter. Others might include:

- ☛ The experience of the management team
- ☛ The level of existing competition
- ☛ Industry dynamics
- ☛ Regulatory concerns
- ☛ Territory
- ☛ Fees and other contract terms
- ☛ Litigation
- ☛ Failure rates
- ☛ Required vendors
- ☛ Candidate fear based on their lack of experience

The list is virtually endless. So before you have that first conversation with a live prospect, give a lot of thought to how you want to handle objections and questions about anything that might come up.

Positioning vs. Competitors

As part of interacting with candidates, one question you will certainly need to answer will be why the candidate should go with you rather than one of your competitors. Most serious franchise prospects will consider six or more franchises at some point during the sales cycle, so positioning your concept against these competitors will be vital.

The first key to positioning is to understand the specific companies against which you are competing. Again, the key is to ask. "Which other concepts are you considering?" is a perfectly acceptable question, and most prospects will not hesitate to provide you with that feedback.

Once you understand the nature of the competition, you should always respond professionally. Never denigrate your competition—even if you believe them to be far inferior to your own franchise.

The best way to respond is to point out how your system is different—and the reasons for those differences. Be sure to highlight the negatives as well as the positives. For example, if you have a higher royalty rate than a competitor, you can rest assured they will point that out. And if they are good, they will quantify exactly how much money that increased royalty will cost the candidate over the life of the relationship.

So don't leave it to your competitors to bring up these issues. Tackle them head on. You might start with, "One of the things we feel sets us apart is the level of service and support we offer our franchisees." Then, after discussing the specifics of their support vs. yours (backed up by verifiable sources), say, "We feel that added support gives our franchisees a greater opportunity to thrive. But in order to provide that added support, of course, we need to staff our organization differently, so our royalty is a little higher than theirs." Then go on to outline some additional advantages of your franchise.

We're assuming here that you have benchmarked your franchise against direct competitors and know the details cold. Moreover, we're assuming you used that benchmarking in the structure of your franchise program and have structured a unique selling proposition (USP) into your offering. If you haven't, you should.

Sometimes, your competitors may be in entirely different businesses. In that case, you will want to focus on big-picture advantages as opposed to more specific benchmarking. For example, assume a prospect is looking at a sandwich franchise in addition to your janitorial franchise. In your sales pitch, you might focus on the low investment costs, the support you provide, your national accounts program, and the ability to grow unconstrained, while pointing out that the sandwich franchisor will always be more expensive and site-dependent. If, on the other hand, you were the sandwich franchisor, you might emphasize the lack of sales skills required, the lack of carrying any accounts receivable, and the fact that you can have a manager supervise the unit, while pointing out the upside-down days and nights you might encounter in the janitorial business.

So while you never want to take a negative approach during the sales process, part of your job is to be sure you draw a clear distinction between the advantages of your franchise and the disadvantages of your competitors.

Financial Performance Representations in the Sales Process

As anyone who has ever been involved in franchise sales knows all too well, the single most frequently asked question in franchising is, "How much can I make?"

So if you choose not to use an FPR, how will you answer this perennial question? For most franchisors, we advise that you reply something like this:

> *"The success you have within our system will be affected by a variety of factors, including the location you choose, the competition in your territory, and the skill set you bring to the table. For that reason, we do not provide earnings information to our prospective franchisees but instead suggest you do your own due diligence to determine what you believe you can achieve in this market by talking to our franchisees, doing market surveys, and conducting your own competitive analysis in your local territory."*

It would seem this answer would go over like a lead balloon. But while the number of franchisors who choose to make an FPR in Item 19 of their FDD is a moving target, recent studies that the iFranchise Group has conducted have not shown any positive correlation between using an FPR and faster franchise sales.

From the outside looking in, the ability to sell franchises without giving any revenue numbers often seems unbelievable for many new franchisors. Why would anyone buy a business without knowing what they could earn? But as most veterans of the franchise sales process will tell you, numbers don't sell. Stories do.

Sure, great numbers are part of some great stories, and being able to use numbers in the sales process certainly makes the job easier, but the fact that so many

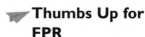

Thumbs Up for FPR

While we believe the decision to use an FPR needs to be based on several factors that will vary from one franchisor to the next, our overall inclination is to recommend them whenever possible, for the reasons discussed below.

franchisors have sold so many franchises without an FPR just reinforces this point.

Think back to your startup days. If you started like most entrepreneurs, no one ever told you how much you could expect to earn with your business. And yet, because you had faith in your abilities and in the concept itself, you jumped in with both feet.

In fact, each year, about 7 percent of the working-age population in the U.S. is actively trying to start a business and each year, more than 600,000 new businesses are formed. And with the exception of perhaps 30,000 franchises that received FPRs, virtually none of these new business owners were told how much they could earn.

So if new franchisors do not need an FPR to sell, why should they even consider using one?

One of the primary reasons for a franchisor to use an FPR is that it makes the story easier to tell. Especially for inexperienced franchise salespeople and new franchisors that cannot fall back on franchisee validation, an FPR can be a huge help in the franchise sales process. Franchisors with direct competition may also find themselves at a disadvantage in the sales process if they fail to use them.

Another reason FPRs are valuable is that the information will give candidates more complete information with which to make an informed business decision about moving forward with the franchise. This is particularly beneficial if the candidate does not have industry experience. Without access to historical financial information from the franchisor, the franchisee may develop unrealistic expectations about how his business will perform—creating issues later on when he fails to achieve those results.

But for many, the biggest reason to use FPRs is their ability to reduce potential liability. This may at first seem counterintuitive. In making these representations, you might think the franchisor is opening the door for potential lawsuits if franchisees fail to achieve the financial performance discussed in the FDD. But since a well-documented, properly prepared, historically based FPR can be factually verified, it can eliminate the cocktail napkin claims that are often the basis for allegations of improper earnings disclosures, making allegations of fraud very difficult, if not impossible, to prove.

Of course, FPRs are not for everyone. In some instances, historical performance is simply not representative of what a franchisee can realistically hope to achieve—perhaps because of a unique location, a long tenure in a community, locations in a region far from where the franchisee would be opening, or modifications to the business model that might make company operations atypical of what a franchisee could expect. In other cases, perhaps a franchisor desires to keep its financial performance out of the public domain, either out of fear that competitors who saw this information would gain an advantage or that potential *future* competitors might be encouraged to join the fray.

And, of course, some franchisors may choose not to use them because their financial performance simply does not stack up well against their competitors. This is not always a bad thing. For example, they may have lower revenues but also a lower level of investment—which could result in a better ROI, or, at minimum, an ability to get into a marketplace that might otherwise be financially beyond the reach of a new franchisee. Other franchisors may offer incremental services, support, or financing, which might reduce the franchisee's return but make the business more manageable from an operational or financial perspective.

The bottom line is not always the bottom line, in other words. And while it is certainly a part of any franchise story, it is up to each franchisor to decide how it can best tell the story of what makes them unique.

Validation: Getting Your Franchisees Involved

As a franchise salesperson, you should expect that at least 80 percent of your prospects will be reaching out to your existing franchisees to get their take on your system. And, since you do not want your candidates to have unrealistic expectations as to financial performance or their role in day-to-day operations, you will certainly want to encourage this. Many franchisors actually tell their prospects that validation calls are an integral part of the sales and qualification process.

The best franchisors will make sure their prospects have every opportunity to learn about the experience of existing franchisees through video endorsements on their website and endorsements featured prominently in their brochures. They may even post their franchisee survey results or hire a public relations firm to spread the word. And, of course, they will put franchisee referral programs in place.

Meanwhile, just about every publication aimed at prospective franchisees advises them that one of the most important steps in their due diligence is to talk to the franchisor's existing franchisees. So before you begin to promote your franchisees' satisfaction as part of your sales process, you need to be sure they are actually satisfied and can be counted on to give prospects glowing reports. If you are not held in high regard by your franchisees, changing that attitude becomes your first and most important job. And while that is often easier said than done, franchisee satisfaction, properly promoted, will generate far more franchise sales than the best marketing plan ever could.

Bear in mind that some franchisees may be fearful of additional franchise sales, especially if they think it may lead to more franchisees near their territories: "What if they come into my market? Will they compete with me? I don't want to be too enthusiastic if a prospect calls me . . ." In addition to this understandable fear, some franchisees feel obligated to sound objective, not overly enthusiastic. After all, they are being asked for advice. So when a prospect asks, "What don't you like about your franchisor?", they feel they must come up with something negative.

The best franchisors understand this and make an active effort to educate their franchisees about the benefits of selling the brand: more advertising power, more buying power, increased brand recognition, an ability to build a larger and more professional support organization, and a greater valuation for the franchisee's business when it comes time to sell. These franchisors also make sure their franchisees understand that they are part of the sales team. Ideally, their enthusiastic referrals to friends and acquaintances will help generate numerous no-cost and high-quality franchise sales leads, a dream component of every good franchise marketing program.

So it's essential to train franchisees in the sales process and actively reinforce the unique benefits of the brand and system on an ongoing basis, so that a discussion of these benefits becomes second nature to them.

But the franchise salesperson's job does not stop when it comes to educating franchisees on the benefits of providing strong validation. She must also prep the candidate on how to conduct his validation research.

In most franchise organizations, the candidate will likely encounter a variety of responses when he contacts franchisees. As such, franchisee satisfaction may fall along the bell-shaped curve some of us had to deal with in statistics class. If franchisees in your organization are likely to be found throughout that bell curve, make sure your candidate knows that in advance—otherwise the luck of the draw could stop validation efforts after a single unfortunate call.

Too many franchise sales professionals simply play Russian roulette with validation, hoping the candidate never encounters a bullet. But holding your breath and wishing for an empty chamber is not a strategy.

The sharp franchise sales professional will recognize this in advance and guide the prospect through the process by explaining that he will likely get a variety of responses. Depending on the system, she may want to candidly state that some franchisees are more successful than others. And, to the extent that the franchisor knows the reason for this underperformance, the salesperson should coach the prospect on how to get to the root of a poor performer's problems.

Franchisors should also recognize that the way in which a question is asked will often frame its answer. A franchisee with expectations of earning $150,000 a year might tell a candidate he is operating well below his financial expectations and that he is very disappointed, when, in fact, the $100,000 the franchisee is earning far exceeds the *candidate's goals*.

Some franchise salespeople will try to avoid this problem by providing candidates with a list of questions they should ask. And while a candidate should be encouraged to ask whatever questions he would like, specific questions designed to elicit realistic answers may help him better understand the life of a franchisee and the benefits of becoming one.

You may also want to advise both your candidates and your franchisees to dig deep in the interview process. Both you and the candidate should encourage franchisees to expound on answers—especially if the answer is a negative one. Perhaps a franchisee did not achieve her desired performance for a reason the candidate could control—location, sales skills, capitalization, industry knowledge, etc. Once the candidate knows why a particular franchisee has underperformed, he can judge whether he will likely encounter the same difficulties.

Keep in mind there are other ways besides phone calls in which franchise candidates can receive validation from existing franchisees. These include video testimonials, which you might place on your website or on YouTube, or share during Discovery Day. If many of your franchisees are continuing to expand within your system, sharing that data with candidates is a very strong measure of validation. Additionally, if you're using a third-party firm to conduct periodic validation research on your franchisees, you can also share those reports with your franchise prospects.

Don't Ask the Internet to Do Your Sales Job

For all its benefits, keep in mind what the internet is not.

An email or an autoresponder is never a substitute for a phone call or a face-to-face meeting. And the written word, because it lacks tone and feedback, can easily be misinterpreted.

The internet cannot sell. It cannot build relationships. It cannot measure quality at the unit level. And it cannot increase trust between the franchisor and its franchisees.

The best franchisors in this modern age of franchising are those who not only recognize how to leverage the internet, but also understand when they shouldn't even try.

As Robert Stidham, my partner at Franchise Dynamics, has been known to say, "If a computer could sell, I would build myself the world's greatest program and sit back and collect the checks."

Franchise Sales Approaches

When it comes to franchise sales, there are several alternative approaches you can take as a new franchisor. You can elect to sell franchises yourself, hire an industry professional, or outsource your sales. Like many business decisions, there are no definitive right and wrong answers, but instead advantages and disadvantages to each strategy, which I have outlined below.

Do-It-Yourself

The alternative chosen by most new franchisors, at least in the beginning, is to take the responsibility for franchise sales themselves. This has several key advantages:

- ➤ It allows the new franchisor to gain a firsthand understanding of the franchise sales process and develop it as a core competency of the new organization. Should an outside sales professional be hired in the future, the franchisor's experience in selling franchises will make it better equipped to manage the new hire.
- ➤ It allows the new franchisor to keep its initial out-of-pocket costs to a minimum when starting its franchise program.
- ➤ With little or no validation from existing franchisees, many early candidates will base their decision on their trust of and respect for the franchise's founder. If the founder is actively involved in the sales process, the candidate will have a better opportunity to get to know him and his vision for the future.
- ➤ In adopting a DIY strategy, the franchisor does not need to spend time interviewing and hiring staff and does not run the risk of staff turnover.
- ➤ It allows them to grow more conservatively—more aggressive sales alternatives, with their associated increases in overhead, typically fund that overhead by selling more aggressively.

Another key advantage of this strategy is in the logistics of a rollout. Remember, on your first day as a new franchisor, you do not have any (or very many) franchise sales leads. If your launch plan is based on selling one franchise per month, your marketing only needs to get you about 50 leads per month. And remember, it takes between 12 and 14 weeks to close a franchise sale, so when you get started, you will only need to make a couple of calls per day (plus some follow-up calls with qualified prospects). So initially, most new franchisors simply do not need a full-time franchise sales resource.

Of course, the DIY strategy may not suit your particular skill set, and you may lose sales as a result. Moreover, it may divert your efforts from your core business (and from the support and service you would otherwise provide franchisees), potentially causing you harm in the long run. For these reasons, the DIY strategy is often viewed as a short-term alternative when initiating a franchise program.

Alternatively, the new franchisor can attempt to train an existing staff member with no prior franchise sales experience. That may lower incremental expenses, but it can also distract your internal staff from their current duties, so this version of the strategy has some of the same disadvantages.

If that staffer does not work out, not only does the franchisor have to find another salesperson, but it is also likely that much of the franchise marketing done over that time has been wasted. The franchisor must hope it can fill the position quickly before its current leads get stale.

The Franchise Sales Professional

Hiring a franchise sales professional can be the next logical step for some franchisors. If the salesperson has a track record of success, you will benefit from the experience and training she has gained elsewhere. The primary benefits to this strategy include:

- 🐦 She is likely to be more productive than the DIY approach, which is even more important when considering the Present Value of a Franchise.
- 🐦 You will be developing an internal resource and core competency you can control directly.
- 🐦 Typically, commissions paid to salaried salespeople are lower than commissions to outsourced sales professionals. Thus, at higher levels of productivity, they can be more economical than outsourcing.

That said, there are some difficulties associated with hiring from the outside.

A franchise sales professional who is accustomed to high earnings may not want to work with an unproven franchisor, particularly if the company plans to sell fewer than 20 franchises each year. A good franchise salesperson can sell 25 franchises or more per year (depending, of course, on the nature of the franchise). Such a pro will wonder whether the new franchisor is committed to franchising over the long haul. Moreover, she may be uncertain whether the franchisor can fund the marketing necessary to generate an adequate number of leads.

Then there are the costs of recruiting and relocating a franchise sales executive, along with associated overhead expenditures. Employee benefits and FICA alone can add 30 percent or more to their salary. You may also need to hire an assistant to handle inbound leads, send out packages, and organize and maintain compliance files. Then there are the associated expenses (desks, computers, contact management software, etc.) and office space.

There are also issues of

> ## ➤ Look for Experience with Smaller Franchisors
>
> I often caution new franchisors to be wary of hiring franchise sales professionals who have worked exclusively with larger franchisors. While their background may be impressive, selling for larger franchisors (which may generate highly motivated leads based on name recognition alone and whose prospect profiles are very different) is nothing like selling startup franchises.

performance. If a franchise salesperson fails to work out (or if she quits), you will be left without a key resource in this vital position. And in the interim, you may be forced to resort to the DIY strategy or to going dark while you recruit a replacement.

Outsourcing

Many franchisors come to rely heavily on outsourcing. When they start out, franchisors will almost invariably outsource the development of their legal documents and their ongoing legal compliance to a law firm. They will often outsource some portion of their payroll and accounting needs to an accounting firm and perhaps a payroll processing company. And frequently, they will outsource their consumer and franchise marketing efforts to an ad agency or public relations firm.

The most recent outsourcing trend in franchising is the emergence of franchise sales outsourcing (FSO) organizations that will handle every aspect of the franchise sales process on the franchisor's behalf. An FSO will typically take responsibility for franchise marketing input, initial lead handling, database input and maintenance, materials distribution, trade show attendance, preliminary lead qualification, disclosure, Discovery Day, document management and preparation, and both pre- and post-franchise sales closing support. In fact, the only aspects of the sales process an FSO does not handle is approving candidates, executing contracts, and accepting franchisee fees on behalf of the franchisor.

These organizations have a number of advantages:

- ☞ FSOs can free a franchisor's time to focus on existing operations and the success of franchisees.
- ☞ They do not require extensive training, you do not need to pay a recruiter to locate top performers, and they can start almost immediately since they do not need to provide notice to their previous employer.
- ☞ They allow the franchisor to avoid virtually all the startup costs associated with creating an internal sales department.
- ☞ They allow a franchisor access to more experienced salespeople, as sales pros will not have qualms about joining established outsourcing companies.
- ☞ They have additional staff they can use to replace any salesperson who quits or is let go, so you will not need to worry about going dark.
- ☞ They can scale franchise sales, as they have the incremental staff to take on greater sales commitments when the franchisor is ready to get more aggressive.
- ☞ They typically have a lower fixed cost than hiring a sales professional, reducing out-of-pocket costs and risk.
- ☞ The best outsourcing firms mystery shop their sales force, carry their own insurance, and will even contractually commit to certain levels of sales.

Yet these organizations are not without controversy and are certainly not the right solution for every franchisor.

One downside to working with FSOs is their potential costs. The top FSOs typically take a monthly processing fee combined with a commission for every sale. And while the monthly fee is usually much lower than the salary you would pay a full-time salesperson, the commission is substantially higher. This low-fixed-cost model reduces overhead, but the higher associated commissions can make them more expensive at certain levels of sales.

In considering costs, remember that FSOs are not responsible for lead generation—so you will still have to spend just as much on franchise marketing.

Likewise, FSOs are *not* brokers. While both are paid commissions, FSOs begin their work where the broker leaves off (and, in some cases, they may even get leads from brokers). Brokers are paid for leads, but only if those leads wind up closing; FSOs get paid for closing them. So if you were to employ both, you would have to pay two commissions.

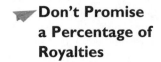
Don't Promise a Percentage of Royalties

Some FSOs ask for a percentage of the ongoing royalties and possibly an actual equity position in the franchise company. These arrangements create a substantial financial burden on the franchisor, and we always counsel against them. A franchisor that chooses to outsource sales should only engage an FSO that will not encumber long-term revenue streams—otherwise it could pay forever for a sale made decades earlier.

There are other considerations apart from cost. Outsourcing your franchise sales activities does not allow you to build an internal core competency around the franchise sales function. And, of course, there is also the question of how much control you can exercise over an outsourced organization. While the best outsourcing organizations will bring you only pre-qualified leads and take your direction, ultimately, they are not your employees. There are limits to how much authority you can exert over them.

THE BOTTOM LINE
It's a Numbers Game

Regardless of the sales strategy you employ, the bottom line is that franchise sales is largely a numbers game. As we saw in the Franchise Sales-Quality

Control Cycle (see Figure 6.1 in Chapter 6), there are six basic factors affecting franchise sales:

1. Concept and Value Proposition
2. Offer/Structure
3. Marketing Plan
4. Message and Materials
5. Advertising Expenditures
6. Sales Process

Assuming the other five elements are in place, franchise sales proficiency is a function of applying proven systems and techniques consistently. And while the average close rate in franchising is low compared to most other types of sales, ultimately, it is a *process*—and as such it can be duplicated again and again with predictable results.

In developing your sales plan, remember there are more costs associated with franchise sales than ad budgets and sale commissions. Most important, a successful franchisor will always focus on the concept and value proposition, because the single greatest factor in long-term franchise sales success is franchisee validation.

So once you have a strong sales process in place, the ultimate question you should be asking is not, "How fast can I sell?" Given the need for franchisee success, the question should instead be, "How fast SHOULD I sell?"

CHAPTER 12

The Franchisee– Franchisor Relationship

"The currency of leadership is transparency."

—HOWARD SCHULTZ, FOUNDER, STARBUCKS

Some people liken the relationship between franchisor and franchisee to a partnership, but in fact, it is nothing of the sort. In a partnership, your interests are aligned with your partner's. And while the best franchise systems actively align franchisor interests with those of their franchisees, the franchisor's financial interests are met by increasing franchisee revenues, while a franchisee's interests are met by increasing profits.

Others liken it to a marriage. But again, it is unlike (most) marriages in that the franchisor has almost all the power in the relationship—at least when it comes to brand standards.

At the same time, it is not like a traditional employer-employee relationship, where you have all the power. As a franchisor, you govern by contract. You cannot hire, fire, or discipline the way you would with an employee.

Perhaps the closest analogy is that of a parent-child relationship. Your franchisee starts out dependent on you for everything, gradually becomes more independent, perhaps grows rebellious, but is ultimately required to follow the rules you set.

As a franchisor, you have both the right and the obligation to enforce system standards, but your franchisees are independent business owners who can call their own shots on day-to-day operational decisions that do not impact brand standards.

Thus, you must pay particular attention to the franchisor-franchisee relationship from the start if you are to create a long-term and mutually prosperous business. In the end, the franchisor is creating a community in which franchisees and the franchisor team have many shared interests and needs. The community thrives if the franchisor can maintain trust, sound leadership, and transparency—and if franchisees actively engage with the franchisor and one another to make the system stronger over time. In many of the highest-performing franchise systems, the franchisor's principal role is as much about accumulating and sharing best practices from franchisees as it is about anything else.

Sources of Conflict in the Franchise Relationship

As a franchisor, you should address and resolve conflict as quickly as possible. In doing so, it is important to realize that the interests of the franchisor and the franchisee are not always perfectly aligned.

- 🠻 Deep discounting, for example, may help you generate more royalties, but it may reduce profits for the franchisee.
- 🠻 Requiring certain qualifications for the franchisee's employees (or certain numbers of staff in various positions) may improve service (and the brand story), but it may also raise the franchisee's labor costs.
- 🠻 Product standards and designated vendors may improve a customer's overall experience, but franchisees may see these standards as unnecessarily increasing their operating costs.
- 🠻 The franchise organization needs to enforce overall system standards, which puts it in the role of policeman, judge, and jury.

▼ Market saturation allows for better advertising, more buying power, and, ultimately, increased royalties—but the individual franchisee will see each new franchisee in his market as a source of competition.

Understanding these sources of conflict is at the heart of good franchisee communications. The best franchisors will try to look at issues through the eyes of their franchisees. That's not to say a franchisor cannot discount, enforce standards, or fully saturate markets—but its decisions need to balance the interests of both parties if the system is to thrive.

The Importance of Franchisee Success

Let's go back to the concept of the Present Value of a Franchise for a minute.

Failing franchisees cost more to support and provide less (sometimes nothing) in royalties. They do not validate well. They often do not follow the system in an attempt to save money (buying substandard products to cut corners, etc.), which can degrade your brand.

Happy and successful franchisees validate well, which helps you sell more franchises. They will tell their friends and family about their success, generating more franchise leads. They will spread the word on social media and elsewhere on the internet—increasing both validation and lead flow. They will usually follow the system—and presumably, that will make them more successful. And generally speaking, the more successful they are, the less they will need from you in terms of support (which reduce your costs) and the more they will pay in royalties. They will interact with you and contribute ideas. Happy franchisees rarely sue.

And, of course, they buy additional franchises.

The Hockey Stick Effect

One of the often-overlooked factors of franchisee success is what we call the hockey stick effect. If you sell five franchises in your first year, six in your second, and seven in your third, you may very well find it easy to jump to 15 sales in your fourth year. Why?

Partly because you are getting better at the franchise sales and marketing process. And partly because of franchisee validation and perhaps increased leads from referrals as the word of your success spreads.

But another factor comes into play as well. By year three or four, if you are doing things right, you may find the franchisees from years one and two are now looking to open additional franchise locations. They have started paying down their debt, they have grown comfortable with the system, and—if they still have a high regard for you and for the franchise—they begin to see multi-unit ownership as the logical path to future success.

And if you are doing things right, the hockey stick keeps going up. By year five or six, your growth could accelerate even further. Not only will your year three or four franchisees start buying second franchises, but early franchisees with multiple locations will gain access to increased capital from their banks and open their third and fourth franchises.

To make the hockey stick effect work for you, of course, you will need to do several things right. You will need to focus on franchisee success. You will need to maintain good franchisee relations. And most important, you will need to coach your franchisees on how to grow their businesses.

For many business owners, the biggest step they ever take is not when they first open for business. Instead, their biggest leap is growing from their first unit (where they can oversee the business directly) to opening their second. Making this leap will require your franchisee to understand that they are going to take a step backward (hiring and training a manager to replace them in the first location, incurring additional cost) so they can take two steps forward when they open their second location. They need to recognize that while they may sacrifice short-term profitability (and perhaps put off buying that new house, car, or boat), in the long run they will be building something more substantial that can run without their day-to-day involvement. But your franchisee will need to make a commitment to training. They will need to make an effort to secure additional financing— and a renewed leap of faith that they are not risking too much, when the easy decision might be to take some of their chips off the table and enjoy the fruits of their labor. And they need to understand it will take improved skills on their part as they transition from running a single location to multiple-unit management.

The best franchisors will institutionalize the hockey stick effect by working with franchisees from day one to begin growing their businesses. Your field support team should not just be policemen—they should focus on helping your franchisees expand. They should be working with your franchisees to develop annual business plans that will address issues such as developing their management team, building their balance sheet for access to further credit, and adding the resources necessary to grow.

Be a Good Parent

Sometimes being a great parent means you cannot be a best friend.

While you will certainly want to maintain great relations with your franchisees, one of the most important things you must do as a new franchisor is establish the boundaries of the relationship. The franchisee needs to understand that your first role is to guard the system and the brand so all franchisees can continue to thrive. As such, you need to communicate and enforce brand standards and be willing to discipline those who do not follow them. Your franchisees also need to realize that not every decision you make will benefit all franchisees equally. Sometimes the greater good of the system needs to supersede the desires of a few. You can't please all the franchisees all the time.

At the same time, discipline cannot be meted out to franchisees as if they were your employees in a corporation. If you try to give a franchisee the "it's my way or the highway" speech, you will quickly find yourself with alienated franchisees and on the road to real trouble. And if you try to dictate certain employment practices, you may find yourself creating co-employment issues—and potentially creating some liability in the process.

Franchisees are proud business owners, and as such, you should always communicate with them in a professional manner. While you will want to be firm on issues involving brand standards, you will need to be sure they understand the nature of the standards you are enforcing and provide an opportunity for their opinions to be heard. As a franchisor, your decisions on brand standards should be law—but you would be well-advised to avoid making any major decisions in a vacuum.

Almost all the things you require your franchisees to do should be for their benefit as much as yours. Your primary goal is for your franchisees to succeed. If a franchisee is not complying with your requirements, the appropriate way to address the issue is to explain why her actions are to the detriment of her business and perhaps other franchisee-owned businesses as well. One of the worst things a franchisor can say to a franchisee is "because it's in the operations manual." Instead, show the franchisee how following your standards can help her increase revenues, reduce operating costs, maximize profits, and enhance the resale value of her business. And rather than having all the information come from you, rely on examples of best practices that have been put in place by other franchisees within your system.

Effective Communication Is Key

The key to successful franchise relationships is trust. And trust starts with communication.

First and foremost, you must create a win-win relationship with your franchisees. Communicate openly and honestly with them, and be as concerned with their profitability as you are with your own.

The ancient Greek philosopher Zeno said we are given two ears and one mouth for a reason—the best communicators, and the best franchisors, use them in roughly that proportion. And they know communication must flow up as well as down.

The best franchisors diligently provide their franchisees with frequent, useful communication, which means more than the occasional email, newsletter, or perfunctory visit from their field representative. Today, it is all too tempting to rely on the internet for communications, but depersonalizing the franchisor is a big mistake. Time and again, well-intentioned emails or texts ignite firestorms when they are misinterpreted. Do not make the mistake of believing an email can substitute for human contact. When your franchisee made the leap, at least part of their investment was in you. They bought into your ability to help them grow a business.

Relationships are built with dialogue, so it is important to encourage dialogue in every aspect of your relationship with your franchisees. Good franchisors are careful to create multiple venues for constructive dialogue. Annual conventions, regional meetings, and advisory and advertising councils all provide for this two-way communication.

To be effective, however, the communication needs to be more than frequent. It needs to be honest. While there are some things you may choose not to share with your franchisees, the key to a long-term relationship is trust. And trust starts with transparency. Get caught in a single half-truth, and you have destroyed trust forever.

Finally, to be effective, you have to genuinely care about the success of your franchisees. Good franchisee relationships start with a franchisor that is, first and foremost, committed to franchisee success. That commitment, more than anything else, needs to permeate the franchisor organization at every level.

If your franchisees do not sense your commitment, the relationship can quickly become adversarial. If, on the other hand, your franchisees see you breaking your back to help them succeed, there is almost nothing they won't do for you. Even failing franchisees are reluctant to sue someone they really like—especially if that individual has demonstrated a real commitment to their success.

We often advise our clients on best practices in franchisee communications. Some of our recommendations include the following:

- ▼ Whenever possible, take calls from franchisees rather than letting the calls go to voice mail.
- ▼ If possible (once you have created a staff organization), have a dedicated franchise support line where a receptionist answers calls rather than having all calls go into an automated attendant loop.
- ▼ If you get a message from a franchisee, always respond the same business day. Unless the message involves a simple issue, default to calling the franchisee rather than responding via email.
- ▼ Each day, pick up the phone and call at least one franchisee you haven't spoken to in a while. Ask how they're doing, how their family is, and what else your team could be doing to support their business.
- ▼ Never speak negatively about franchisees to an employee in your company. If you or other people on the management team say

negative things about franchisees in front of other employees, that
tells your staff they can do the same thing. Communications relating
to franchisees should always be respectful.

⚲ Use a technology platform to track all communications (e.g., copies
of emails, summaries of phone calls) with franchisees. Maintaining a
record of all communications will provide valuable information to
staff members when they prepare to interact with franchisees, and it
will be important should a dispute ever arise with a franchisee.

⚲ Appoint one person in your company as the communications manager, and have all system wide communications filter through that
person to ensure consistent tone and accuracy of information.

Using Franchise Advisory Councils

One of the most important elements to support positive communications
is the Franchise Advisory Council (FAC). Almost every healthy franchise
system has an active advisory council program.

Let's look at what constitutes a good FAC—and what makes for a bad
one.

A good FAC is:

⚲ Generally established by the franchisor
⚲ Designed to facilitate communication between franchisees and the
franchisor, and between franchisees themselves
⚲ Meant to provide a vehicle for franchisee involvement and leader-
ship
⚲ Run with a specific agenda
⚲ Responsible for communicating its minutes with franchisees
⚲ Governed by bylaws that address such issues as communication,
confidentiality, composition, term limits, and purpose

A good FAC is *not*:

⚲ A decision-making body
⚲ A negotiating body
⚲ A vehicle for franchisees to forward their personal agenda or resolve
individual franchisee conflicts

And FACs can be:

- ▼ Made up of elected members or have members appointed by the franchisor
- ▼ Chaired by the franchisor or franchisee delegates
- ▼ Attended (or not) by franchisor management
- ▼ Paid for (travel, food, and lodging) by the franchisor

Franchisors, for their part, are often afraid that open communication may encourage franchisee unrest. The flaw to this thinking, of course, is the assumption that franchisees will not find a way to communicate about any possible dissent without these tools. It is far better for the franchisor to hear about potential problems and address them before they become major issues, and FACs provide that opportunity. The last thing you want is to discover your franchisees have

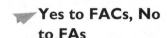
▼ Yes to FACs, No to FAs

Franchisee Associations, unlike Franchise Advisory Councils, are typically formed by dissatisfied franchisees to oppose or negotiate with a franchisor. Many franchisors will not recognize independent associations, and will only communicate to the franchisees as a group through FACs.

formed an association without you. That is usually a sign that something is wrong and they have excluded you from the process of resolving a grievance. Whatever comes next will not be pretty, and it often involves legal counsel representing the association.

A FAC is most often made up of franchisees who are elected by their fellow franchisees. FACs typically meet between two and four times per year, and their bylaws (covering eligibility, voting rights, limitations, etc.) can vary considerably. But the subjects that are typically discussed rarely differ: consumer marketing and advertising, new products and services, and any issues of concern to the franchisees in general. In effect, the franchisees act as delegates on behalf of all the franchisees in the system. In larger systems, the franchisor may use a series of regional FACs that will feed into an overarching FAC so all the franchisees feel they are getting an opportunity to participate. In some FAC programs, all franchisees in the system (or region) are invited to attend meetings.

Caring for Top-Performing Franchisees

Ray Kroc once said of his McDonald's franchisees, "My best ideas came from my franchisees. Why? Because my franchisees were talking to my customers every day and some of them were listening to what they have to say."

Kroc knew that the key to success in franchising was making his franchisees successful. Top franchisees require less support than other franchise owners in their system. As a result, the franchisor may elect to visit their locations less frequently and shift support resources toward franchisees who are struggling.

While this may sound sensible, it is actually a mistake to neglect top franchisees. The franchisor should recall that the highest-performing franchisees are also paying more royalties and advertising fund contributions. Because they're strong operators, it's likely they have the potential to continue growing their business. If their franchise generated $1.5 million last year, the franchisor should help them grow the business to $1.6 million next year. They don't need less support. They may need a different *level* of support than some other franchisees in the system. And it's incumbent upon the franchisor to help them increase revenues and profits as much as any other franchisee.

Trust, But Verify

In many ways, the internet has been a tremendous boon to franchising. Intranet sites, blogs, chat rooms, emails, enewsletters, real-time reporting, and online training have made communication faster and more frequent. And these tools have unquestionably improved a franchisor's ability to train and coach franchisees.

But it is not without its drawbacks. The ubiquitous and sometimes intrusive nature of the internet, combined with the franchise company's need to maintain system standards, can all too easily transform a franchisor from the friendly beat cop into a menacing Big Brother in the eyes of a franchisee. Real-time access to the franchisee's POS system, remote video, and form-letter emails can substitute for dialogue—and in the process create an us vs. them environment.

So where is the middle ground?

The key to successful franchise relationships is trust. As a franchisor, you need to trust that your franchisees are paying all required royalties and properly reporting revenues. You enter into your contract trusting that they will adhere to brand standards and follow your systems. But, as Ronald Reagan often said, "Trust, but verify."

So at what point are you going too far with that verification?

First, understand that verification is in the best interest of franchisees as well. Franchisees suffer when brand standards are not met. They suffer when other franchisees cheat, as that means less advertising funds and royalties to support the franchisee community.

In short, it is a question of transparency.

If, for example, you use mystery shopping to uncover violations of standards and under-reporting of revenues, your franchisees should know about it. Hide this from your franchisees, and it will foster distrust and conflict.

Making Themselves Heard

Strong franchisee relations will necessitate that your franchisees respect your leadership. They will want to know that you have a vision for the brand and are executing against that vision.

At the same time, franchisees want to be heard. And, in fact, the best franchisors make a point of knowing how their franchisees feel. Having spoken with hundreds of franchisors, I can say with some certainty that very few of them conduct any meaningful research on franchisee attitudes and opinions. Instead, they rely on their gut instinct.

Unfortunately, gut instinct is often biased by our perceptions of the job we are doing and how people feel about us. Moreover, your franchisees may be guarded when talking with you or your representatives. Perhaps they believe candid comments will not yield positive results. They may prefer to avoid confrontation. But whatever the reason, franchisors can sometimes be surprised at how their franchisees view them.

So be sure you actively listen to what your franchisees have to say. Solicit their feedback on a regular basis. Conduct formal surveys if need be to supplement other feedback mechanisms. You may even choose to mystery shop your franchise validation to hear what your franchisees are saying to your prospects.

THE BOTTOM LINE

Lock the Contract in a Drawer

The key to success in franchising is successful franchisees. Without that, no franchise system can last. Put their interests first, and they will become the raving fans that build successful brands.

There is a significant correlation between successful franchise systems and good franchisee relations. And while it is certainly easier to keep successful franchisees happy, it takes more than that. It takes trust. It takes leadership. It takes transparency. And most of all, it takes communication.

Good franchisee relations start and end with good communication. In our digital age, it can be all-too-tempting to fire off an email to respond to a nettlesome issue rather than picking up the phone. It can be appealing to believe that technology can reduce the frequency of field visits and face-to-face training.

But in the end, people have relationships with other people, not their computers. So focus on building relationships with your franchisees the same way you build relationships in your own life.

And remember, while the franchise relationship is contractual in nature, if you are ever forced to bring out the contract and cite chapter and verse, you have already lost. The best franchise contracts are the ones you put in a drawer and never look at again.

Chapter 13

Putting It All Together

"I didn't build Auntie Anne's alone. That would have been impossible. From the very beginning, we had a team around us that was exceptional. Our company was successful because of the dedicated people who worked for us."

—Anne Beiler, Founder, Auntie Anne's

If you have made the strategic decision to franchise, you now need to make some more tactical decisions on the question of *how*.

Regardless of how the franchisee makes money, the franchisor has two roles in life: selling franchises and servicing franchisees. And of the two, ensuring the success of the franchisee is more important.

DIY Franchising

Entrepreneurs are, by their very nature, resourceful and self-confident. Especially in young companies, they routinely substitute hard work and ingenuity for growth capital. Chances are they started their business without outside help. So why shouldn't they do the same when they begin franchising?

When these prospective clients ask me why they can't develop their franchise program without outside help, they are often surprised to hear the answer:

Of course they can.

The problem is they're asking the wrong question. The more important question is whether they *should*.

Starting a new franchise program takes time and substantial effort. Done right, it requires competitive research, a well-conceived strategic plan, sophisticated financial modeling, an operations manual, training programs and videos, a marketing plan, brochures, adapting your website, and a properly designed and executed sales strategy.

Where do you find the time to do this when you are already putting in workweeks that would make the average masochist blanch?

If you (or your staff) take the time out of your 60-hour week to do this, something has to give—usually the core business. A part-time effort that conserves your time will delay your market entry. And as the months pass, the window of opportunity may be closing. Competitors are not sitting on the sidelines waiting for you to catch up.

Of course you could hire additional staff, but the chances of finding someone with all the diverse franchise skills needed (research, writing, financial analysis, legal documentation, operations and training, brochure design, website design and optimization, video production, and sales) are remote. And even if you can find people with this combination of talent, many of these skills are necessary only after you start your franchise program.

However, you can outsource much of this work to consulting firms and law firms, whose full-time jobs are to satisfy those needs. And assuming you choose wisely, these resources will have the experience and the team to complete these diverse tasks much more quickly. While you focus on your business, your new team does the heavy lifting—and gets you to market faster in the process.

Aside from the element of time, the decisions you make will have a profound impact on your ability to succeed. We talked about royalty determination earlier in this book. But despite its importance, all too many franchisors take a cursory look at their competitors and pick a number— never taking the time to analyze the implications of their choice. "Me too" is not a strategy—it is a shortcut for people who are unwilling to put in the time needed to do it right.

Whether by design or by chance, every franchise program is unique. Some will feature unique products or services. They will use different vendors, have different costs, and target different consumers. Franchisee revenues, salaries, growth plans, philosophies regarding support, and competitors will differ. And companies will vary relative to their stage in the franchise growth cycle—more established franchisors will have very different internal resources and a very different cost structure.

Several times each year, we conduct research on franchisors in a competitive segment, and after reviewing their FDDs, it becomes clear that multiple companies have essentially copied one another's business strategy. While franchising best practices should be followed when structuring a franchise offering, some companies have clearly adopted the attitude that if a particular competitor appears to be doing well, the business decisions they've incorporated into their FDD must be right. But even if they're right for your competitor, they may not be right for your business. Proper business decisions can only be made after evaluating the many unique aspects outlined above.

Entrepreneurs, whose "ready-fire-aim" personalities and lightning-fast decision making are legendary, never want to hear that developing a sound strategy will take weeks of research and financial modeling. But when they realize the impact of those decisions, the need for this more systematic approach becomes readily apparent—in all aspects of franchising.

Operations manuals and training programs may seem like an easy DIY project. But their role in brand maintenance and liability protection is vital. While many people believe they can write, even good writers rarely have the requisite expertise to draft an operations manual that adequately protects against liability while maintaining brand standards. Being a proficient writer is not enough. Generally it is not how you say it, but knowing what you should and should not say.

Franchise marketing provides more relevant examples. Without access to historical data on what does and does not work, a neophyte's alternative is to learn by costly trial and error. Of course, they can measure and refine and measure and refine, and eventually get it right—if they do not run out of money first.

And while a beautiful brochure never sold a franchise, poorly designed brochures lose sales all the time. This does not even account for the possibility that one of the eight states that regulate franchise advertising might reject a brochure after it is printed—or for the liability that can accrue from a badly worded brochure.

Unfortunately, many of these issues aren't readily apparent when launching a franchise—and some may not become apparent for years. Franchisees will never complain that the royalty is too low. A faulty operations manual doesn't have a warning label about impending doom. It simply ticks like a time bomb. A poorly designed lead generation plan is camouflaged behind the salesperson's excuses. And often, inertia will carry the franchisor for years, until one day it runs into the proverbial brick wall.

The reason to use experts is the knowledge that their experience will allow you to avoid a mistake, grow faster, and operate more profitably.

Why Hire a Consultant?

In short, you hire outside experts, even if you are a larger company with access to internal resources, for the following reasons:

- *To avoid mistakes.* Often, when mistakes are incorporated into a franchise program, you may not even know about them for years, and it could have a huge impact on your long-term profitability.
- *To gain insight.* Advisors bring insight from their work on literally hundreds of businesses.
- *For liability protection.* Franchising is a highly regulated field. Good advisors know where the mines are buried and can help you avoid potential disaster.
- *For their regulatory knowledge.* Your advisors should have intimate business knowledge of what legal hoops you need to jump through.
- *For their institutional knowledge.* The best advisors will systematically collect information (on media effectiveness, close rates, etc.) that their clients can use.
- *For greater speed.* While your internal staff would need to wrestle with other priorities, when you hire an advisor, your franchise program will be their priority.

➤ *For advisor leverage.* Your advisors should have been down this road before—putting them in a position to leverage off the knowledge they have gained in the past.

➤ *For your ability to leverage.* You and your staff can continue to focus on what needs to be done with your business while your advisors complete tasks that are one-time-only.

➤ *To reduce risk.* Ultimately, it is all about decreasing the chance of failure in a new business model.

➤ *To improve results.* And, in conjunction with that reduced risk, it is about improved franchise sales, increased revenues, and lowered expenses.

Choosing Your Consultant

To take advantage of these benefits, it is imperative to choose your advisors wisely. The problem is that every consultant you interview will tell you they are the best.

When making your final decision, you should compare firms on criteria such as quality of people, diversity and relevance of experience, track record, breadth of service offering, institutional knowledge, reputation, references, location, and price. These criteria, more than anything else, dictate the success you can expect with a franchise consulting firm.

Integrity

In evaluating potential franchise consultants, the first thing you should look for is integrity. Be very wary of any consultant who tells you to franchise before evaluating your business, goals, and resources. Franchising is not right for everybody, and those who tell you it is may be more concerned with their own welfare than yours.

Quality of People

When you hire an advisor, what you are really paying for is the quality of the people they have on staff. The quality of a consulting team is a direct reflection of their ability to do great work.

The quality of the consulting team can often be seen on their website. Try to find answers to the following questions:

- How many people does the firm have? If it has a limited staff, you may want to ask what will happen if your consultant falls ill or goes on vacation.
- Do they have experience working with franchise companies? If not, what experience do they have that might possibly be relevant?
- Have they ever run franchise companies at a senior level (CEO, president, EVP, etc.)? McDonald's has more than 440,000 employees, and most of them would not have the experience to be good consultants.
- Who, specifically, will be working on your engagement? If your consulting firm has good people at the top but farms out the work to someone with little or no experience, it is of slight value to you.
- What educational credentials do they have? While MBAs, Ph.D.s, and CFEs (Certified Franchise Executive) should not be the measure of a consultant, these advanced degrees and certificates can indicate how highly your consultant values his ongoing education process.
- Are their people "real"? Some companies post bios of friends on their website to make them appear experienced—but a quick check of LinkedIn will reveal that many of these consultants may work elsewhere. Likewise, be wary of firms that show a lot of consultants if they do not list their address (or if a Google search of their address shows that they are working out of their homes).
- Are they hiding something? I am always skeptical of consultants who talk about their experience at "a major franchising company" but do not disclose the name of that company on their website or on LinkedIn. Why should their prior employment be kept a secret?

If you do nothing else, be sure you have a good understanding of the people who will be working for you before engaging any firm.

Diversity and Relevance of Experience

From the standpoint of "fit" with your organization, you should also look for a consulting firm that has the kind of experience you need. For example:

☛ Do they have hands-on experience in your industry segment (food service, consumer service, business-to-business, health care, retail, mobile-based franchising, etc.)?

☛ If you are a startup, do they have experience in running startup operations? Someone who has never worked in a pure startup franchise may not have the experience to guide you through the process from the ground up.

☛ Do they have hands-on experience in franchise sales? If you fail to sell franchises, you will never be a successful franchisor. So be sure your team has this vital skill set.

Remember, the team's quality is a reflection of the organization's philosophy toward providing excellent services. If an organization does not hire the best people, you can assume they are not committed to providing the best service and support.

Track Record

Ultimately, the past is the best predictor of the future, so look at a firm's track record of client successes. In doing so, however, it is important that you look beyond the client list on a company's website.

Some consultants stretch the bounds of reason when listing their clients—with some including "clients" who did no more than simply attend a seminar held by the firm. Other companies will shoot video testimonials of clients raving about the firm while they are still in the ether of their first trade show—but years later, they have yet to sell a franchise.

So be sure to check their references, and ask about more than their experience. Ask about the success that they have achieved.

The basic rule of thumb: If a firm cannot demonstrate they have made their clients as successful as you would like to be, you should probably consider another firm.

Breadth of Services

A full-service consulting firm will offer a variety of services. The most comprehensive firms in the industry will offer:

☛ Competitive structural research

- ☞ Strategic planning
- ☞ Financial modeling
- ☞ Organizational analysis and planning
- ☞ Operations manuals
- ☞ Training curricula
- ☞ Training video development
- ☞ Online learning systems
- ☞ Primary research into buyer profiles
- ☞ Franchise lead generation plans
- ☞ Franchise sales brochures
- ☞ Website development and adaptation
- ☞ Search Engine Optimization
- ☞ PPC management
- ☞ Public relations services
- ☞ Outsourced sales services

This breadth of services is important for two reasons. First, if you are looking for a long-term relationship with your consulting firm, you will want a firm that can serve your needs both now and in the future. This philosophy should also extend to other vendors, such as architects, equipment suppliers, distributors, technology providers, etc.

More important, a greater breadth of services allows companies to cross-pollinate among disciplines. If, for example, your firm lacks knowledge of franchise marketing and franchise sales, the franchise structure you recommend may work great in theory, but not in the real world. The reverse is also true. A consultant skilled at marketing may structure a program that is easy to sell but a disaster to implement.

Institutional Knowledge

One of the big advantages to working with consulting firms is their accumulation of data that can be of use to you. If, for example, your firm collects media-specific information on cost-per-lead, close rates, and cost-per-sale, this information is likely to save you quite a bit of money on advertising for franchisees.

Firm Size

Another factor worth considering is firm size. Larger firms can put more resources on your engagement and move more quickly. Hiring a larger company also means if one of your consultants quits, retires, has health issues, or is run over by a bus, the firm can quickly replace them without delaying your engagement.

Peer Review

Another advantage to larger firms is the ability to get multiple sets of eyes on the key decisions driving your strategy. The best such firms will typically have formal peer review programs that ensure all decisions are scrutinized by multiple consultants for the best results.

Location vs. Expertise

Being close is an advantage but generally not a necessity. Often you must make a trade-off between location and expertise. So ask yourself whether you want the best team in your local market or the best team in the world—knowing that the latter may be somewhat less convenient.

In the age of connectivity, having someone right around the corner is less important than it was several decades ago. Cell phones, email, text messages, and online meeting platforms have all but eliminated the need for a local presence. And virtually all consulting firms will insist on visiting your business early in the planning process. So generally, choosing a distant firm will not cause any problems with communications or quality.

After all, when you hire a brain surgeon, you want the best. Not the closest.

Along the same lines, consulting firms must decide whether they will maintain all their staff in a central location or employ consultants in multiple markets. The latter model will allow the firm to hire the best consultants available, while the former will provide the convenience of a central office. Again, the need for a central office housing all your consultants is generally not much of a concern given the ease of modern communications—so hiring the best is usually the preferred alternative.

Reputation

Today, checking on a company's reputation takes an hour on the internet. Deciding which consultant to work with is simply too important to neglect this step. Spend an hour on Google and LinkedIn searching the name of the company and the names of its principals.

And, as mentioned above, be sure you check the company's references.

Price

As we have seen, a good consultant will help you make more money—either by helping you sell more franchises, avoid the wrong franchisees, improve your franchise structure, eliminate litigation, or decrease expenses. So obviously, if price were not a concern, everyone would always choose the best consultants available.

But few of us have the luxury of being insensitive to price.

That said, the best consultants generally offer a variety of ways in which you can work together and have some degree of flexibility in the pricing process.

> ### ▼Apples to Apples
>
> It is important when comparing prices to be sure you are comparing apples to apples. You may find, for example, two consultants offering strategic planning advice, but on closer examination, only one of them includes competitive analysis and financial modeling. So be sure you read the fine print.

The Need for Expert Franchise Legal Counsel

Creating the legal documents required to franchise is not something that can be done by your brother-in-law or your real estate attorney. Franchise law is very specialized and, considering the patchwork quilt of laws across the U.S., highly complex. So once you have settled on a consultant, you will also want to hire a franchise attorney.

Make sure you find your consultant first. The reason is simple: Your consultant, if she is good, will not only tell you how to franchise, but will also tell you if franchising is the right expansion strategy for you. Hiring a franchise attorney before settling on this strategy is a waste of time and money.

Moreover, finalizing your business decisions prior to engaging counsel will serve to make your lawyer's time more efficient—thereby reducing your legal costs. In fact, many attorneys will reduce their fee based on the fact that you have retained a consultant.

Generally, a consultant can provide recommendations for an attorney who will best suit your needs. The best consultants will have worked with a variety of different firms that they can recommend.

Note: Some consulting firms provide franchise agreements and disclosure documents and will tout the advantages of getting everything done under one roof. In the legal community and elsewhere, this is widely frowned upon.

By contracting with an experienced franchise law firm from the start, you:

- ⬗ Avoid conflicts of interest
- ⬗ Enjoy attorney-client privilege
- ⬗ Avoid having to pay for legal documents twice (once for their creation and once for their review by outside legal counsel)
- ⬗ Can use a law firm for legal proceedings (such as franchise closings, transfers, negotiations, etc.)
- ⬗ Know the firm that developed your legal documents is properly insured in the highly unlikely event of a problem

Regardless of what you decide, be sure the individual lawyer you will be working with (not the firm) has the level of experience you need to ensure your documents are bulletproof.

Choosing a Franchise Lawyer

Aside from finding a good consultant, choosing the right franchise attorney is one of the most critical decisions you will make as a franchisor. The documents your attorney crafts and the advice she provides can make or break your franchise program. But how do you go about finding the right attorney?

Unfortunately, the legal profession is highly competitive. And with the hundreds of thousands of franchises that have been sold in the U.S. in the past decade, many attorneys who are not franchise specialists can claim to have worked on franchise documents. While they may be able to throw around the names of top franchise companies, their experience may be limited to reviewing an FDD or working with a franchisee on a nonfranchise-related issue. So while an attorney may represent himself as having franchise expertise, in fact his experience may fall far short of what you really need.

While there are more than 1 million attorneys in the U.S., probably fewer than 2,000 have any real franchise experience. Of those 2,000, there are perhaps 200 who are a good fit for a new franchisor looking to franchise their business. So how do you make your choice?

The best way, of course, is to receive one or more referrals from franchise professionals. If you would like a referral to a qualified franchise attorney, the iFranchise Group is happy to do so regardless of whether you choose to work with us. And since we never take referral fees from these attorneys, you can have confidence that these referrals will be objective.

Should you choose to handle the search yourself, the first and most important factor is experience. Check the attorney's website to see if "franchise law" is listed as a separate practice area. Then look at the lawyers in their franchise practice group. Do their bios talk only about franchising or do they list other areas of expertise, such as general contract law, real estate, estate planning, etc., as a part of their practice? Do they list franchise publications? Do they list franchise-specific honors (being named to the *Franchise Times* list of Legal Eagles, for example)? How long have they been practicing franchise law?

Again, it is the experience of the individual franchise attorneys you need to be concerned with—not the firm's reputation. So be sure you check their credentials.

Once you have identified the attorneys you would like to consider, ask them probing questions based on what is important to you as a prospective franchisor. Below are some areas you need to consider:

⬥ *Franchisor vs. franchisee experience.* Your franchise lawyer needs to have experience on the franchisor side of the equation. If a franchise attorney does the majority of her work for franchisees, she may be too pro-franchisee with her advice. In addition, if she does all her work on the franchisee side and does not regularly draft FDDs (a question you should ask anyone you are interviewing), she is unqualified.

➤ *Transactional vs. litigation focus.* A transactional attorney will focus his practice on preparing your franchise legal documents. If your franchise lawyer does not have some focus on the transactional side, he will not be as efficient at preparing your documents. The advantages of working with a franchise attorney who also has a litigation practice are that he can represent you, if needed, in a lawsuit, and he *may* be more focused on preventing litigation in the drafting process. The disadvantages, of course, are that he is not as specialized, and during a trial, he may be almost impossible to reach (if one person does both). As discussed earlier, the threat of litigation can be minimized in a well-run franchise operation, so this may not be much of a consideration.

➤ *Flat fee vs. hourly.* Since FDDs are fairly predictable, many franchise attorneys on the transactional side will work on a flat-fee basis, as they have enough experience to know how much time the average startup franchise program will take. The advantages to working with a flat-fee franchise lawyer are that her fees are predictable and can often be financed over a few months. The disadvantage is you might occasionally (rarely, in our experience) pay more than you would if you were charged an hourly rate. Most transactional attorneys are looking for a long-term relationship, so they will often discount their initial fees to establish the relationship.

➤ *What's included?* If you are working with a flat-fee attorney, make sure you know what is included in the flat fee and what is not. Otherwise, you are likely to compare apples to oranges. Does the fee include any franchise registrations? If so, how many? If not, what are the costs per registration? Does the fee include a review of your franchise operations manual or your franchise marketing material? If he is an hourly billing attorney, will he bill you for his travel time? Who will be doing the work, what is his experience, and what are his billing rates?

➤ *Industry-specific knowledge.* In a few industries (nonregulated service businesses), prior industry segment experience is not extremely important. But in many industries (ranging from food service to senior care to home improvement to education), a knowledge of the additional regulations that impact the business can be very helpful. And in some industries that have complex regulatory concerns (medical franchising, health-care franchising, dental franchising, etc.), this industry-specific knowledge is vital. In areas like health-care franchising, for example, there are probably fewer than a dozen franchise attorneys with deep industry expertise.

▼ *Firm size.* A larger firm can bring more resources to your engagement and can do more for you outside the franchise realm. At a larger firm, your franchise lawyer can bring in a specialist who can help with other transactions like trademark work, real estate, and other needs. Larger firms may have more connections within the franchise community and will often have formal educational programs that allow them to "cross-pollinate" when new ideas or issues arise. On the other hand, larger firms may delegate some of the drafting work to associates (not partners), who are less qualified than the partner you interviewed. While this allows them to work at a reduced fee (associates charge lower billing rates), it may make them less familiar with your documents when questions arise. So the specific franchise attorney who will draft your FDD will be an issue. A smaller firm or sole practitioner will provide you with more (or exclusive) access to a partner-level attorney. The downside is that there is no backup if the partner is run over by a bus, has a health issue, or goes on vacation. Accessibility may be more of an issue. And, of course, there are midsize firms that fill the gap between large and small.

▼ *Price.* There is often a correlation between firm size and price. Larger firms generally charge more, as they have larger overheads to support and often pay their attorneys more. Generally speaking, we do not recommend that price should be the sole criterion for attorney selection, as the small difference in price can often make a big difference in quality (and results!). So be sure that increased price brings you added value. Focus on quality and fit first.

▼ *Accessibility.* All attorneys, in our experience, tout their accessibility. It is not always true. Perhaps more important than accessibility is communication style. Some franchise attorneys prefer email and some prefer phone contact. If you have a preference, you should ask.

➤ *Location*. This is not much of an issue, as transactional attorneys can practice anywhere. Some lawyers do have occasional educational events at their offices, providing an opportunity for networking and learning. Closer is nicer, but again, it is largely irrelevant in your ultimate decision.

➤ *Personality*. In most instances, you will be working with your franchise attorney for years. So if you do not like them, don't hire them.

Again, it is generally best to wait on the decision to hire a franchise attorney until *after* you have worked with a franchise consultant to determine the feasibility of franchising. In that way, you can be sure you are not paying for legal advice for a franchise program that ultimately will not work. And since the best franchise consultants will tell you whether your concept is franchisable without charging a dime, this is often the most economical alternative.

Building Your Team

In most new franchise systems, the management team is very lean when it first gets started. Jerry Wilkerson, the founder of Franchise Recruiters, Ltd., tells about how when he first attended franchise shows, Subway founder Fred DeLuca would work the booth next to his, and afterward they would flip to see who would buy drinks.

So if you are like most new franchisors, you will start with your existing team and will likely wear many hats on day one.

As you grow, your primary cost of doing business will almost always be personnel. The salaries of your team will, in effect, be your cost of goods sold. And, as we saw earlier when discussing structure and speed of growth, your staffing will be determined by the strategic decisions you make early in the process.

Your decision to franchise will require your existing team (even if it is only you) to stretch. Franchising will add new responsibilities in the areas of franchise marketing, franchise sales, franchisee training, field supervision, advertising fund management, and management.

The timing of staff additions is also critically important. Depending on your desired speed of growth, you may have to hire slightly in advance of need to provide enough time for training before your team is immersed in the day-to-day operations of the franchise. Once questions regarding the timing and training of each new hire are resolved, you should also develop an outline of the minimum qualifications for each new position.

Your Time Commitment When Launching a Franchise

While the staffing of your new organization may sound daunting, there is some good news: Your time commitment when starting your franchise will *not* be overwhelming—in fact, much the opposite. Now, I do not mean to imply that franchising does not require a commitment on your part. Ultimately, franchising will become a full-time business.

But when you first start franchising, it is not like you are jumping into the deep end of the pool. It is more like gradually walking into the ocean—first getting your feet wet, then your ankles, then your knees, until eventually you are swimming.

The process of transforming your current business into a franchise that is ready to launch takes about four months—perhaps a little longer if you are in a registration state. And during that time, you will continue to concentrate on your existing business—with an occasional day where you will focus on franchising.

Up until the date of the launch, your consulting and law firms should be doing most of the heavy lifting. Your primary role at that point will be to provide background information on the concept, make decisions on structure, and review the materials your team develops on your behalf—plans, financial projections, manuals, marketing strategies, and legal documents—to be sure you agree with them and understand their implications.

Then, once you are ready to launch, you will switch gears. But even then, your role will start gradually and evolve over time. A hypothetical example may best illustrate the evolution of your role.

Let's say, for example, that you are planning to sell about 12 franchises per year at the start. Let's further assume you have chosen to sell individual franchises (not area development or area representative franchises) and are starting from scratch without any existing leads.

If we assume a 2 percent close rate under this scenario, you will need to generate about 50 new leads each month—or a little under two each business day.

So on day one of the first month, you will have to make one or two calls. About 68 percent of the time, you will just leave a message. About 70 percent of these leads will be disqualified on the first call. Then, at least from a franchise standpoint, you are done for the day!

Your role will continue like that, gradually growing to maybe an hour a day over the first month or so, as you fill your pipeline with prospective franchisees. By month three or four, you should be close to selling your first franchise (12 to 14 weeks to close on average). And that is when your job as a franchisor will expand again.

Once your first franchisee is signed, you will need to schedule and conduct training. Some of that training will invariably be on the job, where your new franchisee will essentially serve as unpaid labor while learning the business. But there will certainly be another aspect of training, where you will need to spend time with your new franchisee in a more formal educational setting. This will perhaps be the first full-time work you will conduct as a new franchisor.

At this point, you will have spent four to six months developing your franchise program, another four months exclusively in a sales role, and perhaps a month or two combining sales and training.

If you continue to do things right, you should be close to signing your second franchisee, and the training cycle will start again, requiring you to conduct training every month or two. Ultimately, you will likely train multiple franchisees at the same time.

Depending on the staff you have to assist you with training, this is when you might first consider hiring. At this point, you will have recaptured some of the capital you invested in your franchise program (via franchise fees), and you can count on royalty revenue in the near future. So you would generally look for someone who can replace you in the role for which you are least suited.

Some new franchisors delegate to a new hire. Some promote from within and hire a replacement for existing unit-level operations staff. And some turn to outsourcing.

As you continue to grow, you will likely have additional needs, depending on how you plan to support your franchisees. For example, you may choose to develop advertising campaigns on their behalf. You may do product research and development. You may assist in the purchasing process. And you will likely need some incremental accounting and tracking. This generally does not require staffing in the first few years of a franchise program.

So while you may choose to wear a lot of hats when you get started, by the time you need a full-time staffer on the franchise side, you may well be able to pay for it out of the fees and royalties you are generating.

Outsourcing

Many franchisors elect to outsource one or more job functions in the early stages of franchise system development. Outsourcing is often an appropriate strategy in the early stages of growth, when cash flows do not yet justify hiring new staff. Likewise, when a specific skill is required and the expertise is not available in-house, outsourcing can be an invaluable tool. As we have discussed previously, some of the functions you may consider outsourcing include:

- Marketing
- Public relations
- SEO and social media
- Franchise sales
- Accounting
- Legal services
- Real estate
- Construction
- Consumer marketing

Each of these functions can be readily outsourced—either as a short-term, stopgap measure or on a long-term basis, depending on your goals and your plan for growth. So you will certainly want to explore these options as part of your strategic planning process.

Choosing Your Team: Bazooka or Peashooter

When you're in the process of hiring consultants and lawyers, all of them will tell you they're the best. And while we have discussed how valuable a team of professionals can be, ultimately you will need to decide whether you should work with the team you feel is the very best, or one that is less expensive but still capable.

Do you really need a bazooka? Or will a peashooter do?

I recommend hiring the company you believe is the best, even if it means paying substantially higher fees, simply because you can enjoy considerable financial benefits (as well as reduced risk) when you work with the best. Revisiting the concept of the Present Value of a Franchise, consider the following:

- ❧ If the strategy or competitive positioning developed by a consultant results in a single additional franchise sale, over the life of that franchisee you could receive hundreds of thousands of dollars in royalty revenues, rebates, product sales, and advertising fees.
- ❧ If a more detailed fee analysis results in a 1 percent increase in your royalty rate, you could anticipate tens of millions of dollars in incremental revenues if you were to sell just 100 franchises.
- ❧ If improved territorial recommendations result in one incremental franchise per metropolitan market, you will add tens of thousands of dollars in revenue for each metro market you sell. Forever.
- ❧ If more impressive operations manuals and training programs help you sell a single franchise, there is another huge financial gain.
- ❧ And if those same manuals prevent a single lawsuit, what is that worth—in cash, in time, and in the preservation of your good name?
- ❧ If a consultant's marketing plan can help you sell one more franchise, again that is hundreds of thousands of dollars in revenues over the next ten to 20 years for each incremental franchise sold.

- ☛ If your training in the franchise sales process improves your close rate by only one-thousandth (from 2 to 2.1 percent, for example), a franchisor trying to sell 12 franchises per year would sell an additional franchise every 20 months.
- ☛ And what is it worth if that same training helps you avoid selling a franchise to someone who will fail?

Frankly, there are dozens of examples like this.

Moreover, when I talk about "one more franchise" above, I think this is a *vast* underestimation of the incremental value a top consulting firm will provide over a smaller, less experienced firm.

Aggressiveness Dictates Cost

In franchising, like any business endeavor, it is important to be properly capitalized prior to initiating your franchise strategy.

For many businesses, the costs of establishing a franchise program are less than the costs of opening a single additional location. And the potential returns of a franchise program are much greater. Yet companies continue to make the leap into franchising without understanding the investment they will need to succeed.

As a general rule, it is important to start by noting that your desired rate of growth will affect the costs you incur. If, for example, your plan calls for you to sell a single franchise to your brother-in-law, who has worked with you for the past ten years, you will need to develop the requisite legal documents and a franchise operations manual to enforce standards and avoid liability. Even if you were to choose a midpriced law firm, you could initiate such a franchise program for less than $50,000—perhaps much less, depending on the team you assemble and how much work you do yourself.

If, on the other hand, you are looking to sell 20 or more franchises in your first year, you will need to budget for increased development costs; more legal fees to get you registered in multiple states; and substantially higher marketing costs, hiring expenses, and other expenditures. Depending on your hiring needs, you could easily top the $200,000 mark.

So be sure you have the appropriate resources, depending on your ability to leverage existing staff and your desired level of growth.

Five Buckets for Franchise Success

As a new franchisor, you will generally have five "buckets" of costs into which you will need to invest: Development, Legal, Marketing, People, and Preparation.

Development Costs

Your first bucket will be development costs—the fees you pay to consultants or others to get you ready to franchise. Depending on your appetite for growth, you may need to develop a strategic plan, an FDD and franchise agreement, franchise marketing materials (brochures, videos, etc.), franchise marketing strategy development, adaptations to your website, an operations manual, and a franchise training program. Development costs will vary based on several factors:

- Aggressiveness of initial goals
- Ability to leverage existing material
- Ability to leverage internal resources
- Services provided by consulting firm
- Consulting firm you choose to work with

As discussed above, these costs could be less than $50,000 or more than $200,000.

Legal Costs

Your legal costs will tend not to vary as dramatically. Regardless of your planned aggressiveness, you will need an attorney to draft your franchise agreement and your FDD. More aggressive rollouts will require a larger number of initial state registrations, adding the cost of preparing these filings as well as state registration fees. Depending on the firm and your plan, your legal costs could run less than $15,000 or more than $35,000. And if you have not done so already, you will need to obtain a federal trademark. An uncontested trademark might add another $1,000 to $2,000 to your budget.

Marketing Costs

At least as important as the marketing materials (which are accounted for in the Development Bucket), you need to budget for franchise lead generation. Depending on the size of the investment in the franchise opportunity, a new franchisor should budget between $8,000 and $10,000 (and in some instances more) per franchise for its franchise marketing efforts. For a franchisor planning on selling 12 franchises in its first year, an annual marketing budget of between $96,000 and $120,000 is not at all unrealistic. Keep in mind that, as a new franchisor, it will take several months to build your initial pipeline of candidates. Unless an existing customer or your brother-in-law is ready to buy a franchise on day one, you likely won't sell your first franchise for several months after you begin your marketing efforts.

That said, from a cash-flow standpoint, you can probably set aside less than a full year's budget. Remember, each time you make a franchise sale, you will recapture some of your advertising expenditures in the form of the franchise fee. And since the close time on a franchise is between 12 and 14 weeks, you can anticipate that some of these fees will be available to offset your advertising budget before the end of the year.

Going back to the previous example, assume you are advertising at a rate that will allow you to sell one franchise a month. If you were

> ⬤ **Remember: Statistics Lie**
>
> From a statistical perspective, there is no guarantee that any given 100 leads will contain two sales. Even with a random distribution of buyers within your lead pool, one would anticipate that any random sample of leads might contain more or less buyers than the average. And of course, you cannot anticipate that you will close at the precise statistical average either. Internal factors such as the quality of your franchise offer; franchisee validation; the quality of your leads, marketing plan, marketing materials, and messaging; and your sales process and ability (along with external factors such as the economy) will all impact your ability to close at a statistically average rate.

to fill your pipeline in the first month, you might anticipate you will sell a franchise in about 12 to 14 weeks.

Of course, there is no absolute predictability to the timing of franchise sales. So with this in mind, it is perhaps worthwhile to think of franchise sales occurring around the middle of a typical bell curve, with a little less than half occurring before the peak of the curve and a little more than half occurring afterward. While the odds of closing this hypothetical sale increase over time, there is always the possibility that the sale takes place at the far right-hand side of the bell curve.

In a situation in which your franchise marketing efforts are ongoing, you could envision a series of bell curves for each successive month—with each having a probability of closing on roughly the same time frame. (See Figure 13.1.)

Stack several of these bell curves together, and the likelihood of making a sale rises with each passing month. So from a cash-flow perspective, the greater your monthly advertising budget, the sooner you will likely sell a franchise. For most new franchisors, a cash-flow budget covering six months' worth of planned advertising is often sufficient.

Figure 13.1: **Time to Close the Franchise Sale**

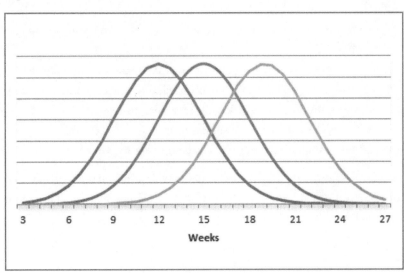

Thus, if you want to sell six franchises in your first year, you might budget for $30,000 in ad spend before beginning to recoup advertising fees from franchise sales. Plan 12 sales in your first year, and you would need to budget between $50,000 and $60,000 to be safe.

People Costs

The fourth major bucket you will need to account for involves the people who will help you implement your franchise program. Many new franchisors choose a rate of growth that allows them to grow without initially adding staff.

Ultimately, your staffing costs will be a function of:

- 🞅 The aggressiveness of your initial goals
- 🞅 Your ability to leverage existing staff
- 🞅 Your ability to free your own time to take on some of these new roles
- 🞅 The degree to which you choose to outsource

Preparation Costs

In addition to the four large buckets above, you will have to account for the various costs associated with creating a new business. Some of these include:

- 🞅 Creating a new franchise entity (if you choose to create a new corporation)
- 🞅 Conducting an opening audit of that company's balance sheet
- 🞅 Duplicating collateral materials (brochures, videos, stationery, etc.)
- 🞅 Any additional trademarks you may need to register
- 🞅 Travel costs for your consulting team
- 🞅 New computers, furniture, and equipment for your team

Depending on the number of brochures you print and the aggressiveness of your planned development effort, these expenses will generally range between $10,000 and $20,000.

THE BOTTOM LINE

You Are Entering a New Business

First and foremost, know that you are entering a new business: the business of *franchising*. As such, you will need to develop two market strategies simultaneously—one for your core business and one for franchising. As a new business, franchisors need to understand that franchising is a low-cost means of expansion—but it is not a no-cost means of expansion.

The business of franchising can be made much simpler by assembling a team of professionals with the expertise to show you the ropes. As major league pitcher Vernon Sanders Law once postulated, "Experience is a hard teacher because she gives the test first, the lesson afterwards." For those willing to pay for the experience of others, those lessons can have a much lower cost than they might otherwise.

CHAPTER 14

Taking
the Leap

*"I learned that you don't get anywhere by
sitting comfortably in a chair."*

—CONRAD HILTON, FOUNDER, HILTON HOTELS

I have a vivid childhood memory of the first time I went to the public pool with my friends. I had learned to swim some years earlier and had been to the beach many times, but the pool, with its high dive, was a whole new experience for me.

My friends, who were far more experienced than I, were old hands at the diving board—running and jumping off the high dive while gleefully shouting, "Cannonball!" Then swimming to the side and doing it all over again.

Soon, I found myself climbing the ladder, about to share in the fun. But as I got to the top of the board and saw my friend fly off in front of me, I suddenly was filled with dread. I walked to the edge of the board and peered down, ostensibly to be sure there was no one beneath me. "Whoa!," I thought. "That is a long way down."

I wanted to turn back, but my friends were already piling up the ladder behind me. And so with a lump in my throat, I screwed up my courage, and like an old pro, went sailing through the air. "Cannonball!"

Those might have been the longest three seconds of my life. But when I came up for air, I swam to the side and ran up the ladder again.

Franchising, in many respects, calls for a similar leap of faith, not unlike my childhood experience—and probably not unlike the experience every business owner has when they first went into business for themselves.

It is new. And it is scary. And there are certain fundamentals that will make the difference between a big splash and a belly flop.

- ⌐ You need to have a successful business as a starting point. Franchising is not a solution to a bad business. It is a means of expanding a great business faster by using other people's money.
- ⌐ Your journey should start with a strong plan that builds a differentiated value proposition around that business.
- ⌐ Quality control and brand consistency will be at the heart of the consumer experience and should be a major focus of your franchise efforts. So do not grow faster than your ability to support your franchisees.
- ⌐ Franchise marketing and franchise sales are a function of applying some basic principles that, when followed, yield predictable results.
- ⌐ Ultimately, the key to your success as a franchisor will be the success of your franchisees. If they fail, you will fail. If they succeed, you will thrive as a franchisor.

Franchising your business is absolutely not right for everyone.

Just because a business can be franchised does not mean it should be franchised. You need to determine if it is the right business strategy based on an examination of your resources, your goals, and your alternatives. You need to ensure that you have the right temperament for the business. And you need to be able to focus adequate resources on your franchise initiative.

Ultimately, a decision to franchise is a decision to start a new business. And your commitment to that business will be the key to its success.

Yes, from the top of the diving board, it looks like a long way down.

But it can be a wonderful and fun journey as well.

Best of luck to you in your expansion efforts, whichever road you choose.

Glossary

Autoresponder Matrix: A sorting mechanism that works with your contact management software to send a customized message to franchise applicants based on their responses to certain questions on your information request form.

Capture Rate: The percentage of people who go to a given page on your website and fill out a lead form providing their contact information.

Confidential Information Request Form (CIRF): A form completed by franchise prospects providing details on their qualifications. This term is preferred to "application" because that can sound too intimidating or appear as if the franchise candidate is applying for a job.

Cost Per Lead (CPL): The cost, in media dollars, for the franchisor to receive a franchise inquiry.

Cost Per Thousand (CPM): The cost to obtain 1,000 impressions with advertising, measured by dividing the cost of an ad by the number (in thousands) of people who saw it.

Federal Trade Commission (FTC): The federal agency responsible for regulating franchising under the Franchise Rule.

Financial Performance Representation (FPR): Previously called an "earnings claim." A representation of sales or earnings that is sometimes made in Item 19 of the FDD, usually based on historical financial performance.

Franchise Advisory Council (FAC): A group formed by the franchisor, generally composed of both franchisee and franchisor representatives, which meets periodically to discuss issues of importance to franchisees, provide recommendations to the franchisor, and communicate these discussions to franchisees as a whole.

Franchise Disclosure Document (FDD): A document much like a securities offering that has 23 specific points of disclosure, which must be provided to a prospective franchisee 14 calendar days prior to the execution of a franchise contract or the acceptance of funds from that prospective franchisee.

Pay-per-Click (PPC): Advertising, often but not always on search engines, in which the advertiser is only charged when the viewer clicks on a specific ad.

Rollovers as Business Startups (ROBS): A process that allows people to access retirement accounts to fund the acquisition of their franchise (or other small business).

About
the Author

A franchise consultant since 1985, Mark Siebert has worked with hundreds of franchisors, from startup operations to corporate giants. In 1998, Mr. Siebert founded the iFranchise Group as an organization dedicated to developing long-term relationships with successful franchisor clientele. He is an expert in evaluating companies for franchisability, structuring franchise offerings, and developing franchise programs. The strategic planning recommendations developed by Mr. Siebert have been instrumental in the growth and success of numerous national franchisors.

During his career, Mr. Siebert has personally assisted more than 30 Fortune 1,000 companies and hundreds of startup franchisors. Some of the more prominent companies he and his companies have assisted include: 1-800-FLOWERS, Ace Hardware, Al Baik (Saudi Arabia), Amazing Lash, Amoco, Applebee's, Armstrong World Industries, ASICS (Japan), Anheuser Bush, Athlete's Foot, Auntie Anne's Soft Pretzels, BBQ Chicken (Korea), Benihana, Berlitz, Betafence (South Africa), Bikram Yoga, BP Oil, Bridgestone/Firestone, Brightstar, Caribou Coffee, Carstar, Charles Schwab, Checkers/Rally's, Chem-Dry, Chevron, Children's Place, Circle K, Claire's Stores, Coldwell Banker, Computer Renaissance, Comfort Keepers, Cosi, Culligan, Dale Carnegie Training, Denny's, Dippin' Dots, DuPont, Edwin

Watts Golf, Einstein Brothers, El Pollo Loco, Fast Acai (Brazil), FedEx Office, Fleming, Game Truck, General Electric, Goddard Schools, Gordon Biersch, Guinness Imports, Häagen-Dazs, Hallmark Cards, Home Depot, HoneyBaked Ham, IBM, IHOP, Instant Tax Services, Interstate Batteries, Jackson Hewitt, John Deere, Johnson & Johnson, Krispy Kreme, Kudu (Saudi Arabia), LA Weight Loss, Lenscrafters, Line-X, Little Gym, Manpower, Massage Envy, McDonald's, Michelin, N-Hance, Nalco, Mobil Oil, Muzak, National Easter Seals, Nestle, Nissan (Saudi Arabia), Oreck, Orica, Paris Baguette (Korea), Payless Shoe Source, Pearson (U.K.), Perkins, Pet Supplies Plus, Petland, Phillips Electronics, Pinkberry, Popeye's, Quizno's, Rita's Italian Ice, Ryder Truck Rental, Saladmaster, Sears, Senior Helpers, Serta, Shell Oil, Shopko, Signature Flight Support, Sonic Drive-In, Subway, Successories, Swarovski, T-Mobile, Texaco, Togo's, Total Nutrition, Towne Park, True Religion, Tyco, the UPS Store, the United States Navy, Van Huesen, Wild Birds (Rovio), Wingstop, Yankee Candle, and Zain (Kuwait). He travels extensively to meet with companies considering franchising, and regularly conducts workshops and seminars on franchising in cities around the world.

Along with helping franchisors expand domestically, Mr. Siebert also has been actively involved in assisting companies in developing international franchise programs. His efforts have been responsible for the sale of numerous international licenses. Siebert has provided franchise consulting services to clients in more than two dozen countries on six continents.

In addition to his role at the iFranchise Group, Siebert is also an officer of Franchise Dynamics, the nation's premier franchise sales outsourcing firm. The consultants at Franchise Dynamics have, during the course of their combined careers, been responsible for the sale of more than 7,000 franchises. Franchise Dynamics has processed hundreds of thousands of franchise sales leads and routinely sells hundreds of franchises for its franchisor clientele every year. Based on its success in franchise sales, Franchise Dynamics was named to the Inc. 5,000, its list of the fastest growing companies in America.

Siebert is also an officer of TopFire Media, the nation's premier digital media and public relations agency specializing in franchising. TopFire

Media provides both franchise and consumer marketing assistance to a variety of companies with assistance in the areas of website development, mobile websites, search engine optimization, social media, pay-per-click optimization, and public relations.

Siebert is also the CEO of iFranchise Group International, the international licensing affiliate of the iFranchise Group. In this role, he provides training, marketing, and other support to consultants serving the U.A.E., Saudi Arabia, Qatar, Bahrain, Oman, Kuwait, Turkey, Egypt, and nine other countries in the MENA region. Additionally, Siebert has personally supervised the establishment of international consulting practices in Argentina, Chile, Japan, Mexico, Spain, Uruguay, Peru, and the Philippines.

A regular on the speaking circuit, he is active on various committees of the International Franchise Association, and was named to the *Franchise Times* list of "20 to Watch" in franchising. Siebert has been a featured speaker on franchising in a dozen countries and has lectured at Northwestern University, DePaul, and the University of Chicago. With a B.S. in Advertising and an M.B.A. from Northern Illinois University, he has published well over 150 articles on franchising in both the United States and abroad, and is widely quoted in the business press.

Index